Human Rights and International Relations

This book is about the impact of human rights on the relations among states. It seeks to bring together in one place an account of the theory of human rights (what they are; where they come from; whether they are universal); a discussion of the part they play in contemporary international politics (including East–West and North–South relations); and a view of what ought to be done about them – especially by the western powers.

The central policy recommendation made by Dr Vincent is that, as a project for international society, provision for subsistence rights has a strong claim to priority over other human rights. Dr Vincent's conclusion about the place of human rights in contemporary international society neither simply endorses the notion of the advance of cosmopolitan values on the society of states, nor rests on the mere observation of the continuing strength of state sovereignty. He shows how the grip of the sovereign state might in fact be tightened by its successful co-option of the international doctrine of human rights.

R J Vincent is a Fellow of Nuffield College, Oxford

The Royal Institute of International Affairs is an unofficial body which promotes the scientific study of international questions and does not express opinions of its own. The opinions expressed in this publication are the responsibility of the author.

Human Rights and International Relations

R.J. VINCENT

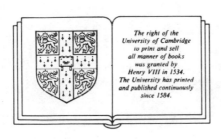

The right of the
University of Cambridge
to print and sell
all manner of books
was granted by
Henry VIII in 1534.
The University has printed
and published continuously
since 1584.

PUBLISHED IN ASSOCIATION WITH
THE ROYAL INSTITUTE OF
INTERNATIONAL AFFAIRS

CAMBRIDGE UNIVERSITY PRESS
CAMBRIDGE
NEW YORK   NEW ROCHELLE
MELBOURNE   SYDNEY

Published by the Press Syndicate of the University of Cambridge
The Pitt Building, Trumpington Street, Cambridge CB2 1RP
32 East 57th Street, New York, NY 10022, USA
10 Stamford Road, Oakleigh, Melbourne 3166, Australia

First published 1986
Reprinted 1988

Printed in Great Britain at the University Press, Cambridge

British Library cataloguing in publication data
Vincent, R. J.
Human rights and international relations.
1. Civil rights
I. Title   II. Royal Institute of
International Affairs
323.4   JC571

Library of Congress cataloguing in publication data
Vincent, R. J., 1943–
Human rights and international relations.
Published in association with the Royal Institute of
International Affairs.
Bibliography.
Includes index.
1. Civil rights.   2. International relations.
I. Title
JC571.V554   1987   323.4   86-14803
ISBN 0 521 32798 9 hard covers
ISBN 0 521 33995 2 paperback

Contents

Preface

This book seeks to bring together in one place an account of the theory of human rights, an examination of the part they play in international relations; and, finally, a view of the part they ought to play – what states, and particularly the western states (which have some choice in the matter), should do about them in foreign policy. The book was begun at the Royal Institute of International Affairs, continued at Keele University and at the Australian National University in Canberra, and completed at Princeton University. In the course of writing it, I have incurred many debts. At Chatham House, I am grateful to William Wallace, from whom the invitation to write this book came, and whose encouragement throughout has been unwavering. Christopher Hill, with whom I shared a room at Chatham House during 1980–1, helped me form the questions the book asks, though he might not recognize either his contribution then or the questions now. At Keele, all the members of the Department of International Relations (and of some other departments) have had parts of the manuscript inflicted on them from time to time, and Christopher Brewin and Hidemi Suganami especially have challenged me to come up with a bolder and clearer statement of my position. Alan James has been a source of consistent encouragement. At the Australian National University, I am grateful to J.D.B. Miller and to T.B. Millar for their intellectual and moral support. At Princeton, Richard Falk has as usual been a starting-place for ideas, and Richard Ullman's international relations discussion group accelerated the production of the manuscript to meet its deadlines, and then slowed it down again by giving me penetrating comments to take into account. The advice of Andrew Linklater, of Monash University, was crucial at more than one point in the argument. And Chatham House's readers, Emanuel de Kadt and William Wallace made important suggestions about the improvement of the manuscript.

There are also the institutions to thank: Chatham House for appointing me to a research fellowship and the Social Science Research Council for funding it under the Personal Research Grants scheme; Keele for allowing me time elsewhere to write; the ANU for the award of the MAIR Fellowship (funded by the Ford Foundation); and Princeton for the appointment to the Visiting Professorship of World Politics of Peace and War, which allowed the completion of the manuscript. To thank, too, for often extremely helpful discussion, are the various places where I gave parts of the book as seminars: the School of General Studies at the ANU, the Johns Hopkins University, La Trobe University, the London School of Economics, Monash University, Southampton University and the University College of Wales, Aberystwyth. Part of Chapter 3 was given as a paper to the 25th International Studies Association Conference in Atlanta in March 1984, and part of Chapter 8 was given as a paper to the Australasian Political Studies Association Annual Conference in Perth in August 1982 (and published in a modified form in *Australian Outlook*, vol. 36, no. 3, December 1982).

A number of individuals made comments or suggestions. Among these I should like to thank Charles Beitz, Margaret Canovan, Roberta Cohen, Michael Donelan, Jack Donnelly, Michael Doyle, David Dunn, Richard Flathman, Tony Godfrey-Smith, Margaret Grayden, Alan Hall, Stanley Hoffmann, Rhoda Howard, Dan Keohane, Lowell Livezey, Donald Markwell, Marilyn McMorrow, Henry Shue and Michael Walzer. Others, who were public officials, I can thank but not name.

Maureen Simkin typed the manuscript professionally and patiently. I thank her for this and for her unfailing cheerfulness, which was catching. Pauline Wickham, the Publications Manager at Chatham House, was very helpful, tireless and encouraging. At home, Angela, Geraint and Gareth put up with the project, celebrated the completion of each new chapter, and were nearly as pleased as I was at its conclusion.

Finally, I want to acknowledge someone who read no part of the manuscript, but whose influence on every page of it will be unmistakable to all those who knew him. Hedley Bull died tragically as the book was being completed. I had hoped with it to make some inroads on his cheerful scepticism about human rights. I hope now that the argument will stand as some small memorial to him.

R.J.V.

Princeton, New Jersey

Introduction

What human rights are is dealt with in Part One of this book. Part Two is concerned with the role they play in contemporary international politics. And Part Three answers the question: what ought to be done about human rights in international relations? The movement is from theoretical analysis, to the judgement of practice, to recommendations about policy. The book speaks of 'we' as though for the whole world. It treats human rights as the universal standards their name implies. And it makes reference to all foreign policy, and not merely to the position of this or that state. But it is a study by someone from the West for a western institution. Accordingly, the policy, if not also the theory and the practice, it has chiefly in mind is that of the western powers (and among them mainly the United States and Great Britain).

This does not mean that it seeks merely to find out what western policy is and give it a highbrow academic defence. Indeed, the first chapter of the book accepts a definition of human rights which includes the claims of individuals to subsistence as well as to security, an acceptance the implications of which the western powers themselves have been reluctant to confront. And, still in the first part of the book, the idea, often associated with the emergence of the Third World from colonial domination, that human rights have to be viewed through the separate prisms of the several cultures that participate in contemporary international politics, is taken seriously as a challenge (though not in the end a successful one) to a western conception of the universality of human rights.

The idea that human rights is a name for what are in fact plural and divergent ideologies is nevertheless continued in the discussion in Part Two of the place of human rights in contemporary international politics – because this is how the debate is often conceived by the participants in it. East and West, North and South, region and region, even non-governmental organization and non-governmental organization, argue with each other not only about human rights, but also about what human rights are about. As a result, the establishment of a global culture of which the idea of human rights is a part is as yet rather rudimentary. But it is not non-existent. And its existence may be consolidated if the 'have-ideologies' cease to squabble about what, from a 'have-not' point of view, are marginal differences about rights conceptions and demonstrate the reality of their commitment to human rights by paying attention to the worst cases – which are not each other.

So the central recommendation for policy that this book makes is that, as a project for international society, the provision for subsistence rights has a strong claim to priority over other human rights. This is a position which is often associated in world politics with the interests of the East (on the ground that it is good at such provision and welcomes the opportunity to say so) and the South (on the ground that its need for such provision is greatest) and not with the West. But the argument (in Chapters 7 and 8) on which the recommendation is based does not derive from any principled conviction that subsistence rights are prior to other basic rights, such as those to security and liberty, or from a preference for the purposes in international politics of the Second and Third Worlds over the First. Rather, it comes from a view of the suffering of the starving and malnourished as the worst offence to human rights in contemporary world society, together with a judgement that international cooperation at least to aid the deprived is less divisive ideologically than certain other possible human rights projects.

There are three things that the book does not argue, which, to avoid confusion later, we should note at the outset. In the first place, it is not a tract promoting the idea of basic human needs either as a substitute for human rights or as the basis of them. It finds a great deal of merit (especially in Chapter 8) in what is called the basic needs strategy of development. And it defends the priority of provision for the right of subsistence in a way that overlaps with the argument for meeting basic needs. But it is not basic needs that produce basic rights. One cannot get at a doctrine of human rights from a theory of animal needs. The needs have to be met because of the right, not the right because of the needs. Liberal political theory has until recently neglected the right to subsistence because, in getting on with the more elevated question of the meaning of liberty, it has tended to take provision for it for granted. When, as in contemporary world society, we plainly cannot take the provision of subsistence for granted, the liberal theory of human rights should play its part in repairing the neglect. And the gap between presupposition and actual achievement is so wide that there is a case for considering its closure a priority.

Secondly, policy is not all that the book is up to, and not everything in it is a preface to recommendation. At least as important is the social mapping it attempts in plotting the advance of world society – as represented by the practice of human rights – on the society of states (Chapters 6 and 8). If, in the course of the seventeenth century, a great watershed was crossed from the hierarchical ordering of world politics to the allocation of individuals to separate and equal sovereign states, the question now often asked is whether another watershed is not upon us. This involves the opening, or reopening, of the frontiers of the sovereign state into a global society of the existence of which the universal culture of human rights is one indicator. The conclusion arrived at on this question (in Chapter 8) is not one that can be cheerfully endorsed either by nationalist defenders of the states-system, or by those who see in the movement for human rights their leverage against the bars of imprisonment in the states-system. But the movement for human rights has at least prompted the asking of this fruitful question about the organization of world politics.

In the third place, this is not a missionary volume (though it might be accused of sermonizing) or a piece of liberation theology calling the world away from its evil ways to join up with a righteous army with the cross of human rights going on before. It is written by a student of international relations who takes human rights seriously, not by an advocate of human rights whose conviction makes him oblivious to his environment. So it does not demand that the temple of international relations be torn down to be replaced by a new structure of world society that would more hospitably accommodate human rights. Its tendency is rather to see what can be done to work human rights into the cracks of international society. This will expose it to the criticism of those who abominate mildness in response to outrage. The reply to this is that we are stuck with the states-system, and with the dangers of its nuclear equipment, and prudence in this environment is itself an imperative if any of us are to enjoy the human right to survival.

Before embarking on this enterprise, I should note the anthropologists' objection to it: namely, that people are interesting, both generally and in point of the rights they ought to and do enjoy, not for what unites them but for what sets them apart. The utility of the concept of culture is to distinguish one society from another, not to describe what they have in common. According to this view the quest for a global culture of human rights is not only dull but also pointless. Finding out what everybody ought to or does have in common produces an abstract and empty 'humanness'. What matters is concrete and substantive 'citizenhood'.

The reply to this is that humankind is itself a project as well as this or that branch of it. This notion has a normative and a positive aspect. The normative aspect of it is revealed in the disposition of moral and political philosophers to reflect on right conduct for the whole of humankind and not just a section of it. Natural rights, the rights of man (as species), and human rights have a built-in push towards universal application, and the deprived have their strategy written for them: insist on your common humanity and the wrongfulness of exclusion from the benefits of membership. The positive aspect of it is revealed in the actual

3

spread of a global culture in virtue of the activities, attitudes and artefacts associated with modernization. The doctrine of human rights is not matched by practice in all, or even some, of the world's societies, but there is nevertheless evidence for the existence of global norms (Chapters 3 and 6). What human rights in both the normative and the positive aspects do to international relations is what this study is concerned with.

Part One: Theory

I   The idea of human rights

The idea that human beings have rights as humans is a staple of contemporary world politics. International conventions, both global and regional, state it, at length and in relation to a large number of rights. People speaking for states proclaim it. Groups other than states assert it in its collective form, sometimes as a way of becoming states themselves, sometimes as a bid for recognition of their group-ness by states. Non-governmental organizations make its observance their *raison d'être*. Individuals *in extremis* appeal to it. Reporters presume it. And scholars try to make sense of it, the more so as more use is made of it in the world they seek to understand.

But it is not an obvious idea, however much its proponents may appeal to its supposed self-evidence as a way of entrenching it. As part of moral discourse, duty might seem more obvious, and is certainly more ancient, than right. Until quite recently, the utilitarian doctrine of the greatest happiness of the greatest number has been taken as a more obvious criterion of moral rectitude than the idea of individual rights. And, as a sociological point, it seems more obvious that individuals are gathered together as members of communities that are less than global in extent, than that they stand together as equal members of the society of all humankind.

Since the idea of human rights is not an obvious one, we should begin with an attempt to make it clear. We start with the idea of rights, go on to what is distinctive about *human* rights, then move to the rights that are typically held to *be* human rights, and from there to the grounding of human rights, and finally, at the end of this chapter, to the place of rights-talk in the language of politics.

RIGHTS

When an Australian says, 'She'll be right, mate,' he or she means that things will turn out satisfactorily in the end, and we should not get too anxious about them. When a teacher puts a tick by a sum, a child knows that this means that he or she has produced the right answer. When a minister advises us to do what is right, we understand that we are being enjoined to follow the course that is morally correct. Of these conditions, feeling all right, getting it right, and acting rightly, it is the last that political and moral philosophers have found the most interesting. But it does not constitute the whole of their subject-matter. For there is not only the question of what right conduct is, but also that of what a right is: right used as a noun as well as adjectivally; a right as something one has as well as right as a description of a moral act. This idea of a right as a moral possession or as 'normative property' is the stock-in-trade of lawyers, and their work has been important in the definition of the concept.[1]

A right in this sense can be thought of as consisting of five main elements:[2] a right-holder (the subject of a right) has a claim to some substance (the object of a right), which he or she might assert, or demand, or enjoy, or enforce (exercising a right), against some individual or group (the bearer of the correlative duty), citing in support of his or her claim some particular ground (the justification of a right). Let us take these in turn.

The subject of a right, the right-holder, might be most obviously an individual. But it might also be a group – a family, a tribe, a company, a nation, a state, a region, a culture, even the globe itself (as in the journalists' cry 'the world has a right to know'). Recently, it has been suggested that not only animals, but also trees have rights, and that coasts, rocks and historic buildings might follow.[3] This is not a controversy we are concerned with in this book, but we may note the proliferation of agencies thought capable of bearing rights.

The object of a right is what it is a right to. This may be negative, 'a claim to a secured *space* in which subjects might pursue their own concerns without interference',[4] or it may be positive, a claim that the space be filled with something. Either way, the object to be protected is an interest whose great importance is marked by the attachment of the label 'right'. This special importance of rights in a social system is conveyed by Ronald Dworkin's description of them as 'trumps':[5] they outrank ordinary interests, and they override the utilitarian calculation of communal advantage.

Exercising a right, the activity which connects a subject to an object, takes several forms, of which we may note the most prominent. There is, first, claiming that the right exists in the sense of a claim as a call 'for the acceptability of something admittedly contestable'.[6] Second, there is the same job done more confidently: asserting or demanding a right. Third, there is claiming in the sense of cashing a right: 'You are Lobby Ludd, and I claim the ten-pound prize for spotting you.' Fourth, there is merely enjoying a right, a relaxed form of exercising. And, finally, there are the more energetic versions involved with enforcement: seeking protection against infractions, and demanding compensation for the damage done.

8

Rights, with some exceptions, are held against someone or something. The right of a lender to the repayment of a debt is held against the borrower (this is sometimes called a right *in personam* because it correlates with a specific duty of a particular person). The right of a property owner to exclusive enjoyment of his or her property is held against any person (this is sometimes called a right *in rem* because it correlates with the duty of no specific individual but with a general duty of non-interference).[7] It is the characteristic of correlativity with a duty that is often held to provide the hallmark by which we may know that a right properly so-called exists.[8] Thus it has been suggested that the attribution of a right is meaningless without the possibility of a correlative duty resting somewhere, such that: 'Right and duty are different names for the same normative relation, according to the point of view from which it is regarded.'[9] The number of exceptions spoil the tidiness of this doctrine, of which we may mention two. There is the famous case of the ten-pound note on the promenade.[10] I have a right to pick it up but so does anyone else. They have no obligation not to go for it themselves in virtue of my liberty. And, from the other end of the supposed relationship, we might have duties of charity, but this does not mean that this or that individual or group has a correlative right to it. But despite this untidiness, the basic human rights we shall chiefly be concerned with in this book are ones which fit the pattern of rights having correlative duties.

Finally, there is the question of the justification of a right. In this regard, a right might at the least be conceived as what you can get away with – by lodging a claim to it in the mind of the public and hoping that no one will come up with an objection to it.[11] But a right as a *justified* claim suggests more than this.[12] It suggests social acceptance of the right as of great importance. Then the existence of the social sanction might be said to entitle the bearer of a right to have certain expectations about its enjoyment. Entitlement then rests on social acceptance of the justice of a claim. The type of justification varies. It might (as we shall examine below) appeal to custom, or reason, or statute, or contract. But the form of the defence of rights remains similar: I am entitled to the right *x* (liberty, property) because of *y* (custom, reason).

HUMAN RIGHTS

What does the addition of 'human' to 'rights' in each of these five elements signify?

It means, in the first place, that everybody has them. The subjects of human rights are not members of this or that society, but of the community of humankind. There is some question about full membership in this community, for example for children, or the insane. And there is some doubt as to whether groups can count as members in the sense of themselves being subjects of human rights. But the basic qualification for holding human rights is to belong to the human race.

Secondly, the objects of human rights, like those of plain rights, are of great importance. But just as rights may be said to override other considerations, human rights may be said to override mere rights. The human right to life may be judged to outrank, in a situation where there is a contest between them, a right under a particular civil law, say, to the use of land. Among trumps, it may be said, human rights are the coloured cards, and this is what is meant by references to human rights as absolute rights. It does not mean that human rights are indefeasible. Even the ace of trumps may be topped by a joker (the right not to be tortured, for example, against the need to know where the nuclear bomb has been planted in the Underground), or by a decision to play another game (the transition, for example, from peace to war). It means only that they are, in general, of the greatest importance.[13]

In the third place, the exercise of human rights might have a more restricted range than that of civil rights. We referred earlier to claiming, asserting, demanding, enjoying, protecting and enforcing a right. In the case of human rights, the assertive end of this spectrum is the more prominent. For, very often, human rights are appealed to when the claims they encompass are not locally acknowledged in positive law. The argument is, first, that they should be so acknowledged. Enforcement would then be the next step. The problem with enforcement is that its absence has led sceptics to doubt the existence of human rights – since they take enforcement to be the mark of any rights in the spirit of 'covenants without the sword are but words'. But it is quite possible to have a right to something without the right being enforced. For, as Jack Donnelly has pointed out, if my car is stolen and the thief is not apprehended, I still have a right to the car. This is what he goes on to call the 'possession-paradox', having a right to something but not having it in the sense of enjoying the object of it, which he rightly suggests is characteristic of human rights.[14]

Fourthly, there is the question of the location of the duties that correlate with human rights. In this regard, it has been argued that there are universal human rights in a strong and a weak sense.[15] Rights in the strong sense are held against everybody else. Rights in the weak sense are held against a particular section of humanity. Everyone has a right to life against everyone else: there is a general duty to respect it. But if everyone holds, say, economic and social rights, it is against a particular government: duties are laid only on the responsible authorities. This formulation reveals a certain liberal habit of thought according to which 'negative rights', such as that to liberty, require only an undemanding non-interference, whereas 'positive rights', such as that to education, require substantial provision. We scrutinize this habit of thought in the next section. Meanwhile, we may note a more recent formulation which places the distinction between positive and negative in the duties correlative to human rights and not in the rights themselves.[16] Thus, all (basic) human rights are said to have three correlative duties: duties to *avoid* depriving, duties to *protect* from deprivation and duties to *aid* the deprived. According to circumstances, the duty-bearers may be different (individuals, responsible nations, exploitative companies), and the particular duty varied (aid in a natural disaster, avoidance of deprivation in a monopolistic market). But basic rights trigger all three kinds of duty.

Finally, what is characteristic of the justification of human rights? It is not an appeal to this statute or that contract, for if the rights in question were written into statutes or contracts, those provisions under municipal law would by themselves be sufficient justification. The justification of human rights moves up one level to regional international law (e.g. the European Convention on Human Rights) or two levels to global international law (e.g. the International Covenants on Civil and Political Rights, and on Economic, Social and Cultural Rights), so that the appeal is that standards internationally recognized should be met by domestic practice. And there is a level above these which is the ultimate justification of human rights. It is the level at which what is appealed to is not any kind of positive law, but is what ought by some rational calculation to prevail. Thus, whereas at the beginning of the last section, we separated rights from right, we now join them together. The space protected by human rights is what it is right that people should enjoy. This is the tradition of natural law from which, we shall suggest in Chapter 2, natural rights and then human rights developed. There is more to be said in this chapter about the grounding of rights in nature. But first what are human rights said to be *to* in contemporary international society?

THE LISTS OF HUMAN RIGHTS

There is some warrant, by virtue of usage at the United Nations and elsewhere, to distinguish among civil and political rights, economic and social rights, and collective rights.[17] Civil and political rights include the rights to life, liberty, security of the person, privacy and property; the right to marry and found a family; the right to a fair trial; freedom from slavery, torture and arbitrary arrest; freedom of movement and to seek asylum: the right to a nationality; freedom of thought, conscience and religion; freedom of opinion and expression; freedom of assembly and association; and the right to free elections, universal suffrage and participation in public affairs.[18] Economic and social rights include the right to work and for a just reward; the right to form and join trade unions; the right to rest and leisure, and to periodic holidays with pay; the right to a standard of living adequate to health and well-being; the right to social security; the right to education; and the right to participation in the cultural life of a community.[19]

Collective rights include those of nations to self-determination, of races to freedom from discrimination, and of classes to freedom from neo-colonialism.[20]

These groups of rights form together a long list. Its very length prompts the attempt to shorten it if the adjective 'human' really is to be applied only to very important rights. One conservative attempt on this task, made by Maurice Cranston, is that which recognizes only the civil and political rights of individuals as human rights properly so-called.[21] They are the most important: plainly, the right to life is superior to that to holidays with pay. And the claims they press are for moral necessities which can immediately be met. Establishing the right to life merely requires legislation against murder. Establishing the right to holidays with pay requires not only the provision of employment, which is beyond some of the world's most advanced industrial societies, but also some substantial fringe benefit. By the standard of what is very important, and what can be achieved now, so-called economic and social rights do not qualify. Human rights are concerned with what must be honoured now, not with what it might be nice to provide for some day.

There is a weak and a strong response to this position. The weak response concedes that economic and social rights are different from civil and political rights.[22] But this is not because economic and social rights are generally less important. The rights to subsistence, and to a form of social security, and to education, and to employment, to quote from Tom Paine's list of the rights of man,[23] are not small matters. Nor should the difficulty of providing for these rights be used to dismiss them as rights. It is hard to achieve a perfect score in defence of the right to security against violence, but it would be odd to argue that this justified the abandonment of the right.[24] The difference between economic and social rights and civil and political rights, according to the weak response, lies in the scope of their universality.[25] Civil and political rights are universal in the broader sense. They are rights held against everyone else. Economic and social rights are universal in the narrower sense. Everybody has them, but they impose duties only on particular governments.

The strong response concedes no general difference between civil and political rights and economic and social rights in point either of their importance or of the scope of their correlative obligations. The right to subsistence (an economic and social right), it argues, is quite as important as the right to security (a civil and political right); starvation is quite as much a threat as violence. Moreover, importance varies as much within the groups of rights as between them, so the problem of priority in human rights cannot be construed as one of deciding between the groups.[26] When Cranston compares important liberty rights with less important economic rights, it is, as has been pointed out, 'no more valid than choosing a very bright yellow and a very dull red to demonstrate that yellow is brighter than red'.[27]

Nor is the distinction between negative and positive rights a helpful one for the establishment of the relative importance of human rights. For the supposedly negative civil and political right to security of life might require a network of 'positive' arrangements – such as the provision of adequate policing – before there is confidence that the right can be comfortably enjoyed. Equally, the supposedly positive right of subsistence might merely require a 'negative' arrangement – such as the withdrawal of interference – in order to allow a person to provide for himself or herself.[28] There is, in this regard, the possibility that the failure to provide for subsistence universally is not an unfortunate accident of international politics, but something which is built into the structure of the system.[29] In any event, the assertion of a right to subsistence might be held to require a rearrangement of things in order to provide for it, and this question is investigated in Part Three of this book.

The doctrine asserting the primacy of civil and political rights seems to assume that all problems in regard to providing for subsistence are taken care of,[30] while at the same time being hesitant to call such provision a right on the ground that meeting it would be impracticable. But it makes no sense to speak of a right, for example to liberty, where there is no reliable expectation about the maintenance of life. And yet we are invited to think of such claims as that to subsistence as aspirations rather than rights. It is reasonable to argue, as Cranston does, that talk of human rights should be restricted to things that are supremely sacred,[31] but not to draw from this the conclusion that all economic and social rights fail to qualify under this heading. Sense cannot be made of a right to life unless it is a right to subsistence as well as to security, and we shall carry this interpretation throughout the argument of the book.

What of collective rights? Can they join the front rank of human rights along with the right to security and the right to subsistence? The liberal answer to this question is that they may, provided that they are derived from the rights of individuals and serve to sustain them. So that, for example, the right of individuals to subsistence might confer rights on a group if the organization of the group were somehow integral to the provision of subsistence to individuals – as may indeed be the case with the supply of such things as clean drinking water. But we shall encounter, in Chapter 3, and again in Chapter 5, the assertion as human rights of collective rights that have no such liberal anchorage. This is a difficulty for a liberal theory of human rights which we merely note here and come back to at the places mentioned.

THE GROUNDING OF HUMAN RIGHTS

Human rights are the rights that everyone has, and everyone equally, by virtue of their very humanity. They are grounded in an appeal to our human nature. What does this appeal amount to?

It might, first, take the form of an appeal to our physical nature. Being human involves, generally, having certain physical characteristics – from the standard number of arms and legs, to the need, say, for food, to vulnerability to violence, to a variety of capacities to reason, learn, make and use tools and so on. From a comprehensive physical profile along these lines, a pattern might emerge showing a set of needs requiring to be met if human survival and well-being are to be assured. Thus Christian Bay argues that, in order of importance, there are 'physical survival needs, social belongingness needs, and individual subjectivity needs', which he then uses as the basis for human rights, defined as any claims 'that ought to have legal and moral protection to make sure that basic human needs will be met'.[32]

The difficulty with the appeal to needs as the basis for rights is that it gives us no formula by means of which to translate one into the other.[33] Thus there is a second, and deeper, appeal not to our physical but to our moral nature. This is an appeal not merely to this or that capacity or need, but to a notion of human potentials in the achievement of which we recognize the concept of human dignity. And because of what has been achieved, we know that certain forms of life, the life for example of a slave, do not accord with human dignity, do not meet the standards required by human rights. It is in this context that human rights are sometimes called 'inalienable'. It is not that they cannot be alienated, but that if they are, the life left is not fully human life. The appeal of human rights here is to the 'good' side of our human nature.[34]

If this second kind of appeal suggests that human rights have to do with reaching for the sky of human achievement, there is a third sense in which human rights, as 'basic rights', appeal only to what is rudimentarily necessary for the enjoyment of a dignified life. Thus Henry Shue sees basic rights as those rights (including the right to subsistence and security) which are essential to the enjoyment of all other rights.[35] And Alan Gewirth has worked out a detailed rationalist defence of basic human rights founded on the proposition that 'Because every human being must have certain goods if he is to be able to act either at all or with chances of success in general in achieving his purposes, *it follows that* he has rights to these necessary goods'.[36] Rights in these formulations are not needs-based, despite the references to what is essential and necessary – for the appeal is to what is essential or necessary for a properly human life, not for the fulfilment of basic needs.

There is a seemingly apolitical quality to each of these purported bases for human rights (what is needed, what is transcendentally moral, and what is basic to the enjoyment of other rights – including political rights). They seek what is basic to our humanity, not to our membership of this or that political community. Or, to put the point another way, they establish the values that all political communities should start by providing for. Thus, in the Declaration of the

Rights of Man, 'Le but de toute association politique est la conservation des droits naturels et imprescriptibles de l'homme. Ces droits sont la liberté, la propriété, la sûreté et la résistance à l'oppression.'[37] This is the natural rights tradition marking out limits beyond which political arrangements cannot go.

However, these limits, as we shall see at greater length in Chapter 2, can themselves be rendered as mere political preferences. For this reason, it has been argued that the modern consideration of the theory of human rights should start not with the natural rights tradition, but with the theory of social justice.[38] The argument for severance from the natural law tradition is based on the view that the continuation of the connection leads to a substantial imbalance and to arbitrariness. The imbalance derives from the traditional natural rights preoccupation with civil and political liberties that we have already noticed in another context. And the arbitrariness derives from the neglect, by the natural rights theorists, of information about the actual position of people in society. The insistence, for example, on the right of everyone to property, looks after the interests, not of everyone, but only of property-owners. The argument is that if the ownership of property in any society is uneven, then this is a consideration to be taken into account when working out the principles of social justice. Rights, on this view, should not place barriers in the path of deciding on the political arrangements which would lead to social justice, but should be the outcome of such a decision. Or, in other words, rights should be apportioned at the end of the process of considering what is socially just, rather than placing limits on that process from the beginning.

The difficulty with this doctrine is that it would tend to narrow the distinction between social justice and human rights, the importance of which we may illustrate in two ways. The first has to do with point of view. A theory of social justice and a theory of human rights might both hold that it is not right to break promises. From a rights standpoint the wrong consists in the damage done to the rights of the promisee. From the social justice standpoint, on the other hand, the wrong consists in the unfairness done to those who, by keeping their promises, maintain an institution from which the malefactor generally benefits.[39]

The second illustration has to do with substance. Charles Fried has described common human nature as not merely 'something which each of us possesses singly, though the possession is identical to all – like different examples of the same coin'; it is also a 'single thing which we all share, like the common thread that runs through each bead in a string'.[40] This simile will do admirably for our purposes. Human rights are the coins, and social justice is the beads on the string. Human rights are what ought to be distributed to everybody whatever their circumstances. The rights that arise from the calculation of social justice have to do with the fruits of common labour, or the security of civil society[41] – from the circumstance of connectedness. Rights from both sources have to do with distribution; but whereas everybody equally gets human rights, only unequal sections of humanity get the other kind (until world society as a whole is itself a civil society). This distinction is one we shall return to in deciding what ought to be done about human rights in Part Three of this book.

Although we might reject the social justice theory of human rights as too inclusive,[42] it scores a hit on natural rights theory when it shows it to be the result of human choice about what ought to be, and not that of some extraterrestrial or at least unworldly commandment. Thinking about, writing on, or acting on human rights involves taking sides even if at some rarefied level.[43] It announces a position. And the position is not one for which one calls up empirical evidence in support of a scientific hypothesis. It is more a judgement which one defends as one defends the excellence of an off-drive. To assert that we all ought to enjoy human rights, and all of us equally, and at least the rights of subsistence and security, is thus more than a wager but less than a proof. It suggests that there are some respects in which human beings should be considered as all of equal worth, and challenges those who disagree to come up with a better view.

RIGHTS AND THE LANGUAGE OF POLITICS

Rights have a place in both everyday and scholarly language which it would be odd, if not impossible, to do without. It has become natural to think of rights as things which rules confer at the same time as they impose duties. Yet it might still be argued that the structure of moral language could remain standing without rights by leaving the underside of duties to do their work. This is the notion of rights as 'merely the shadows cast by duties'.[44] There are at least two difficulties with this view. In the first place, there is the problem of knowing where the shadow falls. If having a right is to be rendered merely as being capable of benefiting from the performance of a duty, then there is a puzzle about the identity of the beneficiary.[45] If X, in H.L.A. Hart's famous example, undertakes to look after Y's mother while Y goes out, the mother might be said to have a right in the sense of being the beneficiary of a duty, but the duty is owed to Y. Secondly, if such rights as that to liberty were to be thought of purely in terms of the duties with which they correlated, then they would have to be expressed in the empty language of non-interference. The pattern of argument, if duties were substance and rights shadow, would be from the duty of non-interference to the right to liberty. This seems both topsy-turvy and misleading. It is because liberty is prized as a value that non-interference is a duty. Putting it the other way around is doing political theory backwards. And it is misleading because the attempted discovery of the content of a right by inference from a duty might miss much of its substance. Freedom from, or negative liberty, might be got at via the duty of non-interference; freedom to, or positive liberty, cannot be reached by this route.[46]

Not only are rights an important part of the language of morals, but they have, too, a unique role within that language. It is to denote a particular moral attitude. The demeanour of someone claiming his or her rights is not that of begging or pleading, and the response if the claim is met is not one of gratitude. Equally, if the claim is not met, the response is not one of disappointment but of indignation.[47] This is because rights are insisted on as part of one's status as a person.[48] They are not favours done by the holders of power to those beholden to it. As Alexis de Tocqueville wrote: 'There is nothing which, generally speaking, elevates and sustains the human spirit more than the idea of rights. There is something great and virile in the idea of right which removes from any request its suppliant character, and places the one who claims it on the same level as the one who grants it.'[49] In the same equalizing spirit, rights are invoked against the situation in which some people are at the mercy of others, not out of pity, but from concern for the same values that underpin our own dignity as individuals. Rights are thus a weapon of the weak against the strong.[50] And they are in the front line of moral evaluation and criticism. As Hart stresses, the question 'by what right?' is asked at the point of actual or threatened interference with established values.[51] And if this interference becomes intolerable, then it is the existence of and the need to vindicate the right that might justify the resort to violence in its defence.

The references to the status of persons and to human dignity show how closely the idea of rights is connected to that of political individualism. This is the classical liberal idea of society as made up of independent, rational beings who make up their own minds about what is best for them.[52] Reason establishes their most important interests as rights, and it is the purpose of political arrangements – the social contract – to preserve them. They are the source of political legitimacy, and it is their achievement in some degree that provides for political order. Sociologically speaking, rights sustain this order by contributing to security, and to predictability: security of life, or liberty, or property, against interference; and predictability through the degree of control that rights provide over the actions of others.[53] And if rights connect in these ways to order, their fulfilment has also been regarded as a prerequisite for progress, as, for example, in John Stuart Mill's argument that the advance of civilization depended on the protection of individual liberty.[54]

There are also difficulties that attach to rights, and we shall examine the classical objection to them in the next chapter. Here we may note three cautions about rights that have arisen in the contemporary discussion of politics. The first caution is against the 'extremism of rights'.[55] Just as nationalism tends to make states reluctant to give an inch of their fatherland, rights tend to make individuals insistent on all that is their due. They become righteous. We should always, this caution holds, keep rights in their place within rule-governed activities and practices. The second caution is against the *self*-righteousness of rights.[56] This is the tendency to call *our* rights natural rights or human rights which others should also benefit from or conform to, when they have their own pattern of preferences in this regard (and no doubt their own tendency to universalize them). The third caution combines the first two. It observes that even in the realm of human necessities there is a variety of priorities in the world's societies and not a singularity.[57] Even in the case of the right to bread, the staff of life, its religious use might conflict with its nutritional use. Rights even in this most basic sense are relative to the social context in which they are embedded.

We shall carry these cautions with us through the argument of the book, and the difficulty for a universal conception of human rights in a culturally plural world is confronted directly in Chapter 3. But even if Michael Walzer is right that in 'matters of morality, argument is simply the appeal to common meanings',[58] the implications of this are not, in the contemporary global society, merely to send us to our various localities to find out what rights mean there. For the project of humankind itself, kept alive in the western tradition (but not only in the western tradition) by the idea of natural law, has in the twentieth century some sociological counterpart. One of our tasks (especially in Chapter 6) is to decide on the advance of the global on the local in the matter of rights.

2 Human rights in western political thought

A characteristic part of the claim that there are such things as human rights has been that they are universal, and that they are not subject to change over time – since they express the essential nature of human beings. In fact, there have always been difficulties with the notion of the universality of human rights. These will be examined in relation to contemporary world politics in Chapter 3, and in relation to the debate within a western tradition in this chapter. But the chief concern of this chapter is with the fact of change over time. Human rights did not just happen, they had to be invented; and their proponents had constantly to defend them against the view that they were chimerical. Even the naturalist account, according to which what we now call human rights were not invented but discovered (or, in an earlier period, revealed), accommodates change by suggesting that the process of discovery is not once and for all. And whether it is a story of discovery or of invention, it is the evolution of the idea of human rights in western thought that is the main subject-matter of this chapter.

This involves going into the history of ideas, but not in Sir Herbert Butterfield's exhausting sense of analysing 'all the mediations by which the past was turned into the present'.[1] The attempt here will be merely to visit the main stations along the way, and to preserve thereby the generality of the idea of human rights. If this does violence to proper historical explanation, the excuse is that our task here is to provide a backdrop to the discussion of human rights in contemporary international politics, rather than to follow a historical path wherever it may take us. The chapter has three parts. The first is concerned with the emergence and evolution of natural and then human rights doctrine; the second deals with the criticism of that doctrine from a number of standpoints in the western political tradition; and the third examines the contemporary debate on the theory of human rights. The conclusion will attempt to establish the place of human rights in contemporary western thought, so that a platform may be established from which an even more general question can be asked, in Chapter 3, about the place of human rights in world politics at large.

FROM NATURAL LAW TO HUMAN RIGHTS

The main stations along the route to the modern idea of human rights are, it might be said, well enough established. First come the Stoics, so influential in Roman jurisprudence, who started the process off by disparaging the parochialism of the classical Greek *polis*, and upholding the idea of a single city of mankind in which the equal worth of all individuals was recognized, and also their participation, on rational grounds, in a great common enterprise. Then, secondly, there is the fortification of both aspects of this doctrine – its individualism, and its conception of a global community – in the Christian gospel of individual salvation, and the actual or potential unity of all people in Christ. In the third place, there is the double-station marking the assault on medieval ideas by the Renaissance and the Reformation: the Renaissance humanists' heroic view of man, which allowed a view of him as capable of the responsibility of bearing rights; and the reformers' view of the obligations of conscience, which led eventually to the establishment of an individual's right to rebel. The great transition in the progressive societies, which Sir Henry Maine characterized as being the change from status to contract,[2] might be rendered, on an individual level, as a movement from duty to right, culminating in the French Revolution and the Declaration of the Rights of Man and of the Citizen. And, finally, there is the contribution of German romantic thought in the nineteenth century, which took exception to what it saw as the extreme individualism and negativism of French ideas about rights, and caused the writers of manifestoes on human rights in our own century to admit group rights on an equal footing with those of individuals, and to try to make sense of positive freedom as well as freedom merely against something. The transition, in this last phase, is from natural rights to human rights, and we shall have occasion to inquire whether this is a matter of substance or merely of labelling.

Greece and Rome

Scrutinized more closely, these stations, so prominent from a distance, begin to lose their clarity of outline. The account of Natural Law, which begins with the Roman idea of a universal system of laws,[3] is in fact dependent not merely on Stoic cosmopolitanism, but also on the earlier Greek discovery of the idea of nature. By opposing what belonged to people naturally – by virtue of their instincts, or their creativity in harmony with instinct, or their final purpose[4] – to the conventions that they happen to have established, the Greeks allowed two kinds of distinction that were important in the subsequent development of the theory of natural rights. In the first place, an ideal world constructed on rational principles from a theory of nature could be set alongside the real one, permitting criticism of the mundane and not mere conformity to what was customary.[5] And, secondly, it meant that what was general, common to all societies because common to all natures, could be set apart from what was particular, relative, to the several societies of the world. It was to this idea of the natural that Antigone appealed in defiance of King Creon's edict that her brother Polynices should remain unburied on the battlefield because he had fought traitorously against his own city.[6] And it was an appeal that showed the incompleteness of the moral community of the *polis*, which was the subject of classical political theory.

In treating justice as a quality that existed in a whole community, a *polis*, Plato, and also Aristotle, had subordinated the good of the individual to that of the state, and allowed him no appeal beyond the *polis* to any wider notion of community. Stoic doctrine, reflecting, no doubt, in the Greek period the Hellenization of much of the world by Alexander the Great, and in the Roman period the imperial integration of diverse cultures, broke open the enclosed community of the *polis* and upheld the individual as an independent moral agent. The master concept, making this development possible, was that of reason yoked to nature. The Stoic ideal of 'living agreeably to nature' had an external and an internal aspect from the point of view of the individual. It supposed that there was a natural order in the world at large, governed by reason, and that it benefited individuals to discover and live in conformity with this order. And, internally, the individual was to subordinate will to reason in order to live a moral life.[7]

While the individual had, in these respects, a central place in Stoic ethical thought, it was not at the expense of the older idea of obligation to community. Virtue was still a social thing. The difference was that the idea of community did not stop at the frontiers of the *polis*, or at any other more or less arbitrary divide. For the community was not one of kinship or neighbourhood, but of reason, and this was universal.[8] The individual belonged to a universal community which existed by nature and whose rules were apprehended by the use of reason.

These are the rules of Natural Law, which Cicero described as 'of universal application, unchanging and everlasting . . . we cannot be freed from its obligations by Senate or People, and we need not look outside ourselves for an expounder or interpreter of it. And there will not be different laws at Rome and at Athens, or different laws now and in the future, but one eternal and unchangeable law will be valid for all nations and for all times, and there will be one master and one ruler, that is, God . . .'[9] In this passage, Cicero foreshadows both the *ius naturale* of Roman law and the Christian idea of a universal law.[10] And Cicero's conception of the equality of men, a single definition applying to all men because all have received the gift of right reason, has been located as 'the beginning of a theory of human nature and society of which the "Liberty, Equality and Fraternity" of the French Revolution is only the present-day expression'.[11]

The Middle Ages

Let us take first the bridge to Roman law. Each of the three divisions of the Roman law had a part in the foundations on which natural rights were constructed. The *ius naturale*, not as a body of law so much as a way of interpreting it, kept alive the idea of a universal and rational standard of justice.[12] The *ius gentium*, in its practical definition as a body of law which applied in cases that might involve foreigners as well as citizens, provided something like the fact of universality to accompany the theory of natural law.[13] And even the *ius civile* – an improbable source for universal rights, being the law which applied only among Roman citizens – also played a practical part in forming the basis of the canon law which applied in the ecclesiastical courts of the Middle Ages. Roman law in this form was 'the law of an international civilization, and relatively universal'.[14]

It may be, however, that it was not by running with the ball of a universal law that Roman jurisprudence made its chief contribution to the evolution of the modern idea of a right, but by providing the wherewithal for a new sense of *ius* (as a right as well as what was rightful) derived from the concept of *dominium* (proprietory power).[15] The ancient doctrine was that under the *ius naturale* everything was held and used in common. There were no natural property rights. Property rights came in by way of the *ius gentium*, which recognized the fact of possession by identifying rights that came to be defended as natural rights in order to defeat the old idea that the *ius naturale* ruled out *dominium*. Then the defence of a right to private property as coming from nature, because it allowed the cultivation that made survival possible, was stretched to include not merely possessions but the faculties of individuals: control over one's life came to be described as the exercise of a *dominium*. And so the natural rights to life, liberty and property (which are associated, as starting-places for political theory, with Locke) were all derived from an idea of possession borrowed from the Roman-law concept of *dominium*, going back, it is argued, to the French scholar Gerson in the fourteenth and early fifteenth century, and before him to the twelfth century. In the course of this process, it is suggested, *dominium* had become a *ius*, and ius *had* taken on an additional meaning: what was rightful, good or just was now joined by a right in the modern sense of a moral possession.

Meanwhile, the canon law of the Middle Ages was raising natural law above its place in Roman jurisprudence, and having it come before positive law in both origin and dignity.[16] In medieval political theory, it was the law which expressed the organic unity of the whole of mankind. The fact of disunity, such as in the division between church and state, was rationalized by reference to a theoretical synthesis at a higher level – the papal claim to overlordship of both the spiritual and the temporal domains.[17] But as the facts, not merely of this twofold division but also of the plurality of independent states, became more and more palpable, the medieval doctrine of unity became harder to sustain. And when it gave way, according to Otto Gierke, it revealed the 'antique-modern' theory, which looked back to the ancient theory of the state, and forward to a new theory of natural law based on the individual.[18] So the 'fundamental fact' at the close of the Middle Ages was the obliteration by the state and the individual of all intermediate groups in society,[19] and it is in the contest between the victors that the western theory of human rights is worked out.

Renaissance and Reformation

The emergence of the individual from the communal cocoon of the Middle Ages is celebrated in Renaissance humanism. Now it is legitimate, indeed it is part of the definition of man, to pursue excellence in everything, to pit human creativity against the hand dealt by fortune, and to accept the glory that goes with success in this enterprise.[20] But if this was the platform from which the idea of the individual dignified by the responsibility of bearing rights as well as duties could eventually be launched, there was before this the extreme reaction to Renaissance *hubris* in the view of man taken by the early reformers. The importance of this, in turn, was first to unshackle the absolutist state, and then to assemble a theory of resistance against it which ended up with individual rights.

Against the humanist view of the dignity of man was placed, in the early Reformation, Luther's idea of his total unworthiness, his fallen nature and his inability to escape from sin except by the grace of God.[21] And along with this miserable estimate of the worth of individuals went a return to medieval ideas that were careless of mere worldly arrangements. 'For what doth it matter in respect of this short and transitory life,' St Augustine had asked, 'under whose dominion a mortal man doth live as long as he be not compelled to acts of impiety or injustice?'[22] This idea was sharpened by Luther to enjoin the obedience of Christians to the secular authorities by reference to St Paul's command, 'Let every soul be subject unto the higher powers. For there is no power but of God; the powers that be are ordained of God.'[23] And this was interpreted to mean that it was wrong to resist even tyrannical rulers; even particularly wrong to do so because tyrannical rule had been established because of the people's sins.[24]

This was the doctrine that legitimized the absolutist state, but it was not a legitimacy that went unchallenged. There were, firstly, the arguments against it already available from medieval and older political theory. From the later Middle Ages came the idea that political authority resided in the body of the people; that the lordship of an individual prince was only a temporary and representative exercise of a power in the polity, an office or function; and that there was a right arising from the popular sovereignty of an assembly of the people to depose

23

magistrates who failed to fulfil their proper functions.[25] And from an older tradition came the Roman private-law power to use force against unjust force, and the injunction of natural law, emphasized by Aquinas, that every man-made law must derive from it and serve to give the moral law force in the world.[26]

In the second place, there were the arguments against absolutism that added to the stock of political theory, and that were worked out in the battle with it. The reformers found themselves at precisely the point at which Augustine had seemed to allow an interest in government – that is, where they were compelled to acts of impiety or injustice. In these circumstances, they came to focus not on the citizen's duty of obedience, but on the ruler's obligation to govern justly. If he failed to do this, it came to be argued, then he may be regarded as having ceased to be a power 'ordained of God'.[27] And from here the way was open to the argument that tyrants are not the institutions of God, but the mistakes of men.[28]

In correcting such errors lay part of what came to be the right of resistance. But it was a duty before it was a right: Christians, according to Calvinist doctrine, had covenanted with God to do what they could to remove evil, and they broke that covenant if they endured a tyrannical prince. The last step from a duty to a right of resistance was taken in the Huguenot struggle against the French government in the late sixteenth century.[29] If the early reformers had insisted on the liberty of princes, who derived their right to rule directly from God, to determine the religion of their subjects, the problem of the later reformers was that of providing the domestic dissenter with a political defence against his prince. Huguenot political theory achieved this in two stages. The first consisted in a constitutionalist appeal to the checks on the power of the monarch, established over centuries, in order to demonstrate to all Frenchmen, and not merely to the Huguenots, the excesses of the present authorities against Frenchmen. And the second returned to natural law. But it was not the natural law that had been exclusively about obligation, but one which took natural liberty as the starting-place for political society. This was taken to be axiomatic, since magistrates were made by people and not people by magistrates, and any infraction of the liberty and security of the people, for which the original contract was said to have been made, was now thought to trigger a right of resistance. So, to the Calvinist doctrine of an individual's covenant with God was added the medieval notion of a contract between the king and representatives of the people, and to a religious duty was added a political right.

It was a right cautiously advanced, and there was, even in the late sixteenth century, still a preference for the language of duty.[30] But in the course of the Reformation the modern sense of right had been established in a usage sufficiently general to include conservative as well as radical thinkers. The Spanish sixteenth-century jurist Francisco Suarez thought the true meaning of *ius* to be 'a certain moral power which every man has, either over his own property or with respect to that which is due to him.'[31] There is in this definition not only the idea of a right as a power over possession, but also the equally modern idea of a right as something which imposes a duty on others. And this allows the notion, absent from classical Roman law, of law as a system of rules connecting up rights and duties.

If the reciprocity of rights and duties means that the content of the law can be got at just as easily from either end of a legal relationship, it is the Dutch jurist Grotius in the seventeenth century who suggests that we should make it a habit to start with rights. In his work, it has been said, the law of nature becomes 'respect one another's rights'.[32] Then his contemporary Hobbes pushes the idea of right beyond legal restraint by calling it a liberty to do or to forbear – contrasted with law, 'which bindeth to one of them' – and allowing, in the form of a right of nature, anything which is necessary to an individual's self-preservation.[33]

In Locke's work later in the seventeenth century, so often taken as the foundation of modern natural rights theory, by virtue chiefly of his impact on the American Revolution, these earlier developments join up. The *dominium* of the scholastic philosophers becomes the right to property, meaning life and liberty as well as mere possession (though a property in one's own person does not in Locke entail a right to enslave oneself, as some earlier writers had argued).[34] The Huguenot theory of popular resistance to a tyrannical prince becomes in Locke an individual right of resisting.[35] And from Grotius and Hobbes comes the notion of individual rights as the starting-place for political theory, the purpose for the achievement of which the social contract is agreed.

The French Revolution and the nineteenth century

Its individualism, together with its rationalism and its radicalism, have been taken to be the distinguishing marks of the theory of natural rights that underpinned the French and American Revolutions.[36] The theory was individualist both in its assumption that individuals came before communities in the imagined history of the state of nature and the origin of civil society, and in its assertion of the priority of the moral claim that individuals had over groups. The social contract catered for both these aspects of individualism by providing the means through which rational and autonomous people could construct a society, and by taking the purpose of the contract to be the better provision for the values of the individuals who agree it.

In political theory of this kind, reason has a prominent part. But by the rationalism of modern rights theory is meant chiefly two things: the idea that reason can act alone in political life without the assistance of authority, or tradition, or God; and the notion of the constructive power of rational thought. This is Tom Paine's retort to Burke's astonishment at the French Revolution. It was not a creation from chaos, but the consequence of a mental revolution. 'The mind of the Nation had changed beforehand, and the new order of things has naturally followed the new order of thoughts.'[37]

In this trust in the power of thought to produce social change lay part of the radicalism of the theory of rights. And beneath this was the more substantial idea of the theory of rights predisposing revolution because it had become detached from the discipline of duty, or even from any legal constraint. So that in the passage from natural law to natural right, from objective principles to subjective claims, it is often reasonably argued, there is a substantial discontinuity in the naturalist tradition even though, as we have seen, the change was effected in a series of small steps.

However this may be, French revolutionary doctrine now took the failure to observe the rights of man to be the cause of all public misery, much as earlier conservatives had blamed the neglect of degree, and later radicals were to find fault with the exclusion of a particular class. The preamble to the Declaration of the Rights of Man and of the Citizen announced that 'ignorance, neglect, or contempt of human rights, are the sole causes of public misfortunes and corruptions of Government'.[38] And while this diagnosis of social ills has been an important theme of liberal political theory down to the present day, it is not one that went unchallenged at the time of its invention – even by the proponents of the theory of revolution themselves. Indeed, Article 3 of the Declaration seemed to come up with a rival doctrine in its description of the nation as 'essentially the source of all sovereignty; nor can any individual, or any body of men, be entitled to any authority which is not expressly derived from it'. In this regard, Rousseau, whose influence on French revolutionary doctrine is clear, has been described as a Janus-like figure in the history of natural law, manifesting its individualism and universalism, but looking forward to romantic German thought in his idea of the general will.[39]

The stress on the community, which the doctrine of general will presaged, weakened each of the three props of the theory of natural rights. The individualism which arrived at the state through social contract theory was set aside by the idea of the state as itself a real personality with the capacity to will and to act. And instead of showing the community to be the outcome of individual decision, the emphasis was on the extent to which the individual was shaped by the community: language, law, morality were all the products of society. 'Individuals pass like shadows,' Burke said, 'but the commonwealth is fixed and stable.'[40]

The rationalism of the theory of natural rights also suffered from the new stress on community. Against a universal natural law based on reason was placed a particular national law based on the spirit of an historical community – the *Volksrecht*, 'the product, in each nation, of the national genius'.[41] Instead of the *ius gentium intra se* (the law of nations within the state), which had expressed that part of any legal system which was common to all legal systems, the new concern was with what set the systems apart from each other, and with ridding them of artificial foreign elements. The revolt of the Nation against *Natura* has been called 'the essence of the revolution in German thought'.[42]

The radicalism of the theory of natural rights went the same way as its individualism and rationalism. The treasure of liberty was a possession to be secured, rather than a prize to be contended for by political exertions.[43] Society required that the inclinations of men 'should frequently be thwarted, their will controlled, and their passions brought into subjection.'[44] Not rights but duties, not nature but convention, not reason but authority: this seemed to be the result of the return to the medieval, or even ancient, stress on the community above the individual.

Certainly, it was the recapturing of the ancient Greek sense of solidarity with the *polis*, the community, that provided part of the incentive for the work of the German philosopher Hegel in the nineteenth century.[45] But this was not to be done at the expense of the liberty of the individual. Rather, individual freedom was to be realized in the political community through a synthesis which provided a view of history as a vehicle for the *Geist*, the cosmic spirit uniting man and society in a larger whole. To the *Moralität* of his predecessor Kant, concerned merely with what individuals ought to do, Hegel added the higher imperative of *Sittlichkeit*, the moral obligation to the community in which there was no gap between ought and is, because is had matched ought.[46] Freedom reigned once this was achieved. And this, it has been said, is the great distinction between the liberal conceptions of the eighteenth and nineteenth centuries: 'The one places liberty at the beginning, the other at the end of the historical process.'[47]

The importance of this, from the viewpoint of the history of human rights, is its elevation of group rights to a dignity equal to or greater than those of individuals. Such group rights as that to self-determination, so important, as we shall see, in contemporary world politics, may be traced back to the French Revolution, but are consolidated in German thought. And the idea of self-determination connects to that of positive freedom, which, in the twentieth-century discussion of human rights, has had an equal claim with that of the negative liberty associated with Locke and the eighteenth century that followed him. The economic and social rights which are often associated with Marx's criticism of bourgeois rights, and which the countries with Marxist-Leninist ideologies lay a special claim to, are in some degree the product of nineteenth-century thought about what is now called positive freedom.

THE CLASSICAL CRITICISM OF THE THEORY OF NATURAL RIGHTS

Before this positive contribution to ideas about rights in the twentieth century came the attack on the eighteenth-century idea of natural rights. It was an attack that began as soon as, some say even before, the ink was dry on the Declaration of the Rights of Man, and it came from all political directions. Here it is intended to look, first, at Burke and Hegel, then at Bentham, and finally at Marx. These authors, taken together, constitute what can be called the classical objection to the theory of natural rights.

Close to the heart of Burke's criticism of the theory was its tendency to turn the complexities of politics into the false simplicity of metaphysical abstraction. Natural rights, so clear and seemingly unequivocal, were foreign to the complex nature of politics, which consisted in manoeuvre, adjustment, and, above all, attention to circumstances, which gave 'to every political principle its distinguishing colour'.[48] Against the 'Rights of Men,' he said, 'there can be no prescription; against these no agreement is binding; these admit no temperament, and no compromise; anything withheld from their full demand is so much of fraud and injustice.'[49] The language of rights deepened the antagonism of political opponents while raising their expectations, and made more difficult the task of the statesmen, which was to bring them together. Worse, the rights of man led down a path to anarchy. They were among the pretexts behind which 'pride, ambition, avarice, revenge, lust, sedition, hypocricy, ungoverned zeal, and all the train of disorderly appetites hide'.[50] From these nobody was safe. The rights of man of the Jacobins were a challenge not merely to this or that ruler, but to civil society itself, and it was out of this fear that Burke regarded the events of the revolution as a European civil war rather than a local French difficulty.[51]

The correct way to think about rights, according to Burke, was in terms of the ancient and indisputable laws and liberties inherited from our forefathers, and this meant particular rights, the rights of Englishmen, not the rights of man.[52] Property rights were the model for all rights, and the agency for their establishment was prescription from time immemorial, 'an *entailed inheritance* derived to us from our forefathers'.[53] And the mechanism for generalizing the prescription associated with property to embrace all rights is that of 'prejudice', the 'latent wisdom' in a community predisposing its members to the established way of doing things without the necessity of submitting it to the test of reason.[54] Rights had a part in this pattern, but it was better that it be discerned than defined, felt as much as thought.[55] Civil society was to be interpreted, not as a collection of right- and duty-bearing individuals who were united by some abstract principle of equality, but as a differentiated community in which wants were satisfied according to ancient rituals, and to which people were attached more by sentiment than by mere advantage. Even if society was a contract, its

28

ends could not be maintained except in many generations, and it was a partnership therefore between the living, the dead and those yet to be born.[56]

Burke, then, brought down the three props of the theory of the rights of man single-handed. Its rationalism was defeated by the idea that commonwealths grow rather than being constructed. Its individualism was confronted by the injunction that mere temporary possessors of the commonwealth 'should not think it amongst their rights to cut off the entail, or commit waste on the inheritance, by destroying at their pleasure the whole original fabric of their society; hazarding to leave to those who come after them, a ruin instead of an habitation.'[57] And its radicalism was weighed down by the attention to custom, and to the wisdom of our ancestors.

In Hegel's writing, there was a good deal to be found that was similar to Burke. There was the same concern to fill in the gap between the individual and the state in the recognition that all manner of intermediate attachments helped bind the community together more firmly than could a mere contract. There was the same notion of society as differentiated and hierarchical rather than uniform and equal. And there was the same fear that the doctrine of absolute freedom would lead to the destruction of the social order. Unlike Burke, however, Hegel was disposed to find the universal rationality behind these institutions, rather than to doubt with Burke that such an investigation was wise.[58]

Hegel did not deny that there were rights of individuals to life, liberty and property. Indeed they formed the basis for man's participation in civil society. But this was not civil society in Locke's sense. Hegel meant by it the system of needs that were met by exchange in the market – and this was a society into which men entered as men, and not as members of a particular community.[59] But political society was about the particular community, and, in regard to participation in this, private rights meant very little. This was because freedom, in the negative sense of the Enlightenment, meant the freedom merely to choose between passions and impulses if there was no control over the contents of choice.[60] And such control, to allow genuine self-expression, required the integration of the independent individual into a larger conception of liberty which could be worked out only in the community as a whole.[61] 'Since the state is mind objectified,' said Hegel, 'it is only as one of its members that the individual himself has objectivity, genuine individuality, and an ethical life.'[62]

So, while Burke upheld the social bond of prejudice almost as a substitute for reason, Hegel sought a reasonable justification of it: not, that is, in the superficial reason of the revolutionaries, but in a deeper sense of history as the working out of reason through individual and collective wills.[63] Nor was his doctrine as conservative and anti-radical as Burke's, since, as Charles Taylor points out, the notion of reason in history could be used on the opposite side as it was by Marx.[64] But Hegel did match Burke's anti-individualism, and, as has been observed, his idea of the real unity of the group looks forward to an important strand in the theory of human rights in the twentieth century.

Bentham, the founder of utilitarianism, was more coldly destructive of the theory of natural rights of the French revolutionaries than either Burke or Hegel. First of all, they had made a simple mistake of philosophical method. They imagined that principles preceded consequences, whereas in fact particular propositions always came before general ones, which were built up on the basis of agreement among the particular.[65] Then the generality of the propositions made it difficult to keep them within the bounds of truth and reason. And this was compounded by another scientific error, that of appealing to abstract propositions for proof of the existence of abstract propositions and so begging the question.[66]

The propositions themselves were simply nonsense anyway. Plainly, men were not born free, nor did they remain so, any more than they were born equal and remained so. All men were born in subjection to their parents; into families unequally endowed, to live lives in a society constructed on inequality – apprentice and master, ward and guardian, wife and husband.[67] So these pretended indefeasible rights were false, and to make matters worse, inconsistent with each other.[68] And the nonsense was not harmless as an improper word might be in a play or a novel, but dangerous because in a body of laws such a thing might be a national calamity: 'out of one foolish word may start a thousand daggers.'[69]

If the theory of natural rights was useless, superfluous and exaggerated nonsense, why did the revolutionaries invoke it? They did so not only to justify the revolution in France, but also 'to excite and keep up a spirit of resistance to all laws – a spirit of insurrection against all governments'.[70] Here, Bentham was as frightened of anarchy as Burke, and as contemptuous of the selfishness of rights as Hegel. Society was held together by the sacrifices that men could be induced to make by those practised in the art of government, and talk of rights parted the cords that held in the selfish passions.[71] There was also an antipathy for France more parochial than Burke's Europeanism: there was nothing in the theory of the rights of man, but if there were it was an English achievement not a French one, and 'the nerve of vanity in a French heart' had led them to suppose that they knew the rights of Englishmen (and everybody else) better than they did themselves.[72]

The reason that rights could be called, if anyone's, an English achievement, rather than a French one, was that here right had arisen as the child of law. From real law came real rights, but from imaginary laws, such as the law of nature, came imaginary rights.[73] Sense could be made of a political system only by reading from government to law to rights and not in the opposite direction. Social contract theory was another piece of nonsense. There was no such thing; contracts came from governments, not governments from contracts.[74]

Marx's objection to the theory of natural rights had more in common with those of Burke and Hegel than that of Bentham, although its thrust was revolutionary rather than conservative. The French revolutionary theory was not a silly mistake, though it might not tell us as much about society as its proponents thought. Rather, it was a theory with a limited application in time and space which had to be interpreted in the light of the political interests it was designed to defend. Thus the rights of man took on their most 'authentic' form 'among those who *discovered* them, the North Americans and the French',[75] and they described the outlook not of all men, but only of bourgeois man.[76]

Bourgeois man was the person participating in civil society in the sense (borrowed from Hegel) that was opposed to political society. And he participated in civil society as an egoistic man 'separated from other men and from the community'.[77] His right to liberty was a right to this separateness, to be independent of others, an 'isolated monad'.[78] The practical application of this right to liberty lay in the right of private property, and, as powerfully argued by C.B. Macpherson, freedom in the liberal theory of rights is a function of possession.[79] Then civil society can be rendered as the relations of exchange among proprietors, and political society as the arrangements made to protect property and orderly exchange. Locke is above all the champion of property, and having derived a right to property from natural law, he then removed all natural law limitations from it.[80] Thus the idea of society based on a contract agreed by individuals guarding their moral possessions becomes *The Political Theory of Possessive Individualism*.

This was a theory that institutionalized separateness. Its definition of human nature had man 'squatting outside the world', whereas 'human nature' always belonged to a particular kind of social man, being the product not of nature but of history.[81] It misunderstood man's character as a *Zoön politikon*, 'not only a social animal, but an animal which can develop into an individual only in society'.[82] Like Hegel, Marx was concerned to reintegrate the civil with the political, and on the pattern of the Greek *polis*, to bring together *l'homme* and *le citoyen*.[83]

In Marxist thought, then, the theory of natural rights is the special language of a group defending a particular pattern of interests. It is a language that, in the eighteenth century, might have been appropriate, and progressive in getting rid of feudal remnants, but its use outside the context is to be suspected as an attempt to make an unequal distribution of property acceptable to the least advantaged. Certainly, it provides no objective standard, as it would in the theory of natural law, by which to judge the strength of any political claim.[84] So, against the rationalism of the theory of natural rights, stands Marx's historicism; against its individualism stands a Hegelian insistence on the possibility of freedom only through community; and to its radicalism is added an insistence on a new revolution that would, in advancing the disadvantaged class, sweep away the debris of the old advantaged one.

The theory of natural rights has, then, come under fire from all points of the political compass. In the conclusion of this chapter we shall have to decide how much of the theory survives the onslaught. Before that, there is the question of the place of 'rights-talk' in contemporary western political theory.

HUMAN RIGHTS IN CONTEMPORARY WESTERN POLITICAL THEORY

We have surveyed the onward march of the theory of natural rights from its roots in antiquity to its radical reformulation in the light of romantic criticism of the impoverished rationalism of the Enlightenment. What is striking about the place of natural rights thought in contemporary western political theory is not the achievement of some great new synthesis, or of some major new discovery allowing us to treat the history of natural rights doctrine as merely its preface, part of prehistory, but the extent to which positions, seemingly well enough established to be transcended, continue to be defended by reference to the tradition which established them. The marching is as much round and round as ever onward. We shall illustrate this by reference to what some have called the revival of natural law doctrine; to the continued taking of rights as a starting-place for political theory; and to the persistent disposition in the largest western democracy to 'take rights seriously'.

Human rights are taken by some writers to be simply the contemporary expression for natural rights, corresponding to natural duties in the classical rendering of the law of nature. Human rights, in this context, have been said to express 'virtually all the requirements of practical reasonableness'.[85] The principles of practical reasonableness are those which make possible the achievement of the end of the basic goods of 'human flourishing' by connecting up nature and reason.[86] These basic goods include life, knowledge, play, aesthetic experience, sociability and religion.[87] Knowledge can be taken as the paradigm explanation of what it is to be a basic good. The good of knowledge is self-evident. We show this when we accept 'finding out' as a sufficient answer to the question of what someone is up to when he or she is pursuing knowledge.[88] And we confirm it by the observation that the sceptical assertion that knowledge is not a good is 'operationally self-refuting': anyone who, intending to be taken seriously, asserted that knowledge was not a good, must himself or herself believe it to be true; but the proposition asserts that the truth is not worth knowing, and therefore there is a contradiction.

Human rights have a part in this account of human flourishing by providing the infrastructure by means of which it is achieved. And they can be accepted as part of natural law doctrine, despite their rather unfortunate associations with 'fanatics, adventurers, and self-interested persons', for three reasons.[89] They stress equality, and make of justice a prominent political issue. They are anticonsequentialist by their insistence that moral worth is to be judged not by the effect of an action, but by whether or not it would be right to do it in the first place according to certain ends that must be respected. And they provide, together, a checklist of the aspects of human flourishing.

Human rights, in this account, not only belong in the tradition of natural law, but also, and more importantly, are part of the working out of the law of nature in the contemporary world.[90] A theory of human rights can also be derived from H.L.A. Hart's much less ambitious idea of the 'minimum content of Natural Law'.[91] Given a number of elementary generalizations about men and the world in which they live, says Hart, it is possible to deduce certain rules of conduct (the minimum content of natural law) without whose observation in some degree social organization would disintegrate. Thus, because of human vulnerability, there must be some rule about the restriction of violence. Because of limited resources, there must be rules which protect the property on which industry is based, and the institutions of exchange involved in the division of labour necessary for the survival of all but the smallest societies. And, because of men's limited understanding and strength of will, there must be sanctions to discipline those who would not voluntarily obey the rules.

There is a weak and a strong sense in which human rights may be said to have a part in this scheme of things. The weak sense consists simply in the application of the logic of legal language. If there is a rule against the use of violence, then the people to whom it applies can be said to have a duty to observe it, and also a right (in virtue of the existence of the same rule) not to be the victims of violence. But here the notion of a right is not doing any work; it is merely a different way of expressing a rule. We may seek the strong sense of a right, in which it does do some pulling of its own, by pursuing Hart into his own qualifications of the doctrine of the minimum content of natural law. It is plain, he says, 'that neither the law nor the accepted morality of societies need extend their minimal protection and benefits to all within their scope, and often they have not done so'.[92] And he illustrates this by reference to slave-owning societies in which to be a slave was to be more an object of use than a subject of rights. Our strong sense of a human right may consist in the criticism of this situation and in the protest against it on the grounds that natural principles ought to apply to all human beings and not, arbitrarily, to a section of humanity only. The appeal here is to the universality and to the equality integral to the idea of human rights.

Whether the content of natural law is minimal, as in Hart, or maximal, as in John Finnis, human rights appear in the theory as a subordinate part of a much larger whole, and thus assimilate with a tradition that predates the eighteenth-century theory of natural rights. Other contemporary theories are closer to that of the eighteenth century either in the sense that they start with rights, or in the sense that they take them to be something out of which a theory can be

33

constructed – and not as simply the name for a function in a moral scheme defined by duties. Robert Nozick's is a theory of the former kind.[93] He takes the rights of individuals to be so strong and far-reaching as to put the state permanently on the defensive as to what it may do: political theory is for him a question of the room left to society by individuals.[94]

John Rawls's emphasis is importantly different from this in that while he ends up with a theory of individual rights, these did not constitute his starting-place.[95] The theory of justice is first of all a theory formulating the principles for the structure of society, for social cooperation: justice as fairness. Rights are assigned 'to fulfill the principles of cooperation that citizens would acknowledge when each is fairly represented as a moral person'.[96] So, for example, Rawls's first principle of justice, by which each person is to have an equal right to the most extensive liberty compatible with a similar liberty for others, is not a starting-place but a finishing-line: it is what rational people, deciding behind a veil of ignorance about their actual position in society, would agree on. Some might suggest that it is no accident that this conclusion arrived at by a liberal writer matches the classical liberal axioms, but the point is that it is not taken to be self-evident.

Ronald Dworkin combines the fundamentalism of Nozick with Rawls's rationalism.[97] He describes individual rights as 'political trumps held by individuals', to be used against the imposition of collective goals, and he suggests that the highest among these trumps is the right to equal concern and respect.[98] Rights-talk has two functions in his theory. One is to present a view, in contrast to the positivists and the utilitarians, of what judges actually do: the 'rights-thesis' holds that judicial decisions enforce existing political rights.[99] And the other is to defend a political theory which takes the protection of certain individual choices to be fundamental – natural – 'in the sense that they are not the product of any legislation, or convention, or hypothetical contract'.[100] In asserting this, Dworkin suggests, he is not alone. The language of rights dominates political debate in the United States, and draws its strength from the 'vague but powerful' idea of human dignity and the 'more familiar' idea of political equality.[101]

If this evidence shows the vitality of that political theory which is disposed to take human rights seriously, theory critical of this position is no less alive. Michael Oakeshott reaches Burkean heights in his denunciation of rationalism in politics, not only in the sweep of his description of all politics today as rationalist or near-rationalist, but also in his conviction that moral education consists more in the acquisition of a habit of behaviour than in the explanation of principles.[102] Though it is not based on utilitarian principles, John Charvet's criticism of the theory of human rights as radically incoherent – because its starting-place in the nature of man divides particular selves from other-regarding selves (which are really social rather than individual) – recalls Bentham in the neatness of its job of demolition.[103] And the Marxist doubt continues both about the value of insisting on rights if the cause of social wrongs is not explained, and about an explanation that would dwell on the part of individual will in the human predicament rather than the real moving forces contained in the class-structure characteristic of particular periods of history.[104]

CONCLUSIONS

The list of objections to the idea of human rights seems formidable. There is no such thing as a human right. Worse, the idea of a moral possession on which it is based is mere nonsense. Every man the sole proprietor of his own person? It is as if, said Bentham, 'man were one thing, the person of the same man another thing; as if a man kept his person, when he happened to have one, as he does his watch, in one of his pockets.'[105] This is perhaps Bentham confusing a fiction with a falsehood, but even if they did make sense, rights start political theory in the wrong place: duty is the firm ground, or the principle of utility. And starting in the wrong place, they remain there: they are negative rather than positive, divisive instead of uniting, abstract where they ought to be concrete.

Abstractness, what Burke called metaphysics, is perhaps the central difficulty with the theory of human rights. It is a feature of the theory which threatens to drive human rights out of the political world altogether. In this respect they share the unworldliness of the Christian doctrine expressed in St Paul's epistle to the Galatians: 'There is neither Jew nor Greek, there is neither bond nor free, there is neither male nor female: for ye are all one in Christ Jesus.'[106] Here is universality and equality but in the kingdom of God, not in that of man. And this doctrine has its secular counterpart in Kant. The freedom of each member of society in a civil state was founded on his humanity.[107] And the moral law which he was bound to obey was found not in the circumstances in which he was placed, but '*a priori* in the concepts of pure reason'.[108] The universalism of this formula, as Hegel said, resulted in emptiness.[109] The moral law stood over against society rather than being part of it.

The suggested solution, as we have seen, was to reintegrate the two, to bring together the empirical part of Kant's ethics – what he called 'practical anthropology' – with the *a priori* part, which he called 'morals'.[110] Thus Hegel's notion of *Sittlichkeit* that we noted above. Moral ideas, in Oakeshott's words, 'are a sediment; they have significance only so long as they are suspended in a religious or social tradition, so long as they belong to a religious or a social life'.[111]

The difficulty with this point of view, as Rousseau saw, was that in practice the *moi commun* (the individual as a member of a particular community) drives out the *moi humain* (the individual as a member of the human race).[112] The integration of society does not take place on the global scale that is required in

35

order to match the universalism of the doctrine. What, in these circumstances is the function of the theory of human rights? It might be to pull the world in the right direction by the strength of moral exhortation: a function that Marx ridiculed. Or it might be to point out the direction in which the species ought to go, as Kant thought, whether or not there was any prospect of it actually getting there.[113] Or at the least, and in relation to the purpose of this present work, it might seek to describe the moral world that confronts the statesman in order that he can make sense of 'human rights in foreign policy' (see Chapters 7 and 8).

But all this is about the positive role that the theory of human rights might play in the construction of some future world society. Meanwhile, there is the critical role. The 'mind of man', wrote Ernest Barker, 'will always demand that the core of justice should be beyond time and space – *quod semper, quod ubique*'.[114] And though it is not beyond time and space, the theory of human rights reflects this demand by providing a body of doctrine which suggests a standard against which what is, what happens to be, can be judged. Its own claim to be authoritative, and not just another variety of 'what is', relies on the observation that it stands outside any particular society or culture (a claim which it is the purpose of the next chapter to scrutinize), and that it endures beyond a single generation. In this latter regard we may notice a strength of the theory of human rights in its capacity to absorb criticism in a way that enriches the theory. Hegel's criticism of the theory of natural rights, we have seen, adds to the doctrine of human rights. The Marxian criticism of civil and political rights turns out not to have buried the theory of rights but to have spawned a new category of economic and social rights.[115]

Finally, there is a sense in which the constructive and critical aspects of the theory of human rights merge in providing the arena for the debate about which political values are of the greatest importance. The argument about human rights surveyed in this chapter is not just about what they are, and whether they are a good or a bad thing. It is also about a debate betweeen different versions of the 'rights-thesis': Rawls and the primacy of liberty; Marx, or certainly some Marxists, and the primacy of equality; and Dworkin on the false opposition between the two and their union in the doctrine of 'equal concern and respect'. The vitality of this debate in world politics at large is recognized and dealt with in Part Two of this book.

3 Human rights and cultural relativism

The argument between those who assert the universality of human rights, at least as claims that ought to be recognized, and those whose tendency it is to see any universalist claim in the context of a particular time and place has carried on in western thought, as we have seen, for at least two centuries. And we sought at the conclusion of the last chapter to defend the notion of a minimum content of universal human rights. The task now is to extend the discussion beyond western political theory to the world as a whole, and to investigate whether a doctrine of the minimum content of universal human rights survives the transition.

The first step in this process is to notice that there is a world beyond the west. namely, that great portion of the globe which is neither west European, nor North American, nor Australasian. And although it is a portion of the globe that may have been westernized, to various degrees, as a result of the dominance of western culture over the past several centuries, this is not a contingency that has emptied all meaning from the distinction between the western and the non-western worlds. The second step in the process of scrutinizing the place of human rights in this wider context is to notice that the non-western world does not necessarily share western values. Indeed the emergence of a good part of the world from the dominance of European imperialism has carried with it a new emphasis on the plurality of values in world politics and on the rediscovery of the deep roots of indigenous culture. The doctrine of cultural relativism was not invented by nationalists throwing off the yoke of empire, but its popularity has been sustained by these movements.

What does the doctrine of cultural relativism entail? In the first place, it asserts that rules about morality vary from place to place. Secondly, it asserts that the way to understand this variety is to place it in its cultural context. And, in the third place, it asserts that moral claims derive from, and are enmeshed in, a cultural context which is itself the source of their validity. There is no universal morality, because the history of the world is the story of the plurality of cultures, and the attempt to assert universality, or even Kant's procedural principle of 'universalizability', as a criterion of all morality, is a more or less well-disguised version of the imperial routine of trying to make the values of a particular culture general. In this regard, such documents as the Universal Declaration of Human Rights, passed by the United Nations in 1948, are futile proclamations, derived from the moral principles valid in one culture and thrown out into the moral void between cultures.[1] They might have some validity if the proclaiming culture was successfully imperialist, and had imposed its values on others by *force majeure*, but the doctrine of cultural relativism at its strongest regards this always as a superficial phenomenon, incapable of eroding the irreducible core of cultural singularity in the various social components of the world.

The protest it utters against imperialism, and the buttress it seems to provide against it, are two of the attractions of the doctrine of cultural relativism. It suggests, with Rousseau, that missionaries are no better than conquerors.[2] Moreover, it seems to carry the fight further, beyond the country which seeks to impose its culture abroad, to any attitude which suggests the assumption of the moral superiority of self. It 'questions any view of morality that ascribes an exclusive and exalted position to the morality of one's own society'.[3] It is against what is now called ethnocentrism, and it sees in moral self-centredness the formula for a constant battle among cultures, each insisting on its moral superiority. To this it opposes a tolerance based partly on scepticism about the claim of any one culture to wholesale moral superiority, and partly on the claim that the 'recognition of cultural relativity carries with it its own values': namely, the acceptance of the 'equally valid patterns of life which mankind has created for itself from the raw materials of existence'.[4] Cultural egalitarianism seems to follow from cultural relativism.

So the argument provided by cultural relativism against imperialism appeals not merely because it is an argument against imperialism, but because it seems true. There is a plurality of cultures in the world, and these cultures produce their own values. There are no universal values. This, to the cultural relativist, is not a problem. It is a solution. How does one cope with the coexistence in the world of value-systems that conflict with each other, or which are not necessarily mutually consistent? One adopts Hume's formula: 'In each city, the rites of that city.'[5]

The object of this chapter is to scrutinize this doctrine. In the first part, it develops an admittedly crude, but for our purposes sufficient, picture of the reality of cultural pluralism in relation to human rights, treating Africa, China and Islam. Then, in the second section, it turns the canvas over, and gives a summary account of the international law of human rights as a body of rules which, in some sense, draws the several cultures together (we shall treat at the appropriate place the question of whether international law is equivalent to 'inter-cultural' law). In the third part of the chapter, we shall examine the senses in which this 'drawing together' takes place. Human rights might be taken as merely a portmanteau term for African rights, American rights, Chinese rights, and so on, so that the term is general but the rights are specific. In Java, according to Clifford Geertz, it is said that: 'To be human is to be Javanese'.[6] Being human is not being Everyman, Geertz goes on, but being a particular kind of man. Thus, if there are human rights, they are the rights of particular people. A second way of drawing the particular and the general together might be to investigate the extent to which the rights of various peoples do in fact overlap, so that there is, as a matter of observation, a core of basic rights that is common to all cultures. And a third way might be to examine the extent to which there exists, in contemporary world society, a single cosmopolitan culture stretched over the profusion of indigenous cultures, so that there is a properly universal level at which the vocabulary of human rights has meaning.

At the conclusion of the chapter, we shall take seriously the Kantian objection that an inquiry of the kind conducted in the third section of the chapter is an example of 'practical anthropology' but not of 'morals', and that one cannot arrive at what ought to be done from observation of what is in fact done. In this spirit, an argument will be developed against the doctrine of cultural relativism in its extreme form, and an attempt made to reconcile the fact of plural values in world politics with the universalism implicit in the very idea of human rights.

THE CULTURAL CONTEXT OF HUMAN RIGHTS

Africa

The Banjul Charter on Human and People's Rights, passed in June 1981 at the eighteenth assembly of heads of state and government of the Organization of African Unity (OAU) devotes its first eighteen articles to the rights of individuals, and only its second eight to the rights of peoples.[7] But it is the idea that the rights of collectivities such as 'peoples' should enjoy at least equal dignity with those of individuals that is often said to be characteristic of African approaches to human rights; and this is reflected in the title of the Banjul Charter. And if priority is to be determined between individual and collective rights, there is a tendency among the interpreters of traditional African culture to find in favour of the latter.[8] Social harmony, it is said, the preservation of the fabric of social life, comes first in African thought, and the threads in this fabric are either the connections among extended families, or other connections modelled upon them. Individuals are not visible in the fabric, only the duties they discharge, the functions they fulfil. To be a person, in traditional African society, is to be incorporated in this way into a group. Personhood, in contrast to individualism in the West, is intelligible only in the group and not against it.

If group values predominate, the language of duty is a more natural usage than that of rights: obligation to the community rather than freedom from it. This too is reflected in the Banjul Charter, which includes a chapter on duties as well as one on rights. And the duties involve not just the recognition of the equal rights of others, but also the promotion of such substantive goals as the harmonious development of the family (Article 29(1)), national solidarity and independence (Article 29(4) and (5)), and African cultural values and unity (Article 29(7) and (8)).

The emphasis on the group, and on duties, connects up to a third strand of African thought which has society organized to meet basic human needs, rather than being the means for the promotion of individual acquisitiveness. Thus traditional African cultures are said to have paid attention to justice in the distribution of social goods in a way that western liberal capitalism has not.[9] This also is reflected in the Banjul Charter, at least in its declaration that fortune, as well as race, ethnic group, colour, sex, language, religion, opinion, social origin, birth and status, should be no bar to the enjoyment of the rights and freedoms it guarantees (Article 2). In addition, there is the assertion in the preamble that it is essential to pay particular attention to the right to development, and that the satisfaction of economic, social and cultural rights is a guarantee for the enjoyment of civil and political rights.

Thus, to refer back to our discussion in Chapter 1 of the establishment of hierarchies of human rights, it might be argued that the tendency of African thought is to turn the western list upside down. Collective rights are first in importance, second come economic and social rights, and third civil and political rights. It is possible to observe this asserted hierarchy at work in contemporary international politics in the goals which African statesmen have set themselves. Thus, in the first place, when Ali Mazrui, in his well-known book, expounded an Afro-Asian, but especially an African, view of the United Nations Charter as a global bill of rights, and opposed it to the great powers' view of the Charter as a minimalist arrangement for the maintenance of international peace and security, the rights he had in mind were the collective rights to national and racial self-determination.[10] And the international community represented in the United Nations General Assembly endorsed these rights in such instruments as the Declaration on the Granting of Independence to Colonial Countries and Peoples (1960), and the International Convention on the Elimination of All Forms of Racial Discrimination (1966).[11] Then, secondly, formal independence for the most part having been achieved, there is the mounting preoccupation with the economic and social right to development, which is reflected in the wider international community in such instruments as the Declaration on Permanent Sovereignty over Natural Resources (1966), and more recently the Charter of Economic Rights and Duties of States (1974).[12] Finally, and most recently, there has been the recognition that, in spite of the importance of the principle of non-intervention in the operation of the OAU, it was wrong for African states to condemn human rights violations in southern Africa and yet remain silent about shortcomings in this regard elsewhere in the continent.[13] The Banjul Charter sprang partly from the crossing of this threshold. And, in it, there is the endorsement of individual rights, as well as of the collective and economic and social rights against which, it has been argued, they have to be judged.

China

In China, as well as Africa, community and obligation have come traditionally before individual and right. In the five basic social relations of Confucian teaching – those between ruler and subjects, parents and children, husband and wife, elder and younger brother, and friend and friend – the connection is one of mutual obligation rather than of reciprocal rights and duties.[14] And in all the pairings, except perhaps the last, the nature of the relationship is hierarchical rather than egalitarian, suggesting unequal duties rather than equal rights.

Rights, when they came, were an import from the West via Japan, and the idea of a right was approximated in the Chinese language by the combination of the word for 'power' with that for 'interest'.[15] But it may be argued that this artificial addition to the language did not change the more organic Chinese conception of law as fulfilling the function of the maintenance of social harmony, which contrasts with the western model of law as arbitration between claims.[16] And the conception of it in terms of its function in a wider system continues to inform the theory and practice of law in contemporary China.

The theory is now Marxist, not Confucian. And law is thought of as an instrument of the policy of the state rather than, as in the West, an 'objective body of authoritative rules'.[17] Human rights, it follows, should be analysed in this light. As the 'natural rights of man', according to Chinese Marxist theory, they had been a powerful ideological weapon of the rising bourgeoisie; and latterly, as human rights, they have been used by the imperialists, the risen bourgeoisie, to slander measures effected under the dictatorship of the proletariat, such as the suppression of counter-revolutionaries.[18] The proletariat, the argument continues, should recognize that human rights had once fulfilled a progressive function, and that the human rights provisions in the United Nations Charter still had an anti-fascist progressive significance. But they should also insist on the realization of communist goals beyond bourgeois rights: the dictatorship of the proletariat, the elimination of private ownership, the emancipation of all mankind.[19] In this regard there were more accurate Marxist formulations than those provided by the language of human rights, and all rights were restricted by certain material conditions and cultural levels.[20] The 'concept of man', Mao said, 'lacks content; it lacks the specificity of male and female, adult and child, Chinese and foreign, revolutionary and counter-revolutionary. The only thing left is the vague features differentiating man from beast.'[21]

Whether or not the reason lies in the vagueness of the features, China has been very cautious in expressing its attitude towards the human rights issues which confront it by virtue of its full membership in the international community of the United Nations. There has been a reluctance to participate in the work of the UN Commission on Human Rights, and a failure to ratify the vast majority of the multilateral treaties on human rights which have been concluded under UN auspices.[22] China's preference is to see the campaign for human rights as part of the wider campaign against imperialism, hegemonism, colonialism and racialism, and to speak not of the rights of man but of those of nations to independence, of races to equal treatment, and of states to development.[23] These are collective rights, not those of individuals, and they impose duties on the currently privileged towards the world's deprived. Human rights should be used as an instrument in the greatest of contemporary struggles for equality among states.

Individuals come last, by a distance longer than in African doctrine. Indeed, there is some doubt about whether they come anywhere at all. For the Chinese render the western (albeit heretical) theory that individuals are constituted subjects of international law – by virtue of the attention paid to human rights in that body of rules – as just another variety of imperialism, a pretext for intervening in the internal affairs of the socialist states.[24] And the attention paid to the rights of individuals in the Chinese constitution itself is apparently nullified by the article which reads: 'The fundamental rights and duties of citizens are to support the leadership of the Communist Party of China, support the Socialist system and abide by the Constitution and the laws of the People's Republic of China.'[25]

Islam

In Islam, too, the community, this time the religious community of Muslims, comes before the individual. The Muslim community is 'a compact wall whose bricks support each other.'[26] And the wall must stand on its own without any external buttress. The part of the individual in this community is not merely to act so as to ensure its preservation, but also to recognize that it is the community that provides for the integration of human personality realized through self-abnegation and action for the good of the collectivity.[27]

So in Islam, also, the language of duty seems more natural than that of rights, and obligation is consolidated by its being owed to God. Rules of conduct for all Muslims were laid down by Allah, and communicated through Muhammad, and Muslims do service to God through obedience to these rules. The fundamental nature of the idea of obedience to God in Islam shapes the discussion of Islam and human rights so profoundly that rights always seem to be pulled back in the direction of duties. Thus the assertion that the 'essential characteristic of human rights in Islam is that they constitute obligations connected with the Divine and derive their force from this connection'.[28] Thus, also, the reluctance to make a stronger claim for human rights in Islam than that they are the privilege of God, in whom all authority ultimately resides.[29]

If rights are thought of as freedoms, then – to revert to the distinction made in Chapter 1 between positive and negative rights – Islam favours 'freedom to' over 'freedom against', freedom to be or to become over freedom from external constraint.[30] True freedom consists in surrendering to the Divine will rather than in some artificial separation from the community of God. And while it was possible for God's representative on earth, the caliph, to act unjustly, this did not confer on his subjects a right of resistance.[31] In this regard, there has been in Islamic doctrine no 'protestant' revolution of the kind we paid attention to in Chapter 2. Rights remain subordinate to and determined by duties.

And, if there are difficulties about the autonomy of rights in Islam, there is a question too about whether they are human in the sense of being applicable to all human beings. Human rights in Islam, it has been said, are the privileges only of a person of full legal capacity – 'a living human being of mature age, free, and of Moslem faith.'[32] Some arrangement might be made for non-Muslims residing in Muslim lands provided they paid the poll-tax, but the rights that were guaranteed in exchange for this – to security of life and property, and freedom of prayer[33] – did not derive from a notion that all humans had rights in virtue of their humanity, but from the need to make practical arrangements for those not of the faith. And, in any event, the freedom of prayer did not extend to Muslims. Religious liberty meant the freedom of non-Muslims to practise their religion unobtrusively in Muslim lands, or to abandon it in favour of Islam.[34] There could be no traffic the other way, for Islam had transcended other religious systems.

Like Christianity, Islam approached the notion, prerequisite to the emergence of the idea of human rights, that there was a unity in mankind which made no difference between an Arab and a non-Arab, a white man and a black man.[35] But, also like Christianity, in St Paul's doctrine that *in Christ* there was to be neither Jew nor Greek, it was the faith that made the difference. The brotherhood of man was for every believer in Islam, just as it was for every believer in Christ. The important contrast between the two religions in regard to their attitude to human rights lay elsewhere. The unworldly strand of Christian thought which had all men equal in the sight of God, and in the world to come, allowed Christian doctrine to detach itself from a particular sovereign, and eventually to give place to the theory of natural rights which saw value in every individual regardless of religious attachment. Islam, not making any distinction between Caesar's and God's, for all was God's, did not allow a theory of religious duty to turn into one of political right.[36]

THE INTERNATIONAL LAW OF HUMAN RIGHTS

Classically, at least in the positivist treatises, international law was a law between states. States were its subjects, individuals merely its objects.[37] Individuals could enjoy benefits from the law of nations only through the medium of their nationality, their belonging to a state. So human rights, which are associated pre-eminently with individuals, and with groups other than states, might have some moral claim to the world's attention, but were not part of international law. Indeed, they seemed to be excluded, by definition, from entering that realm: municipal law was for individuals (among other legal persons); international law was for states (and perhaps for international organizations which were the creatures of states).

Despite the neatness of this distinction between the law within states and the law among them, state practice has always cut across it, and the cuts have become deeper during the course of the twentieth century. For evidence that state practice has always cut across the distinction, it is possible to refer to the body of customary rules forming what lawyers call the 'international standard of justice', which makes states internationally responsible for the treatment of aliens within their frontiers, and also to the right, asserted by a number of publicists, of humanitarian intervention if a state 'shocked the conscience of mankind' by its treatment of its own nationals.[38] For evidence that the cuts have become deeper during the course of the twentieth century, it is possible to draw attention to a range of developments: the Minorities Treaties, a series of treaties associated with the League of Nations imposing international obligations on certain states in regard to the treatment of minority groups residing within their boundaries; treaties giving rights directly to individuals, as in the Convention of 1907 setting up the Central American Court of Justice, the Mixed Arbitral Tribunals established in the Treaty of Versailles to deal with debts owed by Germany to allied nationals, and the European Convention on Human Rights; the work of the International Labour Organization (ILO), which produced standards of treatment for workers; the International Military Tribunal at Nuremberg, which imposed duties on individuals in the international law of war; the provision for human rights and fundamental freedoms in the Charter of the United Nations as purposes which members pledged themselves to achieve; and, finally, the Universal Declaration of Human Rights, the International Covenants on Civil and Political Rights, and on Economic, Social and Cultural Rights, and the several other conventions and declarations on human rights sponsored by the United Nations.[39]

While this evidence can all be marshalled against the doctrine that international law is exclusively a law between states, it is not equally straightforward evidence for the existence of an international law of human rights. This is partly because some of the developments have more to do with duties than rights, for example, the Nuremberg Trials.[40] And it is partly because there are doubts about whether there is any prospect of implementing what is called the international law of human rights. 'Human rights lawyers', it has been said, 'are notoriously wishful thinkers.'[41] These doubts are well displayed in the debate on the lawfulness of humanitarian intervention.[42] The argument takes place at two levels, one of law and one of policy (though it is the view of one side in it that it is not possible to separate the two). On law, those who argue against the rightfulness of humanitarian intervention rely on the strength of the prohibition against the unilateral use of force in the United Nations Charter (especially Article 2(4)), and on what they insist is a total absence of support for humanitarian intervention in contemporary state practice. On the other side are those who regard the achievement of human rights as a purpose of the United Nations Charter that ranks with the pursuit of peace and security, and who are prepared to sanction unilateral action if the collective action envisaged in the Charter comes, as it characteristically has, to nought.

On policy, those who argue against the rightfulness of humanitarian intervention are inclined to observe that it is a doctrine used by the great against the small, that it smacks of imperialism, that it disguises ignoble motives (or, conversely, that it expects too high a standard of behaviour), that it might encourage counter-intervention, and that it is in general heedless of consequences. On the other hand, the argument is that the costs of non-intervention have to be counted alongside those of intervention, and that the doctrine of the doubters amounts to throwing up one's hands and leaving the international community impotent however shocked its conscience. Good policy, in the view of this school, should shape the interpretation of the law, and indeed good policy is part of the definition of what the law is.[43]

This argument continues, and the determination of a position on it must await the inquiry which is to follow. It has been raised here to show the weakness of the hold of the international law of human rights. However weak, it is not non-existent, and the hard-line argument that human rights law is general and aspirational, consisting largely of norms *de lege ferenda* (the law which ought to be made, as opposed to the law which is already made – *lex lata*),[44] while no doubt true, does not do away entirely with the idea of present and general obligation.

There are two ways in which this idea can be said to have force in the contemporary international community. In the first place, there is the view that the Universal Declaration of Human Rights is not merely a resolution of the General Assembly recommending preferred conduct to the international community, but a solemn undertaking which provides an authoritative interpretation of the United Nations Charter, and might even be said to be part of customary international law.[45] This view can be illustrated by reference to the memorial filed by the United States with the International Court of Justice on its claim against Iran in regard to the seizure of the embassy in Tehran.[46] The United States claim relied mainly on agreements signed between it and Iran. But it referred also to alleged Iranian violation of international human rights law. The United States argued that such multilateral instruments as the United Nations Charter, the Universal Declaration of Human Rights, and the International Covenant on Civil and Political Rights had established fundamental principles of customary law of which Iran was in breach. It was legally irrelevant whether the United States and Iran were signatories of the Covenant on Civil and Political Rights because it merely expanded obligations already existing under conventional and customary law.

The second way in which present and general obligation can be established deepens the first by reference to a celebrated legal judgement: that of the International Court of Justice in the *Barcelona Traction* case.[47] The Court drew what it saw as an essential distinction between 'the obligations of a State towards the international community as a whole' and those arising as against another state.[48] The former were by their very nature the concern of all states. 'In view of the importance of the rights involved, all States can be held to have a legal interest in their protection; they are obligations *erga omnes*' (against everyone). And such obligations derived from the outlawing of acts of aggression, and genocide, and 'also from the principles and rules concerning the basic rights of the human person, including protection from slavery and racial discrimination'. The argument here is that there may be, in virtue of *Barcelona Traction*, a part of 'international human rights law which has achieved the position of *jus cogens* – law which is 'binding on all states and also having the status of peremptory norms'.[49]

In conclusion, we may sketch the area occupied by the international law of human rights in the contemporary international community by reference to three landmarks. In the first place, there is the view that the emergence of international human rights law has transcended the old debate between those who argued for an 'international standard of justice' and those ranged against them who insisted on equality of treatment for nationals and aliens.[50] One of the celebrated arenas for this debate was Latin America. European states, and later the United States, were inclined to assert an international standard of treatment which would justify intervention to protect their people and their property in Latin America: and Latin Americans were inclined to allow no excuse for any kind of interference in their internal affairs.[51] In requiring a minimum standard of treatment for all human beings, it may be argued, international human rights law has removed, at least at the minimalist level, the contentious distinction between nationals and aliens. But this is very minimal, bespeaking no sudden cosmopolitanism. For it is next door to an area in which, as J.E.S. Fawcett has pointed out, the domestic jurisdiction of states 'remains largely untouched' – the admission and expulsion of foreigners.[52]

Secondly, there is the view that certain doctrines such as the principle of non-discrimination on racial grounds, and the principle of self-determination, which were formerly dismissed as political slogans that had no part in the law of nations, are now part of customary international law, and even of *jus cogens*.[53]

In the third place, there is the view that what these previous two landmarks indicate is 'the common law of mankind in an early stage of its development', and that international law can be intelligently expounded only if this new *Gestalt* is adopted.[54] The difficulty with this view is that it makes of what might possibly develop, but which has not yet developed and might not, the touchstone for the interpretation of contemporary international law.[55] It is more realistic to render the attention that contemporary international law gives to the individual, and to groups other than states, such as nations and races,* as subsidiary themes to the law between states rather than as developments which have made that law itself a subsidiary theme. And the discussion of humanitarian intervention was designed to show the extent to which this is still true. But the subsidiary theme is established. As Rosalyn Higgins has put it, in relation to the individual in international society, 'There is now a legal yardstick against which the behaviour of states may be judged and a point of reference for the individual in the assertion of his claims.'[56]

A SOCIOLOGICAL ROUTE TO HUMAN RIGHTS?

The official doctrine underlying the international law of human rights, whatever its stage of development and however many the signatories of its covenants, is that it is in principle universal. It does not suggest (except where special regional arrangements have been made, which must then not conflict with general international law) that there are different rules for Africans, and Chinese, and Muslims. And yet we saw, in our discussion of these three cultures, and in Chapter I above, that the interpretation of human rights varies with culture both as to their place in society and as to the hierarchy established among them. And

---

* The state is the body politic, the agency organized for rule, having a defined territory, a population, a government and, some add, sovereignty. The nation is a community, to which individuals feel they belong, established historically by common descent, or language, or culture, or circumstance.

there may even be doubt about whether some societies pay any serious attention to human rights at all – preferring citizen to human and duty to right. What we try out in this section of the chapter is the three purported solutions to the problem of bringing the universal and the particular together that we noted at the outset.

But it is appropriate before that to deal with the question of whether 'human rights in international law' and 'human rights in cultural perspective' are commensurable. Can they be brought together through the level of analysis of the society of states? It is true that not all (or even most) considerable cultural groupings surface in the society formed among states, and that some of the most disadvantaged cultures may be so precisely because they are excluded from it. Nor is there any straightforward matching of cultures with states. Nor, indeed, is culture a precise enough concept for us to know this – as is revealed by the acceptability of our using it to describe a continent (Africa), a country (China) and a religion (Islam). But plainly some states see themselves as carriers and defenders of a particular culture in world politics, and China and the Islamic states are examples of this. And our task here is merely to ask what kind of barrier this presents to the establishment of universal rules, or, to put the question the other way around: what, if any, are the ways over the barrier?

Human rights as particular rights

Our first suggested solution to the problem of asserting universal human rights in a culturally plural world was to treat the expression 'human rights' as one that all or most societies recognize, but which they define in terms of the values of their particular society. To be human is to be Javanese. The enjoyment of human rights might result only from participation in a real community, and not from some abstract connection to human society as a whole. Human rights list variety not similarity. Java is different from Ghana, and there is no basis for preferring Javanese conceptions of human rights to Ghanaian ones.

The idea that conceptions of rights vary according to culture is an anthropological commonplace. If it were not true, doing anthropology would lose much of its point. It might seem, then, an attractive solution to allow human rights to take on whatever is the local colour. But this is not a resolution of our difficulty. It is a surrender to the universality of particularism: the *moi commun* again driving out the *moi humain*. The global conceit of calling particular rights general is recorded, but the idea of general rights is not itself confronted.

Human rights as 'core' rights

Our second proposed solution has the merit of confronting this question directly. It asks whether there is in fact a core of basic rights that is common to all cultures despite their apparently divergent theories. This question is consistent with the natural rights tradition. If there are rights whose content can be decided upon by the use of right reason, then since reason is a human faculty the outcome of the process of decision-making should be similar across cultures. The modern investigation of this proposition might take a natural scientific form as in the inquiry into the biological basis of morality.[57] Or it might be based on some sociological hypothesis like Barrington Moore's notion of the unity of human misery, according to which general opposition to human suffering is a standpoint that transcends differences of place and time.[58] Or it might be based more on the refinement of inductive generalizations, as in the concern to 'distill from the multiplicity of philosophies and ideologies and their divergent values any universals that may exist'.[59] What these investigations might be expected to produce, if anything, is a lowest common denominator of basic or core rights, which, if found across all societies, would then have a proper positive claim to the label 'human rights'.

There are difficulties with the ahistorical quality of this mode of inquiry, and also with its wishful character – suggesting that anyone determined to find (or not to find) similarities across cultures will shape the evidence to fit the thesis. But its cross-cultural perspective has given rise to some progressive features in the investigation of human rights in world politics of which we may mention three. The first is the disposition to become aware of and make explicit our own value preferences and implicit comparisons in thinking about human rights abroad.[60] The second is the attempt to marshal data that might begin to reveal global patterns in regard to conceptions of rights, their observance, and their enforcement.[61] The third has to do with measurement: of 'human rights conditions' in general (establishing an index that would reflect all the values in the Universal Declaration);[62] or of performance on particular rights (economic and social rights as approximated, for example, by the Physical Quality of Life Index,[63] and civil and political rights as judged, for example, by Freedom House[64]).

Though it may be a surprise to some of their authors, all of these approaches can be placed in a natural rights tradition – at least to the extent that they do not suppose that cultural relativity disposes of the cross-cultural enterprise from the outset.[65] There is also an inverted form of our second solution which we might notice here. It seeks universal human rights, not in the pursuit of what is common to all cultures, but in the production of a list which takes something from all cultures. According to this notion, human rights that were properly universal would do something for Islam, and for China, and for Africa and so on, rather than relying on the straightforward conversion of western into universal values.[66] The difficulty with this procedure is that while it might reduce the ethnocentrism of declarations about them, it abandons in the process any notion of universal

49

rights. Drawing up a long list to satisfy everybody merely adds variety together. It does nothing to resolve the differences between one item or group of items on the list and another, and it would invite particular societies to consult only their section of the document. It therefore makes no progress beyond our first solution, which had human rights as particular rights. And if a resolution among items were attempted, or an effort made to produce a list that was common to all societies, only an outcome that was reasonable, and not merely the arbitrary product of some political bargain, would deserve respect. This again draws us back to the naturalist tradition, a subject that we shall return to at the end of the chapter.

Human rights in the global cosmopolitan culture

Meanwhile, the third proposed solution to the problem of establishing that there are universal human rights was that there exists in the contemporary world a single cosmopolitan culture which is spread across all indigenous cultures, and which carries to each of them what are, in some at least geographical sense, global human rights. This is the common culture of modernity which has touched, some would argue that it has engulfed, all societies in virtue of the rise of a global economy. States, regions, cities, families, patterns of life, are all shaped by this culture.[67] All over the world individuals have been pulled away by its operation from their traditional attachment to the local community. In these circumstances, the philosophy of human rights can be rendered as 'the natural response to changing conditions, a logical and necessary evolution of the means for realizing human dignity'.[68] Human rights are part of a world social process, the institutional expression of which is the international law of human rights that we considered above. And if international law is, as we suggested earlier, in some degree an inter-cultural law as well, we may appeal to it as evidence for the existence of universal standards of human rights.

There are at least three difficulties with this association of human rights with the emerging common culture of modernity. The first is that there is not one single animal called the 'common culture of modernity'. The process of modernization might be said to produce two cultures, as in the centre-periphery model of it and the idea that it creates a dual economy in developing societies. Or it might be said to produce as many cultures as there are societies, modernization affecting each differently. Or, with particular reference to how human rights are viewed, it might – to adopt Professor Macpherson's scheme – be reduced to three political models based on dominant conceptions of democracy – the liberal-democratic, the communist, and that in the underdeveloped world.[69] Civil and political rights are associated with the first conception; economic and social rights with the second; and collective rights with the third.[70] No one of these is preferable to the others. They simply reflect different priorities in different material circumstances.

The second difficulty follows from the first. If there is more than one culture associated with the process of modernization, then there is no basis for an appeal to that process itself to settle an argument about universal human rights. Calling up the international law of human rights as evidence for the existence of a world cosmopolitan culture of which all societies are part, and whose rules should then apply to them, fails because international law itself is subject to interpretation from the standpoint of this or that culture. The argument that takes place between East and West, and also between North and South, on the question of human rights, which we examine in Part Two of the book, does show some point in Macpherson's distinction between three worlds of democracy.

A third objection to the idea of a common culture of modernity questions not its existence but its pedigree. A common culture does in some degree exist in the contemporary world, but the extent of it is the measure of westernization and not of modernization. It is a species of imperialism, a charge the West seeks to avoid by calling it a world social process, or modernization, or an emerging global social structure. On the matter of human rights in particular, the West employs a similar dodge. What is called the international law of human rights, a seemingly neutral title, is in fact the machine for widening and deepening the legitimacy of western conceptions of the good society. As a result, according to this view, Third World conceptions of human rights must be presented as different conceptions if they are to play any part in the strategy for emergence from western dominance.

Let us take these difficulties with the association of universal human rights with a common cosmopolitan culture in turn. The first argument was the most radical. In its 'three worlds of democracy' form it was that the separate worlds were constructed of different conceptions of rights that were in principle unassimilable. One might allow successfully either for civil and political liberty, or for economic and social equality, but not at the same time and in the same place for both. The flaw in this objection is that it seems to suggest that the three worlds are sealed off from one another, immune to external criticism. This seems doubtful empirically. It may be true that the 'three worlds of democracy' accurately conveys three main tendencies in the world in the interpretation of human rights, but we can observe these tendencies contesting with each other within western and eastern and southern societies, as well as between the West, the East and the South. Moreover, if we take, with Macpherson, Locke to be the captain of the civil and political rights team, Marx of the economic and social rights team, and Rousseau of the collective rights team,[71] these are three great western thinkers invoked in what is now a global contest. That it is possible to characterize the contemporary debate about human rights in world politics by reference to these western figures itself casts doubt on the disposition to have the tripartite division as the more fundamental reality than the contest which makes the division intelligible.

The second difficulty with the argument for universal human rights as part of a common global culture was that this global culture was subject to interpretation by the primary cultural groups, over which the so-called world culture was stretched. Thus the international law of human rights was in reality African, or Chinese, or Islamic, or western, and not some meta-law above the cultures. There is a naive realism about this difficulty. It is tautological that western, or Islamic, or Chinese lawyers interpret international law from a western, or Islamic, or Chinese point of view. It is plainly not true that they regard international law merely as the vehicle for their own cultural freight. A law among nations acceptable to all its members suggests the existence of some common ground, and not merely the outward thrust of domestic preoccupations. This common ground then has some autonomous existence which it is the burden of international lawyers to explicate. They might disagree about it. But this does not sanction the reductionist view that international law can be understood only at the level of the cultures participating in it. For the disagreement might take place within as well as among cultures.

The third difficulty concerned the pedigree of the global cosmopolitan culture. It may be true that the chief fact about modernity is its westernness, and that the international law of human rights, like all international law, is more an export of the West to the rest of the world than of the rest of the world to the West. It may also be true that the emancipation of the Third World requires the uncovering of authentic indigenous conceptions of 'human rights' with which to confront the notions of the imperialists. Ironically, however, it may be argued that the emergence from western dominance is not advanced by the assertion of the cultural relativity of all values, but rather by appealing to certain universal principles, such as that of state sovereignty, to roll back the hegemony of the imperialists. And even if the right asserted is a right to be different, it is one protected by a doctrine long familiar in the western world, namely the principle of self-determination. Moreover, if the countries and peoples of the Third World want something positive from the First and Second Worlds (such as the claims made under the heading of the New International Economic Order, which we shall come to in Chapter 5) in addition to the right to be left alone, there is even more reason to underline the existence of a common moral world in which the weak can make demands on the strong to some point.

These arguments show the utility of acting as if a common moral world existed; they do not prove its existence. But what is being suggested here is that the emergence of the new states, and the associated revival of suppressed cultures, has not in fact meant the jettisoning of western doctrine. What it has meant is, in part, the use of western principles against their authors, and in part the accommodation of a western tradition to these new arrivals. The principle of self-determination may illustrate this process at work. It is a western principle, at least as old as the French Revolution, which the new states used to gain their independence. Since independence (as we shall again see in Chapter 5), they have added racial and economic interpretations to the principle that were not previously associated with it. In this respect, the common cosmopolitan culture has been received and then added to from underneath, not imposed and entrenched from on top. It is possible to interpret the whole of the international law of human rights as an example of the operation of this process of adaption.

A solution?

Let us recapitulate. Of the three sociological arguments which might bridge the gap between cultural pluralism and the singularity of human rights, the first, asserting the universality of particularism, fails by making no real attempt on the task; though, in failing, it serves to remind us that the model of a community in which there is an expectation that rights will be respected is municipal rather than international, local rather than global: Hegel's *Sittlichkeit* rather than Kant's *Moralität*. The second suggested bridge, that of a cross-cultural validation of natural rights theory, seemed more promising, and the naturalist tradition was referred to more than once as a fecund starting-place for thought. The third suggested bridge was a more rickety and fog-bound structure, since it sought general statements about world society as a whole. But one of the main points regarding the tradition of thought about human rights is its involvement in mankind as a whole, and to make sense of it we cannot avoid some global mapping (and we shall revert to this in Chapter 6).

The whole of the discussion of this section has been sociological: how might we find out, by reference to the observation of human action, how to build a bridge between pluralism and monism? But it may be that one cannot get at a notion of universal human rights by this means. To attempt to do so may be a grandiose version of the 'naturalistic fallacy' – deriving statements about how people ought to behave from statements about how they in fact do behave. We pass now, noticing this point, from 'practical anthropology' to 'morals'.

CONCLUSIONS: RELATIVISM AND NATURALISM

The argument of the last section of the chapter was in the spirit of the doctrine of cultural relativism. Human rights must be sought in the practice of the various cultures making up the world, and not in what amount to the political preferences of but one of them. Particular moralities have no purchase on objective truth, and can lay no claim to universality. All we can do as people interested in universal human rights is to record the ubiquity of 'human-rights-talk', to observe the extent to which patterns of human action are repeated in a number of cultures, and to note the extent to which convergence is taking place across cultures.

Recording, observing, noting: these activities seem all to have a non-judgemental quality. They would arrive at universal human rights by the anthropologists' route of participant observation, not the philosophers' route of rational construction. Indeed, cultural relativism has been called by a philosopher 'the anthropologist's heresy'.[72] If a heresy is an unsound or untenable doctrine, what are the reasons for calling cultural relativism heretical?

The doctrine of cultural relativism asserts, we noted at the beginning of the chapter, that rules about morality vary from place to place. This seems an uncontroversial assertion. But if the general moral prescription drawn from it is that we should adopt in each place the rules of that place, this is clear and helpful only if the boundaries between one place and another are clear. When, as in the contemporary world, the downward seepage of a global cosmopolitan civilization has obscured even further cultural boundaries that were previously hardly clear, this aspect of the doctrine of cultural relativism is misleading if not always chaotic.[73] The same difficulty then applies to our second feature of the doctrine of cultural relativism, which was that the way to understand moral variety was to place it in its cultural context. There can be no objection to this attempt at understanding, but much debate about the nature and limits of the cultural context.

It is the third feature of the doctrine of cultural relativism that is the most distinctive and important from a moral point of view. It is the assertion that moral claims derive from, and are enmeshed in, a cultural context which is itself the source of their validity. From this strong version of cultural relativism,[74] two things might be said to follow. The first is that each culture has a pattern of life that is of equal validity to all the others.[75] The second is that moral claims deriving from outside a culture have no validity within it. The first implication seems logically mistaken, the second morally obnoxious.

The moral conclusion to be drawn from Ruth Benedict's assertion that all cultures create equally valid patterns of life is, as Clifford Geertz has pointed out, a strange one.[76] It is that anything one group of people is inclined towards doing is worthy of respect by another. But the mistake of logic takes place prior to the drawing of this conclusion. It is in the assumption that the doctrine of cultural relativism has egalitarian consequences.[77] In logic, the doctrine of cultural relativism cannot rank cultures as equal or unequal. All the doctrine can do is to observe that values are endogenously derived. If the local value is to assert global superiority, that is to say inequality, then no argument from cultural relativism can be mounted against it. The association of cultural relativism with egalitarianism may or may not be empirically demonstrable, but it is not a connection that is logically required.

As to moral obnoxiousness, to assert that moral claims deriving from outside a culture have no validity within it is effectively to withdraw a society from the moral scrutiny of others. The argument that you have to be of us to understand us, and to have a right of criticism, rules out even comment, let alone intervention, on the part of outsiders. This may not be disastrous. The perfect society would not require criticism either external or internal. But the doctrine of cultural relativism can defend imperfect as well as perfect societies, and these are perhaps of greater moral interest. Should the rest of the world have no say about a society in which the rulers practise slavery or starve their people? If this is what the doctrine of cultural relativism allows, then there is some doubt about whether it should be called a moral doctrine at all. It is certainly not a doctrine that has ever been part of the orthodoxy of international society. On the contrary, the international legal doctrine of a minimum standard of justice has never allowed the defence of non-intervention for conduct that has 'outraged the conscience of mankind'.[78]

We began this chapter with praise for the anti-imperialist tendency of the strong doctrine of cultural relativism: its egalitarianism, its reduction of the importance of self. We have now heard from the other side. Its tolerance might be less charitably interpreted as the cowardice of moral abstention. Its egalitarianism might be shown to be unsoundly based. Worse, instead of reducing the importance of self, cultural relativism might on balance inflate it. It might reduce the ethnocentrism of the erstwhile imperialist, but multiply it everywhere else by reinforcing in any culture its adherence to its own tradition.

So despite its progressive association with the campaign against imperialism, what the doctrine of cultural relativity allows in practice is a surrender to what John Stuart Mill called the 'despotism of custom'.[79] It allows the predominant opinion in any locality to prevail whether or not there is any good reason to support it. The despotism is the more remarkable when arbitrary. As Mill again observed, the person who 'devolves upon his own world the responsibility of being in the right against the dissentient world of other people' is never troubled by the fact that 'mere accident has decided which of the numerous worlds is the object of his reliance, and that the same causes which make him a Churchman in London, would have made him a Buddhist or a Confucian in Pekin'.[80]

However true it is that we all tend to devolve upon our own worlds the responsibility of being in the right against others, this is not a reason to withdraw from moral argument in world politics altogether. Otherwise, the argument for human fallibility would beggar every enterprise. At the same time, we have to recognize that conceptions of human rights do vary with culture, and that this is something that has to be taken into account in the making of policy. The problem is to find a balance between insistence on the human rights that everyone ought to enjoy, by virtue of their humanity, and the recognition that the existence, content and importance of these rights is contested. This is a question we dwell on in Part Three of this book, but the initial response to the problem, and a procedure, are again provided by Mill.[81] The response suggests that it is the duty of governments (supposing that they act for societies) to act when they are sure (not absolutely certain, which is impossible) of being right, and that it is not conscientiousness but cowardice to shrink from acting on their opinions. The fact that government has in the past raised bad taxes, and fought unjust wars, is not an argument against taxation, or war when provoked.

The procedure Mill offers concerns how to arrive at what is right, and it consists in rectifying mistakes by discussion and experience. The whole value of human judgement, says Mill, is that it can be set right when wrong, and any conduct worthy of respect is that which is exposed to criticism. What is fixed on temporarily as right is the outcome of the collision of opposing opinions. Even what is wholly true must be contested to avoid its becoming a mere prejudice.

This procedure does not allow the imposition of a moral truth, or the coercion of those not seized of it, in Mill's view, because coercion is only legitimate for the protection of the self and not for the enlightenment of others.[82] But it does suggest a view of the discussion of human rights in international politics as appealing to the empire of reason and not merely to that of power, or circumstance. It supposes, more deeply, that no human being can seriously hold some ethical principle to be right, or imperative, without wishing that others too deem it right, or imperative. '*I* believe in the maxim "Thou shalt not kill", but it doesn't matter if *you* don't,' is a curious moral doctrine. It would be as curious held by societies as by individuals. The debate about human rights between cultures presupposes an anxiety on all sides to win it.

So we have returned to the single moral universe of the natural rights theorists. It may be argued that this is the only world in which it is possible to make sense of an African, or a Muslim, or a Chinese, or a western claim about an order of moral priorities. Each of them would have the world as a whole adopt its particular priorities. If this were not true of any one of them, there would be no reason for the rest to take it seriously. But each of them at the same time accepts that a rational conversation about rights, Mill's procedure, is worth having. The point, put as a point of prudence, has been well expressed in Chinese legal doctrine, in a passage arguing for the reality of international law, and against cultural relativism. The position 'They say they are right, we say we are right,' was detrimental to China's struggle because it would then have no legal right to criticize the infraction of the law by capitalist countries.[83] If the single moral world were not a reality, it would be a good idea to invent it.

We have now defined human rights, asserted a minimum content for them, and presented an argument for the universality of their application. We pass now to the debate on human rights in contemporary world politics, for which our stipulated definitions will be a guide but not a strait-jacket.

Part Two: Practice

4   Human rights in East–West relations

The history of East–West relations in the modern sense of that expression, as the contact between socialist countries and western liberal democracies, is in an important sense the history of a dispute about human rights. In doctrine, equality is opposed to liberty, group rights to those of individuals, economic and social rights to civil and political rights. In practice, the East claims superiority in the actual provision of such rights as that to work, and to an adequate standard of living for all, while the West claims to do better on individual freedom, civil liberties, freedom of information and the other values associated with an 'open society'. The debate continues, at the level of both theory and practice, and it may be argued that it is the different priorities of East and West in the matter of human rights, and therefore their different modes of organizing society to meet them, that provide the reason for the dispute between them.[1]

The dispute, in our modern sense, begins with the Bolshevik Revolution. It is true that some roots of contemporary Soviet human rights doctrine can be traced to the communalism of Russian village society necessary to individual survival.[2] It is also true that the Decree on Peace of the revolutionaries in power in November 1917 recalled the attachment of the French Revolution to the principle of national self-determination.[3] But nation was to give way to class as the instrument of liberation, and the dictatorship of the proletariat was to be established to govern in the interests of the oppressed. The individual might be, ultimately, the beneficiary of this liberation, but it was to be achieved through the community and not against it.

Liberation involved the ending of capitalism, which was the instrument for exploitation of class by class. And since capital had no country, but was actually or potentially universal, the campaign against it had to be fought on a global scale. The implication of this for Soviet foreign policy seemed to be that it would consist of permanent struggle until the revolution was successful everywhere. The establishment of the Communist International to organize the international revolution suggested that this implication had been grasped. But at the same time the Soviet Union had to survive from day to day in a world overwhelmingly hostile to the revolution. The need to provide for the security of the Soviet state, and also to champion the revolution which made the state legitimate, imposed on the Bolsheviks a dual foreign policy: coexist with capitalist governments by agreeing, among other things, to non-interference while encouraging the revolution among their peoples.[4]

This was not a dilemma unique to the Soviet Union. Its principal western adversary from the Second World War onward shared in the discomfort of a revolutionary tradition. The truths that the American revolutionaries held to be self-evident were not just for Americans but for all men, and any men anywhere deprived of the rights to life, liberty and the pursuit of happiness had a claim to American attention. But, owing to the limitations to its power, in reality the United States could not move ahead simultaneously on all fronts towards the Americanization of the world.[5] Just as in Soviet doctrine, the call to intervention on behalf of that liberty which justified the establishment of the revolutionary state is combined with a reciprocal arrangement for non-intervention between governments.[6]

In the Cold War, the ideologies of human rights held by the Soviet Union and the United States met head on, and the contest was the fiercer for the strength of conviction on both sides. The ideas of the protagonists about human rights were not mere preferences which outsiders could take or leave, but commitments the spread of which both measured progress in the contest between the superpowers and, in turn, strengthened or weakened the domestic legitimacy of their governments. This chapter explores the contest, first by examining what is at issue in the argument about human rights, and then by describing the attempt of each superpower to see its attitude to human rights make progress on the territory of the other. It will then look at alternatives to the policy that has actually been pursued, alternatives that might make more or less of human rights in foreign policy, in order that a judgement can be made in conclusion about what ought to be done as well as what is done.

THE ISSUES

There is, first, a disagreement about where human rights come from. In Marxist-Leninist doctrine rights come from law, which comes from government, which reflects the underlying economic relationships of any society.[7] In capitalist society, the content of what are called human rights will reflect the interests of the capitalist class; in socialist society, those of the proletarian class. Where the two kinds of society exist together, there cannot be equal rights to, say, liberty, to both parties, because it is the nature of capitalist society to extinguish the liberty of the masses. Thus, in the transition to socialism, the proletariat has rights, but not the bourgeoisie; the people have a right to liberty but not the oppressors.[8]

Given this division into exploiters and exploited, it is difficult to find a place in Marxist-Leninist theory for *human* rights except when the expropriators have been expropriated, and all are free in socialist society. But if a notion of human rights can survive during the transition, it is in the form of a theory of desert, or of need, rather than that of a theory of worth regardless of circumstance, the notion that informed our discussion of definition in Chapter 1. Those who do work that is socially useful acquire thereby human dignity and human rights.[9] This is in sharp contrast to the western natural rights tradition, which deals out rights to people because of their very humanity, and not because they deserve them, or happen to be located in a particular class, or find them useful in the struggle against an oppressor.

Because rights in Marxist-Leninist doctrine derive from a fundamental economic relationship, from the place of the individual in a pattern of production, it is not surprising that economic and social rights are taken to come before civil and political rights, and this is the second disagreement between East and West. The primary liberty in the socialist countries is economic: the freedom from exploitation that is delivered by having power in the hands of the working-class. The absolute right to work is the mark of this freedom, different in kind from the freedom in the West to choose one's exploiter or to be unemployed.[10] And in the Soviet constitution there follow the rights to leisure, health care, pensions, housing, education, and the use of cultural achievements.[11] Only after these is there mention of such classical bourgeois rights as freedom of speech, of the press and of assembly.[12] And because of the fundamental nature of the achievement of emancipation from capitalist exploitation, these civil and political rights always remain subordinate to it – they cannot be used against the socialist system which guards the primary freedom.

Against this stands the almost unconditional liberty of western political theory, the right of each individual to pursue his or her own purposes free from the interference of others, subject only to the equal freedom of others to pursue their purposes. So powerful is this idea in the West that even the moral sceptics feel its attraction. If there are any moral rights at all, says H.L.A. Hart, there is at least one natural right, the equal right of all men to be free.[13] All civil and political rights flow from and are made sense of in terms of this proposition, and they are in a quite different league from the economic and social rights of Soviet doctrine, which are really political preferences rather than moral rights. Thus, even when western politicians concede, as they did in the United States during the Carter Administration, that there might be a 'right to the fulfillment of such vital needs as food, shelter, health care and education',[14] it continues to take second place to libertarian values in both theory and policy.[15]

Liberty in Marxist-Leninist doctrine is achieved through the group, the proletarian class which acts to end exploitation. This constitutes the third important difference between East and West in the matter of human rights. The state, which is the buttress of liberty in Marxist-Leninist doctrine, is, in the West, the threat to freedom against which individuals must constantly be on their guard. The state in the East plays an active part in the provision of rights, not merely in the sense that it lets citizens know what rights circumstances allow them to have, but also as a direct producer of them. A commitment to such economic and social rights as those to work, to leisure and to health care, taken seriously, requires the substantial involvement of the group: they cannot be achieved by individual endeavour alone.

In assigning, thus, a crucial role to the group, Soviet doctrine shares the characteristics of African, Chinese and Islamic conceptions of human rights that were surveyed in the preceding chapter. It follows that, as in these instances, community and obligation seem to come before individual and right. The group as the grand provider itself has rights in virtue of which the individual has correlative duties. But this is not a call for self-abnegation. Observing duties to the group is the best way of looking after individual rights. The two things pull in the same direction. This doctrine is regarded with the deepest suspicion in the liberal West, where the guarantee of liberty is thought to lie in setting limits to the power of the state rather than adding to it.

All these disagreements, about where rights come from, which have priority, and whom they belong to, are illustrated in the argument between East and West about dissidents in the Soviet Union. Dissent is not a new phenomenon in the Soviet Union, nor is it something which began in Russia only after the Revolution.[16] But its modern phase can be traced to Khrushchev's famous initiation of 'de-Stalinization' in 1956.[17] The prominent landmarks since have been the arrest and trial of Sinyavsky and Daniel, the closed trial of Bukovsky and Litvinov's distribution of his final statement, the flowering of the Democratic Movement,* including the establishment of its unofficial journal the *Chronicle of Current Events*, the establishment of Helsinki Monitoring Groups after the Conference on Security and Cooperation in Europe, the expulsion of Solzhenitsyn, and the internal exile of Sakharov.[18]

Dissent has taken a number of forms, including, according to one classification, repatriatory dissent (Jews, Tartars, Germans, Meshketians), indigenous national protest (the Russian objection to persecution of orthodoxy), separatist demands (Baltic states, Ukraine), the demand for religious rights (Orthodox,

---

* This 'movement' was a loose coalition of different groups among the intelligentsia that were united by their interest in the publication of the *Chronicle of Current Events*, in liberal reform, in the rule of law, in civic education and in a measure of pluralism in Soviet society. See Peter Reddaway, *Uncensored Russia* (London, Cape, 1972).

Catholic, Protestant), the establishment of groups pursuing economic rights, and professional groups pressing for freedom of creative inquiry.[19] None of these forms of protest on its own, it might be argued, is of particular significance, but the same cannot be said of their coalescing into a Democratic Movement united by a commitment to law as the instrument for the achievement of civil rights, and by insistence on freedom of opinion and expression.[20]

The least sophisticated reaction of the Soviet government to the dissident movement is to call it names. The dissidents are, variously, renegades, slanderers, parasites, extortioners and hippies.[21] Those lionized in the West are recognized in the East for what they really are: a 'defender of the nation' in reactionary circles abroad is known at home as a 'hardened, habitual thief'.[22] It is suggested that there is gleeful applause for the Soviet government among segments of society other than the intelligentsia when the latter is put in its place.[23]

That there is a logic behind the name-calling is revealed in the more sophisticated Soviet reaction to the dissidents. There is, first, the idea that the rights of Soviet citizens did not drop from the sky, but were produced by Soviet society. Accordingly, constructive criticism was a right of all citizens, but not anti-Sovietism, which dwelt on only the negative aspects of society and failed to recognize its achievements. Some concrete reason must underlie this wilful omission on the part of the dissidents, such as their surrender to their western paymasters.[24] In the second place, socialist society, through its provision of economic and social rights, had liberated the mass of the people and not just the bourgeoisie whose values were reflected by the dissidents.[25] And, third, but implicit in the previous two notions, there is the idea of the primacy of communitarian values achieved in the socialist transcendence of the self-interested egoism of the bourgeoisie.[26] The self-interested egoism of the dissidents allied them with anti-socialist interests outside the Soviet Union, from which their protest really sprang, and coming thus from outside the system they deserved no protection within it.

Reflected in a western mirror, the view of the dissidents is different. Renegades and parasites become outstandingly courageous individuals on whose qualities the possibility of progress in the Soviet Union depends.[27] The appeal that the dissidents make for liberty, and for freedom of information, cannot fail to gather a western audience, especially in the United States, which was founded for the protection of such universal human rights. The idea that the achievement of a minimum standard of economic and social welfare for the great mass of the Soviet population might justify the extinction of freedom among a minority which still finds proper cause for protest on the ground of liberty is anathema in the West. It supposes that the human right to liberty, which everyone has, vanishes as soon as a group seeks to sacrifice it for a supposedly greater value. The barrier of human rights here collapses just at the point at which its strength should be greatest. And there is, finally, the fear on the right in the West that the celebration of the achievement of communitarian values leads up a one-way street to a totalitarianism which seeks 'to break all social bonds except the ones it has created'.[28]

These disagreements between East and West on the matter of human rights have not been the subject just of a conversation between the blocs. There have also been attempts, by both sides, to shape the human rights policy of the other, or at least to have some influence on it. It is to human rights in this context that we now turn.

THE ISSUES IN INTERNATIONAL POLITICS

It was suggested above that it is possible to interpret the whole of East–West politics in terms of a dispute about human rights. But in the recent history of East–West relations the question of human rights has been associated above all with the Final Act of the Helsinki Conference on Security and Cooperation in Europe of 1975.[29] This agreement gave roughly equal space to questions relating to security in Europe and the Mediterranean, to cooperation in the fields of economics, science and technology, and the environment, and to cooperation in humanitarian and other fields. This shape, it seems, was formed primarily by a deal done between a Soviet Union anxious to legitimize existing European frontiers, and thus its hegemony in Eastern Europe, and a West anxious to extract a price for this recognition of what was already an unchallenged fact.

The deal was symbolized by the juxtaposition, in the Declaration on Principles Guiding Relations between Participating States, of Principle VI on non-intervention, with Principle VII on human rights. The non-intervention principle contained an extensive definition of the action from which the participating states were to refrain, including direct or indirect, individual or collective, armed or unarmed intervention in internal or external affairs. The human rights principle included in its title the freedom of thought, conscience, religion or belief, and went on to produce a list of rights and freedoms longer than that comprising the types of intervention disallowed by the preceding principle. In the Final Act itself, these two principles enjoyed equal status along with the other eight: sovereign equality, refraining from the threat or use of force, inviolability of frontiers, territorial integrity of states, peaceful settlement of disputes, equal rights and self-determination of peoples, fulfilment in good faith of obligations under international law, and cooperation among states. In practice, the issue of human rights between East and West has been an essay on the rival claims of Principle VI and Principle VII.

In the western view, Principle VI was no barrier to the international discussion of human rights in the Soviet Union, or indeed to monitoring them, negotiating about them, or using influence to improve them.[30] This view was based on two grounds. In the first place, human rights were now a matter of international concern in virtue of the existence of a body of conventional and customary law on human rights that was referred to in the Final Act.[31] So the plea of an area of domestic jurisdiction which the principle of non-intervention was designed to protect was not in this context acceptable. And, secondly, the classical conception of intervention in international law consisted not in any kind of interference in domestic affairs, but only in dictatorial interference which sought coercively to subordinate the exercise of sovereign rights to foreign interests.[32] The implication of this is that lesser action than dictatorial interference is not illegal. It is true that the Final Act was, by the explicit agreement of the parties, not a treaty creating legal obligation, but, in the western view, the fact that it did not add to international law could not be used in an attempt to subtract human rights obligations from it.

Not a treaty, the Final Act was nevertheless an agreement which the parties undertook to implement.[33] And they undertook, also, to meet again to discuss implementation and other matters. This happened in Belgrade in 1977, and in Madrid from 1980 to 1983. And a review conference specifically on human rights took place in Ottawa in 1985. As a result of Helsinki, and these follow-up conferences, a new bureaucratic task for all participating governments has been that of monitoring implementation at home and abroad, in order that ammunition is provided for both defence and attack of the record of fidelity to the Final Act. And the matter has not been left to governments. Parliaments, political parties and private organizations have also been involved, and Helsinki Monitoring Groups have been established in the East as well as in the West.[34]

Though western governments have been involved in monitoring performance in all sections of the Final Act, public and press attention has been chiefly on its human rights provisions, both Principle VII, and the measures for humanitarian cooperation in Basket III. The latter include provision for more human contact (family reunification, travel on business and tourism, meetings among young people and sport), freer information (circulation, cooperation, working conditions for journalists), and enhanced cultural and educational cooperation. Under these heads, the human rights issues which have received the greatest attention in the West include the search, arrest and trial of human rights activists and the misuse of psychiatry in their punishment; the continuing Soviet view of the right to emigrate as a privilege to be granted by the authorities rather than a matter of individual choice; the jamming in the Soviet Union of western radio broadcasts; and the Soviet denial that there can be cultural cooperation and exchange 'without boundaries or barriers'.[35] Saddest of all, in terms of what the West wanted from the Helsinki process, has been the harassment, arrest, exile and imprisonment of members of Helsinki Monitoring Groups in the Soviet Union and Eastern Europe.

The Soviet response to all of this was to insist at every turn on the principle of non-intervention. This did not involve a denial that human rights were a matter of international concern: the Soviet Union had after all gone along with the inclusion of human rights and fundamental freedoms as one of the principles governing relations between the Helsinki participants. But it did involve a denial that any foreign government, group or individual had any business overseeing the process of implementing human rights in the Soviet Union, or in Eastern Europe generally: this was a matter for the sovereign jurisdiction of the states concerned.[36] Interference with implementation was thus illegitimate whether it came in the form of a protest by a United States president, a declared wish by a congressional Helsinki Commission to inspect implementation in the Soviet Union, or a move by a Helsinki Monitoring Group to convey bourgeois propaganda to the East.

What the Soviet Union objected to in general about the western attitude to Helsinki was its lack of any semblance of balance – characterized by the obsession with the dissidents. Too much attention was given to Principle VII compared with the other nine principles. Basket III was emphasized at the expense of the other two, where the Soviet record was arguably better than that of the West. Within Basket III the western focus was on such matters as freedom of information rather than on, say, cultural contact – where again the record of the socialist countries was said to be superior to that of the West.[37] And on the matter of freedom of information itself, the West showed its bias by using such freedom to abuse the Soviet system, rather than seeking, in the spirit of détente, to cooperate in the exchange of information to achieve mutual understanding.[38] The dissidents, after all, were a tiny, isolated and atypical section of socialist society.

When the Soviet Union invoked the spirit of détente, something different was meant from when the same invocation was made in the West. And at the centre of this difference lay the disagreement about the place of human rights in international politics. In the West, the phase of détente ushered in by the Helsinki agreement was thought to consist in a new style of international relations as a result of a relaxation in ideological tension between the blocs, and a new subject-matter of human rights added to the old concerns with trade and security.[39] These developments would be visible in the gradual opening up of the closed societies of Eastern Europe and the Soviet Union. If détente were not to result in a relaxation of this kind, then what was it for? It is this point of view which connects together western attitudes which are, in other respects, widely divergent. The Jackson–Vanik Amendment of 1974, which sought to link the extension of most-favoured-nation treatment to the Soviet Union to freer Jewish emigration; the willingness of the Carter Administration to utter specific protests about official offences against human rights in the socialist countries; and Henry Kissinger's quiet diplomacy on particular human rights issues: all have a liberating purpose, however modest.

For the Soviet Union, détente also meant a relaxation of tension, but this was to take place between governments, not between societies. The ideological struggle was to continue unabated. But this was to take the form of a 'comparison of ideas and facts and a dispute over the intrinsic values of a particular system and must not be turned into a conscious incitement of mistrust and hostility, the falsification of reality or, least of all, subversive activity'.[40] The western human rights campaign was not ideological struggle, but psychological warfare of just this subversive kind, and it breached the principle of non-intervention.[41] Détente consisted of businesslike relations based on the non-intervention principle, and the Soviet Union played a noble role in international relations as guardian of this principle.[42]

The result of these different interpretations of détente is that what the West takes to be the evidence of its working – progress in its conception of human rights – is taken by the Soviet Union to be the very thing which undermines it because it seeks to subordinate Soviet domestic affairs to foreign interests. And what the Soviet Union takes to be the evidence of its working – strict adherence to non-intervention – is taken by the West to be a surrender to Soviet imperialism in, for example, Afghanistan and Poland. It follows that when the West has pursued its interest in détente, its intentions have been perceived as hostile by the Soviet Union, and this has led to a counter-attack on what is held to be the dismal human rights record of the United States and others: unemployment, racial discrimination, lawlessness, the impending police state.[43] And when the Soviet Union has pursued its interest in détente, the West has rehearsed its interpretation of the principle of non-intervention as excluding, above all, armed coercion across international frontiers, and has threatened to bring progress in other Helsinki areas, such as trade and credits (Basket II), to a halt.

These unintended consequences of the inclusion of a human rights component in western foreign policies have led many to despair of such a programme. The Soviet acceptance of Principle VII at Helsinki, thought by some to be 'something of a miracle',[44] turns out to be less a matter for western self-congratulation than was thought at the time. In the conclusion to the chapter we shall have to explore whether it is worth continuing with a human rights policy of the kind that has been discussed above. Meanwhile, there are alternative views to consider, including the one that would have such a policy better not embarked on in the first place.

Practice

We have examined that period in East–West relations in which the foreign policies of western states generally, but especially the policy of the United States, took account of human rights not as something which, in the end, we all believe to be a good thing, but as something in regard to which we wanted something from the Soviet Union and its East European allies. Policy on human rights did not have to take this form. That it did in the United States might be attributed to the need for a new domestic legitimation of foreign policy after Vietnam, a need which was reflected in congressional concern with human rights from the early 1970s, and later in the election of a president determined to give human rights a prominent part in making foreign policy. That it did in Europe might be attributed to the realization that certain concrete concessions might be won from the Soviet Union on the pattern of the four-power agreement on Berlin of 1971. But in neither case was it true to say that circumstances allowed no other policy than the one followed. We shall consider here three alternatives: the policy which excludes human rights altogether on the ground that they get in the way of the working of the society of states; the policy that places the interests of the dissidents above every other consideration according to the ancient maxim *fiat justitia ruat caelum* (let justice be done though the heavens should fall); and the policy which, in steering a course between these two, nevertheless makes more of human rights even than was done during the Carter Administration in Washington.

The policy that seeks to exclude human rights altogether is not necessarily an immoral or an amoral one. In the version of it that has been called 'the morality of states' it seeks to uphold such conventions of diplomacy as the principle of non-intervention on the ground that the interests they defend are of greater moral weight than those of individuals, or groups within states.[45] Unless the order which the states enclose, and protect by such instruments as the principle of non-intervention and that of the balance of power, is preserved, then there is no prospect of the achievement of justice for groups and individuals within the state. Order precedes justice. And order in such a rudimentary society as that formed between states is placed under threat if the statesmen make too many demands on it, such as the expectation that it is competent to act in the matter of human rights. The human rights policy which, misjudging the extent of solidarity among states, sets out to improve the international order by enriching the quality of justice within states, might end by placing at hazard the minimal order already achieved.

This is because states, which are disposed anyway, in Burke's phrase, to equivocate, scuffle and fight, might find in a human rights policy not only another issue to dispute about, but also one full of destructive potential. The initiating state will be suspected of having ulterior motives. Even if this were not

70

so, the target state will resent the intrusion: it comes from abroad, and it smacks of moral imperialism. It is unlikely that outside influence could disrupt a domestic pattern of conduct. But if the intrusion were substantial enough to achieve this, then it is unlikely that any wrong would have been righted without equally substantial and not necessarily positive side-effects. Worst of all, disputes about human rights raise fundamental ideological questions which, once out of the bag, prompt the disputants to show that they mean what they say: not a formula for peaceful coexistence. Hence the appeal of the principle of non-intervention: to the guardians of international order because it sets limits to their competition, and to the small states at the opposite end of the international hierarchy as a defence of their independence.

In recent American foreign policy Henry Kissinger is most closely associated with the exclusion of human rights considerations from foreign policy. Sometimes this is rendered as an amoral preoccupation with the interests of the state, which results in obliviousness to the claims of Chilean electors, East Pakistani separatists, blacks in South Africa, and people on the receiving end of oppression and torture in South Korea, or Indonesia, or Brazil, or Iran.[46] But Kissinger himself was concerned to defend the morality of state interests. Security, in a dangerous world, came first. In American relations with the Soviet Union the overriding concern was the prevention of nuclear war, an objective that should not be muddled or undermined by too close an interest in domestic Soviet behaviour. And, in general, a foreign policy that was 'moralistic' in departing from the conventions of diplomacy was liable to turn quixotic, or dangerous, or merely empty: the politics of posture.[47]

According to the logic of the morality of states, there was good reason for Kissinger in 1975 to advise the president not to receive Solzhenitsyn when he visited Washington. In view of this, it is a mistake to declare that the 'impurity of that gesture resonated in the consciousness of those who felt that morality had at least a symbolic role to play in foreign policy'.[48] The question can be made one of competing moralities, and not of morality versus something else. Nevertheless, it is the idea that the universe of free individuals, or of individuals who ought to be free, should trump any rival morality that informs the view of those who argue that the rights of dissidents in the Soviet Union should take first place in the foreign policies of western countries. This is the view most closely associated with Solzhenitsyn himself. The oppressed people in the Soviet Union were the natural allies of the West.[49] Accordingly, détente should aim at concessions to them by the Soviet government, not at concessions to the Soviet government by the West.[50] The proper western policy was to put pressure on the Soviet government to liberalize at home, and to cease disseminating anti-western propaganda abroad. Such a policy would allow the heroic struggle of the dissidents, based on principle and conscience, to bear fruit rather than being overtaken by weak-kneed concessions to the Soviet government. At the least, the West should slow down these concessions. At the most the West should interfere more and more, as much as it could, for the cause of the dissidents.[51] What supposedly reciprocal agreements not to intervene amounted to was appeasement, a sell-out to the interests of the Soviet state, a refusal to stand by the principles of democracy.

The third alternative takes something from Solzhenitsyn and something from Kissinger, and adds a cosmopolitan component found in neither of the others. It shares with the view of Solzhenitsyn the idea that détente is nothing unless accompanied by a democratization of the Soviet Union which will allow liberty to the dissidents. And it shares too with Solzhenitsyn the view that détente should involve pressure on the Soviet government from a unified West, and not merely the relaxation of tension between governments. It is the policy of the Jackson–Vanik Amendment, requiring the Soviet Union to pay a domestic price for economic, scientific and technological help from the West. Among the dissidents, it is the prescription for western policy written by Sakharov. What it takes from Kissinger is the idea that 'the problem of lessening the danger of annihilating humanity in a nuclear war carries an absolute priority over all other consider-ations'.[52] Attacks on this problem, such as the talks on strategic arms limitation, should not be linked to improvement in other areas of East–West relations such as the question of human rights.

The cosmopolitanism of Sakharov is revealed in his doctrine of the indivisibility of human rights. Not only does injustice anywhere diminish mankind everywhere, but it is a threat to justice all over the world.[53] This belief in the reality of a universal community of mankind has given rise sometimes to the assertion of such seemingly absurd propositions as that which looks forward to the United States and the Soviet Union leading the military forces of the United Nations in defence of 'the rights of man'.[54] But there is in it also a largeness of vision not shown either by Kissinger's residence within the world of great powers, or by what has been called Solzhenitsyn's 'Moscow-centrism'.[55]

There are, then, difficulties with each of the three alternatives. Of Kissinger and the morality of states it might be said that by his own realist lights the world has passed him by. Human rights are on the agenda of international politics, and the question now is what to do about them, not whether or not to do anything about them. That Kissinger himself came to recognize this is demonstrated by the increasing attention he gave to matters of human rights during his last years in office.[56] Indeed, in terms of the language used, there was less difference than is popularly supposed between the last year of Kissinger, and the first of Carter. Rhetoric, not substance, no doubt, but there is a sense in which rhetoric shapes substance.

In the case of Solzhenitsyn, there is not only his Moscow-centrism, his obliviousness to world problems which might actually be greater than those of the dissidents, but also his notion that the West has a greater interest in the dissidents than in the government of the Soviet Union. It might be argued that the prevention of the outbreak of nuclear war has more to do with a relationship with the Soviet government than with the rights of the dissidents, and that interference on behalf of the latter should not be allowed to place at risk the avoidance of the former.

The difficulty with the Jackson—Sakharov alternative is that it expects too much from western pressure. As Sakharov himself came to recognize, there was something utopian about the idea of a disinterested concern on the part of western governments for the rights of the dissidents.[57] And, in any event, external pressure might easily produce the opposite of what was intended. Hence the vitality of that strand of thought, among the dissidents themselves, which looks within the Soviet Union for sources of change rather than outside it.[58]

CONCLUSIONS

If human rights in East—West relations is such a minefield, it might be argued, as we have seen, that it is better for the makers of foreign policy not to attempt to negotiate it. A foreign policy of human rights might produce results which are the opposite of what is intended: as, for example, when western attention to the rights of Jews in the Soviet Union allows greater oppressiveness towards them on the part of the Soviet government because they can now be branded as stooges of foreign governments. It might also, as we have seen, complicate the achievement of other and more important goals of foreign policy such as the maintenance of stability in what Kissinger and Nixon used to call the 'structure of peace'. If an agreement about non–intervention is thought by the Soviet Union to lie at the heart of this structure, then western declarations that this principle is no barrier to the scrutiny of the Soviet human rights record are issued largely to itself. The Soviet view of the tract of domestic jurisdiction that is protected by the principle of non–intervention is, as we have seen, much wider than that of the West, and it includes the question of implementation of human rights agreements. Thus any western mention of implementation is, in the Soviet view, an intervention in domestic affairs, and détente is being exploited for the purposes of psychological warfare. Most radically, there is the argument that the doctrines of East and West are so different that there is no common ground between them to begin to inform and justify the intervention of one in the view of the other. Neither side, it is said, can accept the validity of a claim about human rights made by the other, much less accept that it has the authority to act on it.[59]

Let us deal with these arguments in turn. It may be true that prominence given to human rights in foreign policy will produce the opposite of the intended result in the short run: namely, the intensification of oppression rather than its relief.

73

But it is the faith of many dissidents that such oppression is a great recruiting-sergeant for the Democratic Movement, and that the immediate intensification of suffering might give place to reform in the longer term as the greater weight of protest went home.[60] And in any event, Sakharov has argued, it is the cause that recruits, not the likelihood of its success[61] – the implication being, presumably, for outsiders, that right should be supported without too timid a scrutiny of the likely consequences. And if this is an argument of faith rather than reason, reason does not instantly refute it. It is not self-evident that outside pressure is useless, as the advocates of strict non-intervention assume.

As to the argument for the primacy of the stability of the central balance, here too there is the suspicion that it might be used as an excuse rather than a reason for any decision not to recognize human rights as a goal of foreign policy. The capability for mutual assured destruction, it may be argued, has stabilized the strategic relationship between the superpowers in a way that is not likely to be thrown out of kilter by a more vocal western (or indeed eastern) policy on human rights. Certainly strategic stability should have priority, the argument runs, but there is no reason to think that the general run of advocates of more attention to human rights in foreign policy have designs on this priority. Solzhenitsyn is a lonely, romantic exception. We should, in this regard, pay attention to the Soviet doctrine of non-intervention, but not prostrate ourselves before it.

On the question of common ground between West and East on human rights, there are two replies to the view that doubts whether there is any. The first is that it is not a good reason for abstention from right conduct that calls up the fact of disagreement with it. That harassing dissidents is thought to be right by a Soviet government which sees dissent as anti-socialist should not affect our view that it is wrong, though it might affect our strategy in doing something about it. The second reply is that neither side really thinks the argument of cultural exclusiveness to be true. Their ideological disagreement takes it for granted that there is a common universe of discourse between them, and that it is possible for each side to understand the other. And each side, especially when represented by its chief advocate the United States, or the Soviet Union, seeks to persuade the other, by various means, to adopt the better course. Moreover, each side has the capacity to wound the other: the East the West on equality, the West the East on liberty. This capacity reveals the common ground between the blocs as well as what divides them, since the battle is intelligible only in terms of political ideals proclaimed by both of them. In this regard, it is more accurate to interpret the contest between East and West as a schism within a single civilization, a secular version of the earlier religious divide, than as a dispute between civilizations. Indeed, a direct comparison has been drawn between Helsinki and the Treaty of Osnabrück (1648), which created the 'détente' between Catholics and Protestants among the German states, and provided, in particular, for the rights of individuals who were the subjects of Princes of another religion.[62]

Even if all this were granted, a foreign policy of human rights might be objected to on the ground that it is expecting too much of any state to confine itself to the disinterested pursuit of human rights for foreigners. It is more reasonable, it might be argued, to expect a mixture of motives. In pursuing in good faith the rights of Soviet dissidents, the United States might not be too disappointed with a break-up of the Soviet Union which accompanied it. In view of this, there seems to be one of two possibilities. One is a *Realpolitik* of human rights. The charge of ideological imperialism is cheerfully accepted, and the West in foreign policy goes about saving souls for the rights of man. The second is that the West, recognizing the charge of imperialism, and taking it seriously, seeks to detach human rights as far as is possible from the clamour of political debate, and quietly insists on them as what everybody ought to have regardless of their religion, ideology and so on, preferring cases to causes.

In East–West relations (as well as in others), it may be that the latter course is to be preferred to the former, and the theme of detaching the issue of human rights from the exchange of ideological abuse among the powers will be pursued at greater length in Part Three below. But whatever the policy adopted, the West should recognize and preserve its crucial role in the communication of information about human rights in the Soviet Union and Eastern Europe, and insist for this reason on the principle of freedom of information endorsed at Helsinki. If it is true that great writers are the functional equivalent of an opposition in the Soviet Union, the West should at least play the part of providing them with an outlet.

5 Human rights in North–South relations

The debate about human rights in North–South relations is to some extent a rehearsal of the issues in dispute between East and West. Once more individualism and liberty are ranged against collectivism and equality; civil and political rights against economic and social rights. The difference is that the East–West debate takes place between established systems, two varieties of 'have' countries, whereas the North–South dispute is between 'haves' and 'have-nots'. Because of this, there is arguably more vitality in the North–South dispute on human rights. It is not a mere conversation, but a project from which one side looks to gain materially at the expense of the other.

'North' and 'South' are now terms established in the contemporary vocabulary of international politics, but the membership of each group is not always clear. A view from the South might see East and West coalescing into a North which bears all the distinguishing marks of modernity – industrialization, a high standard of living, urbanization, high technology – and which is more remarkable for what its members have in common than for what divides them. But within the North, East and West, and countries within these categories, might be more preoccupied with what sets them apart from each other than what unites them. Certainly, the Soviet Union is anxious to distance itself from the exploitative North. 'It is not the Soviet Union who for ages used to plunder the national wealth of former colonial possessions which nowadays have come to be sovereign states. Therefore the Soviet Union does not bear ... any responsibilty whatsoever for the economic backwardness of the developing countries, their present hard situation, particularly under the conditions of the aggravation of the economic crisis of the world capitalist economy.'[1] The West, for its part, is sometimes inclined to urge the Soviet Union to be more northern by, for example, matching the levels of aid to developing countries achieved by the West, but is more often disposed to assert itself as a different and superior model for southern development. One rather neat version of this disposition is the notion that it is possible to win East–West in

North–South,[2] and the implications of this theme are something to which we shall return.

Nor is the South a homogeneous grouping in world politics. It is not uniformly poor. Not all of it was colonized by the North, and parts of it that were have not all received their independence only recently. Not all of it is non-aligned in the contest between East and West. And not all of it is geographically in the South. But it is a term that has come to stand for the group of states united by the demand for a new international economic order, the so-called Group of 77 of the United Nations Conference on Trade and Development.* And the South so defined locates the North for the purposes of this chapter. It is that part of the North which colonized the South, against which there is a common feeling of grievance and demand for retribution, together with the current exploiters who are said to keep the South still in something like colonial subordination by maintaining an economic structure that benefits the centre at the expense of the periphery. It is, then, human rights in West–South relations on which this chapter will focus, with the East appearing from time to time on the side of the South.

Within the West, the debate about human rights in North–South relations is sometimes treated as a discussion between lawyers and economists in which neither group pays sufficient attention to what the other is saying.[3] The lawyers, well versed in the language of civil rights, come to the discussion prepared to protest against rapid economic development if it prejudices the liberty of individuals. And the economists, whose language is that of growth, take this objective to condone breaches of civil rights. It is put as a question of human rights versus economic development.

This is a rather old-fashioned formulation, which has been overtaken by events. As we have seen, the discussion is not now between rights and something else, but between different versions of rights: particularly civil and political and economic and social. The broader comparison here is between political thought in the West, which, it is said, has emphasized form – constitutions, procedures, who is to do things rather then what is to be done – and socialist thought, which has emphasized substance to the neglect of form.[4] The advantage of the western pattern is the achievement of liberty; of the socialist pattern, that of equality. The disadvantage of the western pattern is economic injustice, of the eastern pattern tyranny. Not surprisingly, the rival patterns extend conceptions derived from their comparative advantage at home into the discussion of human rights in international politics. And this broader comparison is relevant for our present purpose, because of the argument that in the Third World it is the socialist

---

* The name 'Group of 77' derives from the number of Third World States attending the first UNCTAD conference in 1964. There are now about 120 members in the Group.

pattern that is in general preferred because it holds out the prospect of greater equality sooner.[5]

But the discussion of human rights in North–South relations has not rested here. From the idea of a contest between civil and political rights and economic and social rights, it has moved on to an assertion of the priority of the latter. Rather than starting a treatment of the rights of man with Locke on liberty, it might refer to that passage of *The Second Treatise of Government* which has Reason telling us that 'Men, being once born, have a right to their Preservation, and consequently to Meat and Drink, and such other things, as Nature affords for their Subsistence'.[6] And, having started with the right of subsistence, it then seems natural to assert its priority over other human rights such as those conventionally listed as civil and political. The right to eat, it is said, is the most elementary claim.[7] And this claim becomes, in some writings, a requisite or prerequisite for the enjoyment of the rights of man.[8] A person deprived of subsistence, it has often been said, is insulted rather than dignified by a right to vote.

Acknowledgement of a universal right to subsistence has deep implications for the society of states, a subject to which we shall return at the conclusion of this chapter and in Chapters 7 and 8. But the argument of the South, at the United Nations and elsewhere, has moved beyond even this demanding proposition. It asserts not merely the particular priority of the right of subsistence, but also a general priority to economic and social rights over civil and political rights. In its most exaggerated form, it makes the exercise of all economic and social rights a prerequisite for the exercise of all other human rights and fundamental freedoms.[9]

It may be argued that this extreme doctrine is after all only a natural response to the equally extreme doctrine held by some in the West that the only human rights are civil and political rights, and that economic and social rights are mere political preferences masquerading as rights. But, standing at the extremes, neither of these views gets to grips with the important questions that are at the centre of the debate between North and South on human rights and development. When, if ever, is it justifiable to subordinate a particular civil and political right (say, that to freedom of movement) to a particular economic and social right (say, that to an adequate standard of living)? Or is the essential point about human rights that less of one cannot be traded for more of another? When, if ever, should collective rights take priority over individual rights? Do collective rights stand on their own or are they derived from individual rights? If collective rights do have an autonomous status what is their relationship with individual rights?

These are questions that we return to at the conclusion of this chapter. It is the arrival of the South in international politics that has made them prominent in the debate about human rights at the United Nations and elsewhere. Accordingly, we shall first consider southern doctrine on human rights, as it has evolved from the insistence on the collective rights of states and peoples to self-determination, through to the contemporary assertion of the primacy of economic and social rights, which are seen also as collective rights and are now associated with the right to development. The swing here is from political to economic independence. Then we shall investigate the doctrine of basic human needs, examining its individualist thrust, which confronts the collectivism of southern doctrine.

SOUTHERN DOCTRINE ON HUMAN RIGHTS

One of the purposes and principles written into the Charter of the United Nations was 'to develop friendly relations among nations based on respect for the principle of equal rights and self-determination of peoples, and to take other appropriate measures to strengthen universal peace'.[10] The Third World interpretation of this principle of self-determination is notable in three respects, which will provide a structure for this passage of the argument. First, it has emphasized that the right to self-determination imposes a duty on colonial powers to give independence. Second, it has associated practices of segregation and discrimination with colonialism, and has sought the elimination of the first two as species of the last. And, third, the countries of the Third World have stressed the economic aspects of the right of self-determination, that they may freely pursue their economic, social and cultural development, and freely dispose of their natural wealth and resources. In all three respects the North features as the principal adversary.

The Charter of the United Nations was not a rousing declaration of independence for all countries straining under the colonial yoke. It spoke cautiously of an obligation to develop, rather than immediately to grant, self-government.[11] Nor did the overwhelmingly individualist Universal Declaration of Human Rights give much ground for the assertion of the rights of nations and peoples. But in the preparatory work for the International Covenants on Civil and Political Rights, and on Economic, Social and Cultural Rights, the right of self-determination, especially as it applied to colonial arrangements, was vigorously asserted by Third World countries.[12] This vigour was rewarded in the wording of the first article of both covenants, which announced that all peoples have the right of self-determination, and that the remaining colonial countries should promote its realization.

The claim that the right of self-determination was a right properly belonging in the category of human rights, was a development advanced by the Declaration on the Granting of Independence to Colonial Countries and Peoples, adopted by the General Assembly of the United Nations in 1960.[13] It asserted that the

79

subjection of people to alien subjugation, domination and exploitation constituted a denial of fundamental human rights, was contrary to the Charter of the United Nations, and was an impediment to the promotion of world peace and cooperation. Lack of preparedness for independence should never serve as a pretext for delaying it; and immediate steps should be taken to transfer power to the peoples of non-self-governing territories.

Without such a transfer, according to a widespread and often repeated argument of the Third World, the rights of individuals within national groups could mean very little. Individuals could enjoy civil and political rights only if their community did not suffer foreign oppression. Self-determination was the precondition for the enjoyment of all other human rights. First the freedom of the nation and then the possibility of the freedom of the individual.[14] This doctrine of 'external self-determination' has been emphasized in the practice of the United Nations since the drafting of the international covenants, and the Declaration on the Granting of Independence. 'Internal self-determination', the right of people within states to choose their form of government, has been correspondingly downplayed.[15] To the extent that this is true, it is a reflection of the ascendancy of socialist and Third World conceptions of the right of self-determination over those of western countries at the United Nations.

The predominance of the doctrine of external self-determination against alien rule is a feature also of the second aspect of the principle of self-determination, the aspect from which a connection has been made between it and the elimination of racial discrimination. The idea that the institutionalization of racial discrimination is a function of imperialism is made explicit in the General Assembly resolution of 1965, which sees the objectives of the Convention on the Elimination of Racial Discrimination and those of the Declaration on the Granting of Independence being met together.[16] And the point is driven home in the International Convention on the Suppression and Punishment of the Crime of Apartheid, adopted by the General Assembly in 1973, which considers that 'an end must be put to colonialism and all practices of segregation and discrimination associated therewith'.[17] The principle of self-determination should sweep away the debris of colonialism as well as the thing itself.

The third aspect of the right of self-determination stressed in southern doctrine is the economic and social one. There is a basis for this in the Charter of the United Nations itself, which recognized that the promotion of economic and social development was connected to the creation of that stability and well-being necessary to peaceful relations founded on respect for the principle of equal rights and self-determination of peoples.[18] And the connection is made, less cumbersomely, in the first article of both human rights covenants. By virtue of the right of self-determination, all peoples may freely pursue their economic, social and cultural development. All peoples may freely dispose of their natural wealth and resources. And in no case may a people be deprived of its own means of subsistence.

The idea of economic deprivation from outside has become an increasingly important theme of southern international theory, so that in this aspect, as well as the two already considered, external self-determination is thought to come before internal self-determination. It is a theme that begins with the proposition that colonialism itself is an impediment to development.[19] It continues with the idea that economic independence should follow on from political independence, as expressed, for example, in the doctrine that sovereignty should be over natural resources as well as over the territories in which they are located.[20] Then it draws attention to inequalities in the structure of the world economy which were the product of industrialization and of the colonial era.[21] Finally, it observes the extent to which this structure is still in place, providing the means by which the economically advanced countries, notably those of the West, still exploit the weak and undeveloped by managing a system for which they wrote the rules. From this analysis flows the Third World demands for 'pay-back' – the remedying of past and present injustices inherent in the structure of the world economy – and for something more like equality of benefit from participation in the contemporary international economy. These are the normative props of the demand for a New International Economic Order, and their implications are spelled out in the 1974 Charter of Economic Rights and Duties of States. This is a charter for the have-nots. It declares that 'it is not feasible to establish a just order and a stable world as long as a Charter to protect the rights of all countries, and in particular the developing states, is not formulated'.[22]

While this Charter took respect for human rights and fundamental freedoms to be one of the principles that should inform international economic relations, it did not declare that the economic rights of states, and especially of developing states, were human rights. This is the task which the Third World countries have set themselves in the human rights fora of the United Nations since the passage of the Charter. Some groundwork, as we have seen, had already been done. The two covenants on human rights had proclaimed the interdependence of economic and social and civil and political rights, and had seemed to stress their collective aspects in the prominence given to the principle of self-determination. Then in the Proclamation of Teheran, following the international conference on human rights held there in 1968, civil and political rights and economic and social rights were still held to be indivisible, but the suggestion was made that the former might be more dependent on the latter than the other way around. 'The achievement of lasting progress in the implementation of human rights is dependent on sound and effective national and inter-national policies of social and economic development.'[23]

This tilt towards the priority of collective economic and social rights became a substantial list in Resolution 32/130 of the General Assembly in 1977, which set out the principles on which the future work of the United Nations in the field of human rights should be based. All human rights were still 'indivisible and interdependent'. But priority should be given to the rights of peoples and persons affected by apartheid, racial discrimination, colonialism, foreign domination and aggression, and by the refusal to recognize the fundamental rights of people to self-determination and of every nation to the exercise of full sovereignty over its wealth and natural resources.[24] The realization of the New International Economic Order was essential to the promotion of human rights and should be accorded priority. It was in the debate that prefaced the passing of this resolution that the assertion was made by Soviet and Third World delegates that economic and social rights were prerequisites for the exercise of all other human rights.

The next step was to entrench this priority, and this job has been done in the working out of the right to development. One influential view has this right as belonging to a third generation of human rights, following a first generation of 'negative' rights that were concerned with non-interference with individual liberties, and a second generation of 'positive' rights that dealt with social, economic and cultural rights.[25] The third generation was composed of 'rights of solidarity', including the right to development, the right to a healthy and ecologically balanced environment, the right to peace and the right to ownership of the common heritage of mankind.

Implicit in the idea of a third generation of human rights is its natural connection to the two that had gone before. Thus the first generation afforded a basis for the right to development in Article 28 of the Universal Declaration of Human Rights, which read: 'Everyone is entitled to a social and international order in which the rights and freedoms set forth in this Declaration can be fully realized.' And the second generation afforded a basis for the right to development in the idea that economic and social rights could not be secured within states without attention to the order that obtained between them. Both these bases appear in the preamble to the Draft Declaration on the Right to Development of 1983, along with the recalling of a number of other declarations and resolutions on human rights adopted by the General Assembly.[26] In the substantive part of the draft declaration, the right to development 'is an inalienable human right of every person, individually or in entities established pursuant to the right of association, and of other groups, including peoples'. By virtue of the right, every person, individually or collectively, has the right to participate in a peaceful national and inter-national order in which human rights can be fully realized. The right implies the full realization of the right of peoples to self-determination, and its effective enjoyment requires that priority be given to the establishment of a new international economic order.

To recapitulate, we have traced the evolution of southern doctrine by reference to a principle of self-determination which was addressed first to the liberation from colonialism, then to freedom from racial oppression, and then to economic and social independence. In each of these Third World interpretations of the principle of self-determination, we have suggested, the civil and political rights of individuals have had to give way to a prior claim: the collective right of a group to independence of colonial rule; the collective right of a people to ethnic autonomy; and the right of individuals and groups to such economic and social advancement as might make the enjoyment of civil and political rights possible.

The onward march of this southern doctrine on human rights has not been irresistible. The First World, in particular, has consistently insisted on at least equality of status between civil and political and economic and social rights, and has been remarkably successful in keeping alive the idea that human rights are in the end the rights of individual human beings and not of groups. The Third World, for its part, has shown its recognition of the force of this doctrine by not exploiting its majority in the General Assembly to turn international declarations of human rights into more or less straightforward statements of the collective interests of Third World countries. Nevertheless, southern priorities in the matter of human rights are undeniably different from northern ones, and the history of human rights doctrine at the United Nations reflects the change in the balance of power in the Assembly of that organization from the latter to the former.

At the conclusion of this chapter, we shall have to evaluate this change from the point of view of reason as distinct from interest. It will be a task made simpler by the criticism of southern doctrine that is both explicit and implicit in the idea of basic human needs. It is to an examination of this idea that we now turn.

BASIC HUMAN NEEDS

Along with the idea of a new international economic order, the notion of basic needs has come in recent years to be prominent in the discussion of human rights and development. Indeed, it is possible to argue that the dominant doctrine is that basic needs and not human rights should shape the strategy of development. There are several reasons for the attractiveness of the doctrine of basic needs. For one thing, it seems to have a scientific basis not shared by theories of human rights, having been taken as a starting-place for such considerable theories as the functionalist anthropology associated with Bronislaw Malinowski, and the psychology of motivation associated with Abraham Maslow.[27] For another, it seems to make a moral claim that is more urgent than that made by theories of human rights. Classical theories of human rights, it is said, began with man's numberless wants.[28] But wants may be capricious, comparing unfavourably with needs, which must be taken seriously.[29] What is necessary for human life has a stronger claim than what may be gratifying but not necessary. Needs come from nature, wants only from convention.[30] Moreover, the doctrine of basic needs seems to link science with ethics, breaking down the discredited distinction between fact and value, and providing the basis for a universal ethics derived from what is necessary for human existence.[31] All this seems to give basic needs a stronger claim than human rights to our attention and concern.

Indeed, it may be argued, the claim is so strong that it speaks for itself. Needs, or basic needs, or basic human needs, require no definition. Plainly, they comprise what is necessary for human survival – food, at least, and drink. Even if the list lengthens to include, in addition to physiological needs, those for safety, love, esteem and self-actualization,[32] then, it may still be argued, these are all intelligible in terms of the goal of survival. Our concern here, however, is not to take the claims of basic needs doctrine for granted, but to scrutinize them alongside human rights doctrine in the context of the debate about development. This will be done first by consideration of the argument that, in relation to development, the satisfaction of basic needs and not of human rights should be the first criterion. Then we shall consider the view that basic needs might complement without undermining human rights in the pursuit of development. Finally, we shall pay attention to the argument that basic human needs doctrine is a new variety of imperialism.

The preference for basic needs over human rights in the discussion of development is one associated with liberal economists in the West.[33] Their tendency is to treat rights as goals which can be subjected to economic analysis, like any other social goals, and the costs and benefits of attachment to them set out. In relation to development, it is the costs that have struck them more than the benefits. The consequences, for example, of providing for a right to education might be not only the substantial expense, but the creation of a dissatisfied class which cannot find the employment to match its attainment, and the skewing of the economy towards urbanization and away from rural development. In the same way, budgeting to meet a right to social security might lead to provision of curative medicine in towns rather than preventative medicine in the country. The acknowledgement of a right to free choice of employment might have the same effect of promoting urbanization, and the admission of a right to form and join trade unions may, through restrictive practices, allow a small section of a developing society to prosper at the expense of the growth of the society as a whole.

The point here is that many of the human rights which feature in western lists, are rights which are, indeed, associated with the western experience of modernization but which might impede that process elsewhere. The experience of development in Third World countries over the past two or three decades has been such as to question the applicability of western models. In particular, the idea that the benefits of growth in a modernizing sector of an economy would 'trickle down' to the rest of that economy has lost ground to the 'dual-economy' notion according to which a modernizing sector and a traditional sector can exist in comparative isolation from one another. Furthermore, there is less confidence in the market model of development, more talk of the provision of public goods. In both these respects, it is argued, basic needs doctrine may be more appropriate to future development than the idea of human rights, whose currency allowed the situation to become as it now is.

The doctrine of basic human needs, it is argued, provides the platform for an attack on the problem of the dual economy by insisting on provision for all members of a society. It requires attention to the shape of economic growth as well as to the creation of wealth, to distribution as much as to accumulation. Market models might not be appropriate to this endeavour. Such needs as that for uncontaminated water cannot be met in the market-place. From the point of view of balanced development, basic needs are superior to human rights in four respects. They call attention to the objective of development, which is a fuller life for all human beings. They provide a detailed schedule of the requirements for development: health, food, education, water and shelter, as well as non-material needs such as those for participation, identity and a sense of purpose. They are concrete rather than abstract. They have a non-sectarian appeal to all members of the international community interested in development. Human rights talk might be dismissed as camouflage for western interventionism: nobody is against the fulfilment of basic needs.

If this doctrine of the primacy of basic needs can be associated with liberal economists in the West, the idea that basic needs and human rights complement each other, rather than pulling in different directions, can be associated with western liberal lawyers.[34] Basic needs can distil what is fundamental from the lists of human rights. Thus, in one formulation, the virtue of the notion of basic human needs is its use in eliminating those aspects of human rights which pertain only to capitalism (such as the right to property), while adding rights that have been protected heretofore only in socialist conceptions.[35]

If this formulation can be criticized as a liberalism that tilts towards the East, the more classical rendering is that which asks how human rights and basic needs support each other: a compound rather than a distillation. Thus, on the one hand, basic needs might be said to buttress human rights by insisting on a more equitable distribution of wealth and income, by being more detailed and comprehensive, and by spelling out what is basic to human survival.[36] On the other hand, human rights complement basic needs by spelling out the content of non-material needs.[37] A doctrine of basic needs which paid attention merely to brute survival, it might be said, is a doctrine of animal rights and not of human rights. What life is worth living for is the question that informs the lists of civil and political rights. Lawyers add these rights to the basic needs of the economists.

The most ambitious liberal formulation has basic needs and human rights not merely complementing each other, but requiring each other. They are said, as we saw in United Nations doctrine earlier, to be indivisible. The argument that human rights presuppose the fulfilment of basic needs is accompanied by the assertion of a list of preconditions for the satisfaction of basic needs which reads like the classical liberal account of human rights.[38] Broad-based economic development, it is said, cannot be achieved in a repressive environment.[39] Repression and development are opposed to one another.[40] Human rights and basic needs must be met together or not at all.

Common both to the doctrine that basic needs should replace human rights as the first criterion of development, and to the idea that basic needs should complement human rights, is the notion that basic needs take account of Third World claims in a way that human rights do not. There is, however, a third view which has basic needs as a new variety of western imperialism, no less interventionist than the human rights doctrine is sought to displace.[41] Basic needs, in the western thought which informs the activities of such institutions as the World Bank, attach to individuals. Policy that pays attention to the needs of individuals would seek to avoid the road-block of the state in the development of the populations of Third World countries. What this amounts to, it is argued, is an attempt to increase western interference and not to reduce it.

It is the kind of interference, moreover, which, in seeking to bypass the state, aims also to avoid the argument for a new international economic order which is made by and on behalf of Third World states. We have already noted at some length the importance of the idea of collective economic rights for Third World countries expressed in such instruments as the Charter of Economic Rights and Duties of States. Basic needs doctrine, in positing a notion of justice among individuals, allows no room for the notion of justice among states. Indeed, it is suspicious that any such notion is really a disguise for the sectional interests of elites in Third World countries. It is a claim for transnational or cosmopolitan justice and not for international justice. It is deaf, in consequence, to the demand for a new international economic order.

This is to put the matter charitably. It takes basic human needs doctrine to be sprung from a commitment to justice for the populations of Third World countries, while observing that Third World governments have a different conception of justice. The less charitable view is that basic needs doctrine issues a general licence for western meddling in the internal affairs of Third World countries, that it allows First World countries to expand their markets in Third

World countries while slowing down competitive development by them, and that it legitimizes a reduction in aid by putting forward a bogus notion of self-reliance.[42]

There are difficulties with each of these arguments. The economists' view that basic needs have a non-sectarian appeal not shared by human rights is empirically false: basic needs are criticized for their sectarianism. If it is argued in response to this that basic needs ought to have a universal appeal, then this is no different in form from the argument that human rights ought to be universal. Indeed, the attraction of basic needs doctrine, as we shall see in the conclusion of this chapter and in Chapter 8, is not that it somehow finesses the argument for human rights, but that it sets out a programme by which they might begin to be met.

The liberal lawyers' view that human rights and basic needs complement each other is more an article of faith than a statement of a necessary connection. It is possible to point to examples of countries in which the record on meeting basic needs (as measured by the Physical Quality of Life Index[43]) is relatively good, but that on meeting civil and political rights relatively bad (China). On the other hand, it is possible to point to examples of countries in which these records are reversed (India). And there seems to be no clear correlation generally between success in meeting basic needs and success in honouring civil and political rights.[44] It may still be argued that, whether or not meeting basic needs and human rights go naturally together, they ought to be met together, and we come in our conclusion to the view that at some basic level the enjoyment of each is dependent on the other. But this is a conclusion about what ought to happen and not what must necessarily happen (though one might argue that it must necessarily happen if a properly human life is to be lived).

The rejectionist view that objects to the imperialism of basic needs doctrine is weakened if it serves to defend a local system of exploitation. If it is argued in response to this that better a local system of exploitation than a global one, this deprives the local exploited of a protest against their condition which it is the purpose of both human rights and basic needs doctrine to provide.

To what conclusion might we come in this discussion of basic needs as compared with human rights? In the first place, it is true that basic needs doctrine has a programmatic appeal that is not obvious in the lists of human rights. The idea of a hierarchy of basic needs, from physiological to psychological, with each level in the hierarchy requiring to be met before progress to the next level, seems to provide the starting-place for a detailed development strategy: first provide food and water, then security, and so on, working up Maslow's list. Added to this, there is something in the notion of the concreteness of basic needs as contrasted with human rights. If the right to life becomes the need for food, then a society has some notion of what is to be done.

In the second place, however, it is true that basic needs doctrine might, in some respects, subtract from human rights rather than supplementing them. One of these respects is that in which the economists are accused of a preoccupation with material needs at the expense of those non-material needs to which the lists of human rights give expression. Another, and related, respect is that in which the imperatives associated with basic needs may be used to legitimize the activities of an authoritarian elite.[45] It may claim to know what the needs of its population are, and act to meet them in a way that undercuts any protest mounted against it in the language of rights. This is the style of operation of the schoolmaster who knows what his pupils need, and knows too that it does not necessarily match what they want. This returns us to the distinction between what is necessary and what is merely desired, needs being associated with the former, rights with the latter. Libertarians may object to the doctrine of basic needs as a platform from which an assault on the classical civil liberties may be launched.

If these are ways in which basic needs doctrine can be said to add to and subtract from the theory of human rights, there is a third category in which basic needs purport to go beyond human rights but on inspection fail to do so. Thus it is argued that there is a flexibility and adaptability about basic needs doctrine which allows it to accommodate new concerns (such as participation and ecological balance) and to meet the requirements of particular countries depending on their circumstances.[46] In regard to the first of these claims, there is no ground for a distinction here between human rights and basic needs. The history of thought about human rights has been characterized as much by change as by continuity; and the debate about human rights at the United Nations bears witness to the truth of this observation. In regard to the second of the claims about adaptability to circumstance, the same difficulties attend basic needs doctrine as do that of human rights. The idea that human beings have basic needs which require fulfilment is no different from the assertion that they have human rights which impose correlative obligations. In both cases it is expected that circumstances should be managed in order to achieve the objective, rather than that the objective should be tampered with in order to meet circumstances. To put it baldly, basic needs doctrine is an alternative western strategy for Third World development, and not a response to Third World claims.

Accordingly, basic needs strategy might have no greater appeal to Third World countries than western theories of human rights. The Third World states make this plain when they insist – if the language of basic needs is to be spoken – on basic collective needs, or on basic national needs.[47] Then what emerges is a replay of the debate that we looked at earlier between the rights of individuals and those of groups. The individualism of basic needs doctrine is no more acceptable than the individualism of theories of human rights. The problem of how this debate is to be judged is one for our conclusions.

CONCLUSIONS

We saw, in our discussion of southern doctrine on human rights, the progress made in the international community by the idea that economic and social rights were a prerequisite for the enjoyment of civil and political rights. We observed too the headway made by the notion that economic and social rights attach to collectivities before individuals. The point of this was to establish group rights that imposed obligations on other groups: Third World rights, First World duties. Out of this doctrine of external self-determination in its economic aspect came the Charter of Economic Rights and Duties of States, and later the assertion of a right to development.

It may be argued that there is a logic to this move away from classical, western civil and political rights; and it is a logic which its adherents seek to capture by referring to generations of human rights, the one begetting another: negative rights, then positive rights, then 'solidarity' rights. In fact, difficulties attend each step along the way.

The first of these has to do with the assertion of a general priority of economic and social rights over civil and political rights. It would be hard to take seriously, for example, any suggestion that remuneration for public holidays, as an economic and social right, is a prerequisite for the enjoyment of the civil and political right not to be subjected to arbitrary arrest or detention. And even if the point were put more modestly, suggesting a general priority to basic economic and social rights, such as the right to a decent standard of living, it would be by no means self-evident. Should the right to a decent standard of living be generally prior to the right to liberty? This is the tendency of the assertion that 'human rights begin with breakfast'. But the assertion of a right to a decent standard of living itself presupposes a system in which having a right to anything means something, including the freedom to assert the right.[48] So sweeping pronouncements about priority seem doubtful, and the thesis of the interdependence of basic rights more plausible. Certainly, we may doubt the argument often used by Third World states that civil and political rights are claims that can be met once a sufficient standard of economic and social development has been met: there is no guarantee that the one will follow the achievement of the other; it has to be willed.

The second difficulty is with the assertion that collective economic and social rights should have priority over those of individuals. There is a good case for saying that the economic and social rights of individuals can often be met only by paying attention to arrangements made for groups. The provision of clean water, for example, is something that may be achieved only at a social level, and which we have come to call a public or collective good. But individuals drink the clean water, and it is their right to do so that sanctions the collective arrangements. Group rights derive in this way from the rights of individuals. The problem with that part of Third World doctrine which, through the principle of external self-determination, directs our attention to the rights of nations, or races, or states, against some foreign exploiter is that it departs from any necessary anchorage in the rights of individuals. If the human rights debate is narrowed to a focus on this external question, the internal dimension disappears. The obligation to respect human rights is exported. At home, individuals and groups are deprived of the universal language they might use to criticize their own regimes.

This is to take Third World doctrine to a logical conclusion at which it has not in fact arrived. We noted above the extent to which human rights as the rights of individuals have been kept alive in the activity of the United Nations.[49] And it may be argued that there is at least one sense in which Third World doctrine has served to enlarge the idea of individual human rights rather than to diminish it. Its stress on economic and social rights has promoted the view that the right to life is as much about providing the wherewithal to sustain life as protecting it against violence; subsistence as well as security; the right to life as a positive right requiring action by others as well as a negative right requiring merely non-interference. The emergence of the doctrine of basic needs may be interpreted as marking the reception of the force of this idea by the international community as a whole, and especially by that part of it which is officially concerned with development issues: the World Bank, for example, and the International Development Association.

The doctrine of basic human needs does not however displace, or transcend, an older conception of human rights. What it does do, and this is its strength, is to hammer away at that aspect of the right to life – the right to subsistence – which has been neglected. It reminds us of what we have in the past been inclined to forget: that the right to life has as much to do with providing the wherewithal to keep people alive as with protecting them against violent death. Dismal expectations about either of these aspects would not be compensated for by sanguine expectations about the other. At this basic level it is, then, true to say that economic and social rights (the right to subsistence) and civil and political rights (the right to security) are interdependent if something resembling a minimally satisfactory human life is to be lived. The right to life, if it exists at all, is a right to subsistence as well as to security.

If such a right implies, as we have suggested, a correlative obligation, we explore the location of this obligation in Chapter 7. We have seen that, in southern doctrine, that location has already been discovered. We may note, to conclude this chapter, an argument that we in the West should go along with this discovery for reasons of self-interest. The argument goes as follows.[50] The North–South divide is, in the words of the Brandt Report, the great social challenge of our time.[51] The argument between East and West in the North is at a stalemate, and not much change can be expected there. The decisive arena for the

East–West contest is now the South, where a great deal of change can be expected. Given the concerns of the South, which have been described in this chapter in terms of southern interpretations of the doctrine of self-determination, then the activity of the North will be judged in terms of its responsiveness to these claims. So far the Soviet Union has been more successful in associating itself with these claims, while the West has weakened its position by translating its northern argument with the Soviet Union into policy in the South. True policy for the West is to outflank the Soviet Union in the Third World by meeting southern claims rather than resisting eastern ones. This is an appealing policy, because it yokes together idealism and realism. We reach, in Chapter 8, for a higher synthesis of the two which holds out the possibility of cooperation to meet basic rights.

6 Human rights in contemporary world society

Although East–West and North–South relations take up a good part of the debate about human rights in contemporary world politics, they do not exhaust it. The object of this chapter is to come to a view about the place of human rights in world society as a whole. The approach, in the first place, will be institutional. What regimes have been established in regard to human rights at the global and at the regional levels? And what is the contribution of non-governmental organizations in the field of human rights? Then, in the light of this discussion, the next question to be asked will be about the universal values implicit in the expression 'human rights'. What is the evidence that there is the kind of convergence in regard to values in world society as a whole that we tried out in Chapter 3 as a possible sociological route to universal human rights? Might it not be that our regimes cut across rather than reinforce each other?

Finally, we shall need to ask – as a preface to the last section of the book, which looks at what is to be done about human rights in international relations – how differences, in regard both to values and to their implementation, are to be viewed. Do we adopt the shoulder-shrugging formula which observes the plurality of values in contemporary world politics and draws from it the conclusion that there is nothing to be done? Or can we build on our conclusions from Chapter 3, which asserted some political point in a conversation about human rights in international politics? To give these questions some edge, we finish the chapter with some discussion of the nature and direction of change in the impact of human rights on international relations.

HUMAN RIGHTS INSTITUTIONS

Global

In the preamble to the Charter, the peoples of the United Nations determined not merely to save succeeding generations from the scourge of war, but to reaffirm faith in fundamental human rights, in the dignity and worth of the human person, and in the equal rights of men and women and of nations large and small. The kind of language associated with revolutions within the member-states of international society, notably America and France, was now asserted on behalf of world society as a whole. Consistent with this, the United Nations took as its purpose, in addition to the maintenance of international peace and security, the promotion of respect for human rights and fundamental freedoms, and the members pledged to take joint and separate action in cooperation with the organization to achieve this goal.[1] When it is said that this commitment represents a revolution in international politics, two things are meant, the first weaker than the second. The first is that while states still constitute the membership of international society, they have taken on a revolutionary purpose, adding the needs and interests of individuals and groups other than states to their traditional preoccupation with peace and security among themselves. The second is that, in taking on these purposes, states have dissolved international society into a world society in which groups and individuals have equal standing with states.[2]

Assessment of this revolution, in its weak and strong senses, is a task for the conclusion of this chapter. The concern here is with placing human rights on a global map, showing, first, institutions, then principles and finally measures of implementation.

The acceptance of human rights as a general part of the business of international society was signalled institutionally by the establishment – by the Economic and Social Council in 1946 – of the United Nations Commission on Human Rights.[3] It is states that sit on this commission, and progress in it on the question of human rights is constrained by the preoccupations of states and interstate society. But in the year of its own establishment, the Commission appointed a Sub-Commission on the Prevention of Discrimination and Protection of Minorities, whose members sit as experts and not as representatives of governments. Partly because it is uninstructed, this body has become an important agency on the issue of human rights in general, and not just on its official concern with discrimination and minorities. A second set of human rights institutions whose range is global, at any rate potentially, is that composed of committees of review set up under various conventions such as that on the Elimination of Racial Discrimination, and that on the Elimination of Discrimination against Women. The Human Rights Committee, established under the Covenant on Civil and Political Rights, is the best known of these. Then, third, there are the political organs of the United Nations, which have an official interest in human rights, notably the third (social, humanitarian and cultural), fourth (trusteeship) and sixth (legal) committees of the General Assembly. Finally, human rights are entrenched in the global bureaucracy: in the Division of Human Rights of the United Nations Secretariat.[4]

To move on to our second item, what principles would appear on the global map of human rights? Some would. We gave, in Chapter 3, the reasons for rejecting a view of international law as composed entirely of principles for a society of states. The Universal Declaration, the Covenants, the various conventions on, for example, Slavery, the Elimination of Racial Discrimination, the Prevention of Genocide, are all international measures which not merely recognize the existence of a society beyond the society of states, but also seek to constrain the conduct of states towards that society. It is true that the map which sought to depict the principles of this society would be fuzzy, and unevenly shaded, but there would be some point in the enterprise in virtue of obligations that the states themselves had accepted. It is also true that the map would be drawn differently in different societies according to local views about the principles that most mattered in the area of human rights. But again we reviewed in Chapter 3 certain reasons for thinking that there are some human rights principles which have become peremptory norms binding on all members of international society, and we shall return to this question at the conclusion of this chapter.

The final item for the map was implementation. What is called implementation of international human rights instruments is not the kind of process that one associates with a civil service carrying out the will of an elected government. What is most commonly meant by implementation, in the United Nations context, is a system (first developed by the ILO, where it is now the most sophisticated) whereby states parties to conventions report on their fidelity to their engagements, and then a peer group reviews the reports according to procedures varying with the instruments.[5] Finally, recommendations to the states parties may follow, and, much more rarely, international conciliation to resolve a particular problem. Binding measures under the Security Council of the United Nations, or after referral to the International Court of Justice, are rarer still.

Such modest measures of implementation require modest mapping. And modesty might turn to cynicism on two grounds. The first is that where states themselves are the judges of each others' human rights records, we should not be surprised if a kind of freemasonry operated among them, making them reluctant to call each other names in public in case such a policy were to rebound to their disadvantage. Secondly, when name-calling takes place despite this constraint, we should not be surprised if it is directed not at some situation which by an objective measure is the most outrageous, but at those members of the community of states whose hold on their places in the esteem of other is weakest: pariah states like Israel or South Africa. The prospects for the implementation of human rights, evenly, throughout international society, look on this account very bleak.

There are, however, some small indicators of a brighter prospect, arising from the possibility of turning the objection to pariahs to more general account. In 1967, with its eyes fixed on southern Africa, the Economic and Social council of the United Nations passed Resolution 1235 (XLII), which authorized its human rights bodies 'to examine information relevant to gross violations of human rights and fundamental freedoms.' Then three years later, the same Council adopted Resolution 1503 (XLVIII), which, among other things, allowed the Sub-Commission on Prevention of Discrimination and Protection of Minorities to consider communications from individuals on situations 'which appear to reveal a consistent pattern of gross and reliably attested violations of human rights and fundamental freedoms'.[6] The first of these resolutions challenged the free-masonry of sovereign states; the second, the tendency to discuss only the human rights violations that fitted political convenience. This is not to suggest that a bright new day had dawned for human rights with the passage of these resolutions. The dogs that get kicked are still predominantly the dogs that were kicked before. But there is no reason in principle why these bits of international constitutional law should not be turned in other directions as well, and this the West and some Third World countries have sought to do with increasing success in recent years.

Regional

An important idea in the international discussion of human rights is that universal principles might be implemented on a regional basis.[7] The United Nations has directly encouraged the development of human rights institutions at regional level, and the regions in turn have identified themselves as the local bearers of a global burden. This is most notable in Western Europe, America and Africa.

Of the three regions, Western Europe has the best-established human rights institutions. The European Convention on Human Rights, which entered into force in 1953, was not merely the Universal Declaration translated into European. It sought to guarantee rights as well as to state them. For this purpose, a commission and a court of human rights were established, and a further role given to the Committee of Ministers of the Council of Europe. States could bring cases against states to the Commission. The great innovation of the European Convention, however, was the establishment of a machinery allowing individuals to complain to the Commission even against their own governments. The revolution in regard to the membership of international society referred to above might at least be beginning to happen in Europe. And, on the American continent, with the entry into force of the American Convention on Human Rights in 1978, this may also be said of the western hemisphere. Here similar

95

institutions to the European ones, a commission and a court, have been established for the regional guarantee of human rights. Here too there is provision for individual petition. And it is stronger than in the European case for being written into the Convention without the additional requirement of states opting to recognize the Commission's competence in this regard. Africa, in the matter of the creation of human rights institutions, is some way behind both Europe and America. The Banjul Charter envisages the establishment of an African Commission on Human and People's Rights, but the functions of the Commission are to be concerned first with promotion, and then with implementation. In this respect, the Charter follows the American experience.

In the matter of principles, attention to local circumstances in our three regions is added to a core of common values. The local European circumstance is precisely its restrictionist interpretation of the core values, such that they may be rendered as legal rights and not as political aspirations. The European Convention, in A.H. Robertson's expression, restricts itself to the civil and political rights 'necessary in a democratic society', and does not include rights 'one might wish to see guaranteed in an ideal commonwealth'.[8] The American Convention is more ambitious. It lists more rights. It adds duties to rights in the spirit of the American Declaration of the Rights and Duties of Man of 1948. And it incorporates the economic, social and cultural rights which the Europeans chose to hive off to the European Social Charter.[9] The Banjul Charter, as we saw in Chapter 3 by no means abandons individual rights; but it adds to them a rather comprehensive set of duties to family, nation, state and continent.[10] And its stress on the importance of peoples' rights adds to this a collectivist dimension in a way which is studiedly different from the European and American conventions.

Different too, as we have already suggested, is the handling of implementation. Under the European convention, implementation is itself institutionalized. The Commission is empowered to resolve differences, the Court to make authoritative judgements where resolution is not possible, and the Committee of Ministers to supervise compliance with the Court's judgements (as well as having a judicial role itself in certain circumstances). Similarly in America, the Commission has the power to settle disagreements, and the Court to judge infractions of human rights. The Court also has the power to bring any failure to abide by its judgements to the attention of the Assembly of the Organization of American States. Even the Banjul Charter, while not establishing a court, envisages a procedure for amicable settlement, and, if this fails, for reporting to the Assembly of Heads of State and Government. In each case, whatever the institutional arrangements, publicity is central to the process of enforcement.

Non-governmental

Just as regional institutions in the field of human rights have seen themselves as the local promoters of global principles, so non-governmental institutions have taken their cue from the most widely endorsed international declarations. Amnesty International, for example, in its Statute of 1980, has as its object the securing throughout the world of the observance of the provision of the Universal Declaration of Human Rights. In fact, as the Statute goes on to reveal, Amnesty specializes. And there are a number of specialist organizations which, like Amnesty, seek to protect particular human rights: for example, the Minority Rights Group, the Anti-Slavery Society and the International Committee of the Red Cross. There are also non-governmental organizations whose human rights concerns are more general: for example, the International League for Human Rights and the International Commission of Jurists. Then there are organizations not established for the purpose of promoting human rights, but having them as part of their more general concerns, such as churches, trade unions, professional associations and political parties.[11]

The principles which these non-governmental organizations seek to uphold are predominantly those associated with the western list of civil and political rights. Amnesty International concentrates on freedom of opinion, the right to a fair trial, and freedom from torture and the death penalty. The International Committee of the Red Cross is concerned with rights in armed conflict, and with the rights of political prisoners. The non-specialist organizations, like the International Commission of Jurists, have also been primarily concerned with civil and political rights. The Commission's dedication to the universal acceptance of principles of justice has meant the procedural justice associated with the rule of law, rather than with what might be held to be more substantive notions such as distributive justice. The interpretation of human rights as first civil and political rights is true, too, of many of the organizations which become concerned with particular human rights issues from time to time: churches with the liberties of non-whites in South Africa; trade unions with the rights of their fellows in Poland; scientists with the freedom of their colleagues in the Soviet Union. But finally, on principles, we should note that there are a number of western non-governmental organizations which are concerned with economic and social rights before civil and political rights: Oxfam, for example, or War on Want. The point about organizations such as these is that the claim they make to our attention is more in terms of basic needs than human rights. It may be, as we have argued in the preceding chapter, that the most basic needs should be thought of as human rights, but this is not the main flag under which such organizations have sailed.

There is now the question of what these non-governmental organizations do.

Not having even the rudimentary machinery for implementation that is available to global and regional organizations, how can they act to promote and protect their principles in the world at large? In the first place, they can just *have* principles. Principles give point to politics. In order that slavery could be abolished, it might reasonably be argued, someone had first to think it wrong. In order that human rights could appear on the agenda of contemporary international politics, it might equally reasonably be argued, someone had first to think they belonged there.

Then the second step is to agitate for the wider acknowledgement of and adherence to these principles. In the case of slavery, the campaign was carried on in parliament, in political society beyond parliament, and in international society through the lobbying of delegates at international conferences.[12] In the case of human rights in modern world politics, it has been argued, their place on the agenda at all is due in large measure to the energy of the non-governmental groups at the San Francisco conference which established the United Nations.[13] This, of course, was acknowledgement, and not adherence, and it is adherence which is the far more demanding condition. But, even here, agitation has a part: expressing views, drawing up resolutions, drawing attention to violations, urging studies, sending fact-finding missions, protesting misconduct, and so on.[14] In all these respects, non-governmental organizations are the ginger groups of international society.

The third step is direct action on behalf of oppressed individuals or groups. Again, there are not the means available here that are at the disposal of governments, but non-governmental organizations can make a nuisance of themselves by launching letter-writing campaigns, pressing governments for information on particular cases and appealing for improvement, visiting prisons and attending trials.[15] What informs all these activities is the idea that people in positions of authority are more likely to act properly when they know that their conduct is under public scrutiny.

Non-governmental organizations in the field of human rights belong, then, in the liberal tradition of belief in the power of opinion. They believe that standing well in the eye of the public both at home and abroad is important to all governments, though they recognize at the same time that some are more sensitive to opinion than others. They argue that if reputation is something which matters to all governments, then their actions can be affected by pointing out the harm or good that might result from the publicity that will follow certain choices. This is the instrument of Amnesty.[16] And they guard it jealously by insisting on accuracy of information about oppressors and oppressed derived from the highest quality of research. Keeping one's powder dry in this area is minimizing the risk that one is acting on incorrect information. So Amnesty, and the other non-governmental organizations involved in human rights, believe not merely in the power of opinion, but also in the idea that opinion must be founded on truth. From this comes the criticism that we shall return to later that groups of this kind are not political but missionary, and thus confined to the side-lines of the political world, marginal in their impact on it.

HUMAN RIGHTS IN A SINGLE WORLD SOCIETY?

There are, then, in the contemporary world, a number of institutional arrangements that are concerned with the promotion and protection of human rights. It may be said of these arrangements that they constitute international human rights regimes: 'consistent sets of normative and procedural expectations on the part of states'[17] concerning the treatment of individuals and groups throughout the world whatever their nationality. If there are such expectations, it may also be said, with reference to the revolution in international relations with which the last section began, that there has come into being a world society which includes in its membership individuals and non-state groups as well as states, and that the old principles of international society, like sovereignty and non-intervention, no longer have a clear run. In this section of the chapter, we are concerned with whether there is any justification for asserting the existence of a world society in virtue of the establishment of the human rights institutions that were examined above.

Beginning at the global level, an obvious indicator of the extent to which human rights have become a legitimate concern of international society might be taken to be the support given by states to the various conventions. It might be decided, on such a basis, that freedom from racial discrimination, freedom from slavery, the rights of refugees, and the political rights of women were the rights about the existence and importance of which there was the closest to a consensus in contemporary international society.[18] On the same basis, it might be decided that the reduction of statelessness and the international right of correction were the human rights issues that least concerned the international society. But if these indicators are obvious, they are also crude. For signature and ratification of conventions are not the same thing as fidelity to them. As Richard Falk has pointed out, the absence of any real prospect of enforcement makes it feasible for some governments to ratify agreements that they cannot keep, while other governments that might observe them are deterred from becoming parties to conventions by the theoretical possibility of enforcement.[19] So ratification of international instruments may not be even a crude guide to the actual commitment to human rights in contemporary world society.

A second indicator, at the global level, of the reception of human rights in international society is the work of the United Nations on the subject. Of particular interest here might be the extent to which individuals have been able to make headway with complaints against the states whose organization the United Nations is.[20] In the first twenty years of the United Nations, it seemed that, in the matter of human rights at least, international society was successfully defending the principle of exclusive state authority. It seemed to be the rule that the United Nations would take no action with respect to the complaints of individuals against their own governments. The breach in this wall was made by the activity of the United Nations in the area of colonialism and apartheid. In the early 1960s, the United Nations committees on colonialism and apartheid held hearings for complainants and published the complaints.[21] General Assembly Resolution 2144 of October 1966 followed, inviting the Economic and Social Council through the Commission on Human Rights to give urgent consideration to ways and means of improving the effectiveness of the United Nations in the area of human rights. In 1967, the Human Rights Commission acted on this, asking the Sub-Commission to bring to its attention any situation which revealed a consistent pattern of violations of human rights in the area of apartheid and colonialism. It remained only to make this provision apply to any violation of human rights, and by the Resolution 1503 procedure, as we have seen, communications could be acted upon from individuals referring any consistent pattern of violations.

The theme of this story might be taken to be the individual emerging from the shadow of the state, and the states themselves assembled at the United Nations mustering the courage to give and accept criticism of their own human rights records. There are, however, a number of difficulties in taking this as the true theme, of which we may mention two. In the first place, individuals are not all stepping out together from the shadow of the state. Notice can be taken only of consistent patterns of violations – which leaves the victims of random violations internationally defenceless. Secondly, the states in international society still control the pattern of protest at the United Nations. As Richard Falk has again pointed out, it is not severity of abuse of human rights which is the principal criterion of agenda attention.[22] Rather, it is the politics of United Nations diplomacy which allows Israel, South Africa or Chile to be pilloried for human rights violations: another shy at a state which has already been made a pariah is relatively cost-free politically. And while some human rights violations, like those in these countries, are 'supervisible', others elsewhere remain 'invisible'.[23] In the politics of the United Nations, there are untouchables in both senses of the word. So although human rights issues at the United Nations are no longer simply settled in the interests of governments on committees of which they alone are members, the shadow of the state has not significantly shortened. This is a conclusion which is strengthened the further one moves away from the formal human rights institutions of the United Nations. In the debate in the General Assembly about the content of human rights (discussed in Chapter 5), one might find more evidence for competing conceptions of what world society should consist of than for a solidarist conception of what world society now is.

We observed above the notion that human rights arrangements at the regional level are made to carry global standards into all the provinces of international politics. The United Nations has itself encouraged the establishment of European, American, Arab and African institutions for this purpose, and, for their part, the regions have seen themselves as the local carriers of a global message. This benign view of the discrimination between regions in the matter of human rights is made possible by the idea that while the standards are universal, their implementation will be the more successful the closer the attention to local circumstances. States, it is argued, are more likely to accept machinery for implementation if it is established among a group of neighbouring and like-minded countries than if it allows the snooping of strangers.[24]

The benign view of the connection between global standards and regional enforcement is not the only one, and it glosses over large difficulties. There is, first, the well-known problem of the definition of a region. In the second place, there is the uncomfortable fact that neighbourhood is no guarantor of solidarity: Burke's 'grand law of vicinage' does not automatically apply. It may even be the case that such solidarity as has been established on the question of human rights within regions has been achieved against a regional 'outsider': In Europe, Eastern Europe; in the Americas, the communist enemy within; in the Arab world, Israel; and in Africa, South Africa.[25] Third, and most important, the easy distinction between (global) standards and their (regional) implementation seems on reflection an improbable one. This makes of regions mere executives to a global 'legislature'. It seems more plausible that the homogeneity of culture which is supposed to make it possible to consider regions as political units generates principles as well as procedures; and that localities are to be marked off by their different conceptions of rights, and not merely by their different routes to the same basic rights. So regional institutions might pull in a different direction from global ones – which was the point of our inquiry into Africa, China and Islam in this regard in Chapter 3. Moreover, they are likely to pull in different directions from each other, since it is their difference from one another that prompted the setting-up of different institutions within them. It may be argued, therefore, that letting the regions of the world do the running in the enforcement of human rights could end up destroying human rights rather than protecting them. The *moi commun*, even extended to the level of the region, might still drive out the *moi humain*.

The level of non-governmental organization in the matter of human rights might be thought the most reliable indicator of an emerging world society. For here, it may be argued, individuals and groups approach the question of the rights of their fellow human beings unencumbered by a duty to protect this or that political or economic interest. Their principle can be the idea that an offence to the rights of anyone anywhere is at the same time an offence to their own humanity: it diminishes them. Non-governmental organizations acting on this principle might then be interpreted as at once expressing the existence of world society and visibly buttressing it.

Being apolitical, or 'above the fray', detached from any sectional concern, is taken often to be a distinguishing characteristic of human rights non-governmental organizations, and notably of Amnesty International.[26] Dealing even-handedly with human rights violations anywhere is part of its offical doctrine, to which it gives expression by having each of its groups adopt prisoners of conscience from the First, Second and Third Worlds, and not acting on behalf of anyone in their own countries. This appearance of political neutrality, however, may not be reality. There is, first, the argument that Amnesty is in fact dogmatically confined to western liberal principles in its attachment, for example, to individual liberty above any group value.[27] An imprisoned political leader, it is suggested, may prefer to stay in prison to further the interests of group rights than to be released in recognition of individual ones: so there may be no reason for his or her gratitude to an Amnesty campaign to set him or her free. Second, Amnesty is criticized for its conservatism: politically, in its refusal officially to recognize any justification for violent change; and socially, in its elitism, its membership stemming across the globe from the same class as the governments it seeks to influence. This particular variety of social solidarity, it might be said, takes the sting out of any protest. Campaigning for human rights should be a subversive activity, and subversion is not well done by those who are preoccupied with maintaining their apolitical credibility in the minds of the very institutions they should be subverting.[28] The third and most damaging criticism of Amnesty's supposedly apolitical stance is that it is a stance not at all above the fray but in a no-man's-land within it.[29] In criticizing the excesses of left and right, it marks out no position of principle between them, but shifts merely to what happens to be the mid-point in the current debate. Therefore, to be in the centre is not to be apolitical, but to have one's political position determined by others.

The point here is that the kind of transnational society which Amnesty calls up is predominantly a western society with characteristically western values. The criticism, then, is not far behind that it is an organization, and human rights an ideology, which look after western interests while pretending to a selfless concern for the interests of others.[30] This criticism takes two forms, one concerning what the West is seeking to do to the rest of the world, and the other concerning what it is seeking to do for itself. The first is the familiar notion of human rights as cultural imperialism: 'We have defined as fundamental human rights those rights which can be accorded to people in our society without posing a threat to our sociopolitical system.'[31] Change, then, is the duty of foreigners: it is they who must get into step with us. The second form of the criticism is less familiar. It has human rights activism as the opiate of the West, a device by means of which the privileged cope with the existence of the underprivileged, the oppressed. Human rights organizations exist for the benefit of their members, not of victims. If the victims in the Third World were to shape the transnational society of human rights, it is argued, they would bring to it different values, such as those contained in the Universal Declaration on the Rights of Peoples adopted at populist Third World initiative in Algiers in 1976: rights not of individuals but of groups against the oppression of imperialism.[32]

The final level at which the need to inquire whether human rights bear witness to the existence of a world society is that of the state. To what extent have states sought to advance, within their own domains, the values of cosmopolitan society at the same time as defending a right in their locality to be different in some degree from everyone else? And is the area covered by the values they have in common expanding at the expense of the area covered by what makes them different? There are four aspects to this. In the first place, many states have been founded precisely for the purpose of securing for their citizens the human rights that everyone ought to enjoy. The classical examples of this are the United States and France. More recently, a number of new entrants into international society have founded their constitutions on the Universal Declaration of Human Rights.[33]

Secondly, whatever the reasons for their establishment, states are having to come to terms with the expanding international law of human rights, in the sense of deciding on the extent of its domestic application. There is a dispute of theory here about whether municipal or international law should take precedence over the other. There is also the practical question of the use to which international law is put in the domestic courts. In the *Fujii* case in the United States, the plaintiff who had been denied title to land under the provisions of the Alien Land Law argued that, among other things, the law was inconsistent with the principles and spirit of the Charter of the United Nations. The court found that the Charter was not self-executing, and that its human rights provisions lacked 'the mandatory quality and definiteness which would indicate an intent to create justiciable rights in private persons immediately upon ratification'.[34] It may be argued, however, as we saw in Chapter 3, that the customary international law of human rights, at least on the question of discrimination is moving towards the plaintiff's argument about the rights of individuals in *Fujii* and not away from it.

The third aspect is more dramatic. It is that which has the domestic courts of one state upholding the international law of human rights when the offence against human rights was committed by a foreigner in his or her own state. If this practice were to take root, it would indeed be a revolutionary breach of the principle of state sovereignty as received from the nineteenth century, and a clear indication of the existence of social obligations laid upon individuals as humans as well as citizens. The celebrated case here is that of *Filártiga* v. *Peña-Irala*.[35] In this case, Peña, a Paraguayan police inspector, was sued in a United States court by Filártiga, the father of a man Peña had tortured to death in Paraguay. Filártiga's case was that torture was a violation of the law of nations, and that the US court had jurisdiction in the matter in virtue of the 1789 Alien Tort Statute allowing such competence when a tort had been committed in violation of the law of nations. Peña's lawyers argued that torture was not a violation of the law of nations, and that anyway the proper forum for consideration of the case was Paraguay. This argument succeeded in the first instance. But, on appeal, it was found that torture was a violation of customary international law, and that the Alien Tort Statute applied. Judge Kaufman, in his opinion on the case, concluded that 'the torturer has become – like the pirate and slave trader before him – *hostis humani generis*, an enemy of all mankind'.[36] The former United States Ambassador to Paraguay, Robert White, reported anxiety in Paraguay that, if this case was not reversed, no government figure would feel free to travel in the United States.[37]

The fourth aspect of human rights and world society at state level is more ambitious even than this. It is that which has one state not only judging a matter of human rights between a government and a citizen or a group abroad, but also acting to improve it. Action of this kind might range from quiet diplomacy through economic pressure to military coercion, which is a question we come to in the last two chapters of this book. The point here is to notice that the notion of humanitarian intervention, to be both legitimate and potentially successful, presupposes a solidarist society in which it is possible to agree on the values that inform intervention, as well as on the acceptability of policing. Human rights as well established as this would indicate a situation in which what Suarez called the *ius gentium intra se* - that part of the law of nations which described all the values that nations in their domestic law have in common - had expanded almost to obliterate any significant local variation. World society would have arrived, culturally, in the sense of each local society looking like every other.

None of these aspects is trouble-free. The idea that states have established themselves as defenders within their territories of universal principles is something to take comfort from as an indicator of the existence of a world society if the lists of principles to which they attach themselves are similar. This, as we have noticed more than once, is not the case. As to the domestic application of the international law of human rights, it is true that the weight of customary and conventional law is increasingly being felt, but this has not yet turned individuals within states into citizens of the world: by and large they remain at the mercy of their states. The *Filártiga* case provides a glimpse of a solidarist world order of the future, but is not now a reliable indicator of the strength of transnational society. And as for humanitarian intervention, there is, as we recorded in Chapter

3, little ground to include it among the established principles of international law if state practice is the guide to such principles.

Our overall conclusion, in regard to the question of human rights institutions as a measure of the solidarity of world society, must then be modest. At the universal level, human rights institutions are unreliable indicators of commitment to human rights in practice. They play host to the airing of disagreement as well as to recording solidarity. And they reflect the preoccupations of international and not of cosmopolitan society. At the regional level, there is reason to be suspicious of the idea that regions are the agents of universal values and not of regional ones. In regard to non-governmental organizations, their values are skewed in a western direction, and do not faithfully record the views of an imaginary apolitical transnational world beyond the state. Finally, at the level of the state, while there is widespread homage paid to the idea of universal human rights, their content is contested and the prospect of their achievement for the most part remote.

The world society that might be said to exist in virtue of the acknowledgement of and commitment to universal human rights is then uneven and in several places barely visible. But this does not mean that it does not exist at all. We noted, in Chapter 3, the view that certain human rights principles, such as freedom from racial discrimination, and self-determination, have become peremptory norms of international law, and it is no longer controversial to argue that there is a body of customary rules constituting the international law of human rights.[38] If, beyond these basics, it is fair to say that discourse about human rights in international politics is as much about the contest between cultures, ideologies, traditions and nations as it is about an emerging consensus between them, then, again as argued in Chapter 3, there is in the debate among them at least a recognition of the value of a conversation between the cultures. And out of this conversation might come the beginnings of change in patterns of practice in the matter of human rights, a question which we shall investigate in the concluding section of this chapter.

CONCLUSIONS

We have attempted to give some account of the human rights institutions that have been established in contemporary world politics, and to assess these institutions considered as evidence for the existence of a world society: a society which is more inclusive than the society of states, extending its rules to individuals and groups across the globe. To summarize the matter from the point of view of the individual, there is at least access to global institutions both official and unofficial through the United Nations machinery and non-governmental organizations. There is also a regional community available to some individuals. And within the state, there is differential reception of the cosmopolitan values associated with the international law of human rights. We have reviewed the reasons for thinking that this world society is not deeply entrenched, while not simply dismissing it. We might focus our conclusion by referring back to the purported revolution in the purposes of the members of international society, and the deeper revolution in the membership of the society itself – the creation of world society. At least rhetorically, states have accepted the pursuit of human rights as a proper concern of the society they form: they speak the language of the international law of human rights. But for a conclusion as to the tenacity with which the new purpose is pursued we must await the discussion in Chapter 8. On the more profound question of the revolution in the membership of international society, it remains doubtful whether individuals have *joined* the club, as distinct from benefiting from some of its principles and provisions.[39]

This is a judgement about the place of human rights in contemporary world society: a cross-section, so to speak, of that society. There remain two questions for this conclusion: that (linking up with our earlier discussion) of how world society came to take this shape; and that (foreshadowing our later discussion) of whether the direction of change in that society is something we should approve of.

One answer to the first of these questions is circumstance. Attention to human rights might track the capriciousness of human wrongs. Thus the argument that human rights surfaced in international society because of western revulsion at evil done within its midst before and during the Second World War. We may refer also to a contemporary example of reaction to circumstance. The problem of refugees and migrants is a substantial one in every part of modern international society.[40] States, and especially the popular target states for immigrants and refugees, have to form a view about the rights of these individuals however uncomfortable it makes them about undermining the rules of international society. This is not a new problem: the right of asylum is an ancient recognition of it. But the scale and scope of it in the contemporary world is a vivid illustration of the demands that individuals and groups are making of the club of states. Nor are the demands abstract, indicative of some notional transition from international to world society. A connection is often made between a state's observance of human rights and the propensity of its population to emigrate. So one of the reasons for states to be interested in the human rights record, not merely of a neighbour but of another state across the globe, is the interest it has in not suddenly being made a receiver of numbers of unmanageable refugees.[41] An interest in human rights becomes part of the calculation of *raison d'état*. Thus circumstances produce practices which are defended on the ground of interest and harden over time into custom. This is Burke's theory of change: and for him society consists in the conventions that arise from habitual intercourse.[42]

Other theories are less innocent politically. A widespread view about the place assumed by human rights in contemporary international society is that it is the outcome of the grafting of a western tradition onto the rest of the world. The West, in the first place, sets the standards for everybody else. The British Beveridge Report of 1942, it is said, became an international reference standard just as previous items of domestic progress in the West became proposals about how all societies ought to develop.[43] Secondly, it is not merely that the international human rights revolution of the twentieth century followed the revolutions within western countries in the previous two centuries, but that it was shaped by them: it came from this and not another historical mould. So reading modern western history in the matter of human rights is what is required to grasp the debate about human rights in contemporary international politics. The recent argument between civil and political rights and economic and social rights is but a gloss on the old debate about the significance for the world of the American and the French Revolutions, the first being against tyranny and oppression, the second against exploitation and poverty.[44] Americans assumed that the problem of poverty had been solved, and that the task of the revolution was to constitute liberty. The Jacobins, on the other hand, took the revolution to be the solution to the problem of poverty, the new principle to be the welfare of the people. The International Covenants on Civil and Political Rights, and on Economic, Social and Cultural Rights, might be read in this light. In the same way, the recent argument between individual and collective rights can be taken as a gloss on the old differences between Locke and Rousseau.[45] In this regard, Hannah Arendt quotes Robespierre's reversal of traditional political theory: 'Everything which is necessary to maintain life must be common good and only the surplus can be recognized as private property.'[46] The argument here is that the French and the Americans in the eighteenth century created a revolution for all people and not just for themselves, and established the language in which world politics have been discussed ever since.

A third theory of the nature of change in regard to the place of human rights in world society is the opposite of the second. It sees the international law of human rights as an attempt on the part of international society to detach itself from what are purely western values, rather than seeking to entrench them. One way of doing this was discussed in Chapter 3: finding out what values as a matter of observation the cultures of the world had in common, and building on them as the basis for a properly universal conception of human rights. The task here would be, not to trace the imprint of the Enlightenment in the contemporary world, but to stand outside any particular cultural tradition and observe the patterns of values which are shared across societies. Antipathy to torture, or to genocide, it is suggested, might command a wide consensus.[47] The attempt at objectivity in this procedure might of course itself be a product of the Enlightenment, as Peter C. Reynolds says of the subject of anthropology – that it was the institutionalization of a moral injunction to look at other societies 'as if they were created by human beings with as much intelligence and integrity as ourselves'.[48] But if this were the motto for the international law of human rights, there would be little for non-western cultures to object to.

Taken straight, these theories of change are plainly not consistent with each other. But it is possible to run them together in the following way. It may be true that social rules emerge from the experience of coexistence. They may be responses to circumstance. But the circumstances themselves have a context, and it happens that the context of contemporary world politics is predominantly a western one. However, if the modernization which was associated at its outset with westernization continues, even in circumstances of relative western decline, we may call it a universal social process in which it is difficult to identify the particular contribution of this or that culture. In this regard, the international law of human rights may be an expression of this global process, and not merely the American law of human rights writ large. The gradual accumulation of standards of right conduct, expressed in international conventions against slavery, or genocide, or racial discrimination, becomes, in this interpretation, the measure of consensus in an evolving international society rather than the expression of the hegemony of one state or culture within it.

Whether or not this is plausible, there is one thing that these theories plainly have in common. They all seek to give reasons why a particular social pattern prevails, rather than asserting that this or that pattern ought to prevail. And it is only in the light of a calculation of the latter kind that we can judge whether, say, the international law of human rights becoming more entrenched is a good thing or a bad thing. *Filártiga* is progress beyond *Fujii* only if we can assume that cosmopolitanism is an improvement on the contractarianism of the state; that 'civilization' is an advance on 'culture'. Behind this assumption lies a particular kind of progressivist theory which 'regards the state as a temporary association suspended between, for example, a supposed state of nature and a condition which would fully express the human capacity to develop more inclusive social relations'.[49] This assumption will be scrutinized in the next chapter. For the moment we need merely to notice how embedded improvement is in the conversation about human rights. For it is not a conversation of an Oakeshottian kind, an idle conversation in which 'there is no "truth" to be discovered, no proposition to be proved, no conclusion to be sought'.[50] It is a conversation in which each participant, as we argued in Chapter 3, seeks to convince the others of the rightness of a point of view, and to have policy change accordingly. It is to this question of policy that we now turn. We shall examine the theory of the matter in Chapter 7 (what to do about human rights in world politics), and its practice in Chapter 8 (how to do it).

Part Three: Policy

7 Human rights and the theory of international relations

We have now dealt (in Part One) with the theory of human rights: what they are, their evolution in western political theory, the form of their survival in the transition from European to global international politics. We have dealt also (in Part Two) with the place of human rights in contemporary world politics, and with the extent to which they give expression to the existence of a single world society. The task now is to decide what ought to be done. If there are such things as human rights, even if only in the limited senses discussed in Chapters 2 and 3, what, in the light of our discussion of world politics in Part Two, should be done about them? In this chapter, this is treated as a moral question: what attitude should anyone take up towards the issue of human rights in world politics? Then this discussion informs the directly practical concern of the last chapter, Chapter 8, which is to ask what governments, and particularly western governments, should do about human rights in foreign policy.

There are a number of senses in which it might be said that the theory of world politics – theory here as reflection on the public arrangements that ought to be made for the government of humankind – should start with human rights. The first is definitional. Human rights are the rights that everybody should have by virtue of his or her very humanity. Any political theory that disregarded them, therefore, would make the mistake of overlooking a political axiom. If this seems at the same time glib and doctrinaire, a second reason for starting the theory of world politics with human rights is an historical one. It is that, at least since the seventeenth century, human rights or natural rights have been a conventional liberal starting-place for political theory, so that in pursuing reason we would be following tradition. The difficulty with this is that it puts history in the ascendant when the point of natural rights is that they should stand above it. And this is the best reason for starting with natural rights: they fulfil the function once fulfilled by the theory of natural law in putting certain claims about how humans are to be treated beyond the whims of tyrants, but within realist estimates of the limits of the possible. They shape the content of claims that any decent government should respect.

What is this content? There is at least a common vocabulary. It is, to be sure, a vocabulary which states and others use to disagree among themselves as much as to agree, not least about the meaning of such phrases as 'human rights'. But if this fact alone were taken to rid the discussion of human rights in international politics of any point, it would also make a dispute about the meaning of words in, say, an English language seminar, pointless: when the dispute is precisely the point. Certainly it is the exception rather than the rule for states to claim, in their conversation about human rights, that the coexistence of several sometimes competing conceptions of human rights rules out the continuation of the conversation.[1] We saw, in Chapter 3, a realist Chinese defence of its continuation: stopping it would allow the opposition to get away without even a criticism of its policy.

But are there rights in common, in addition to a common language in which to discuss them? On the affirmative side, as we have seen, there are minimalist and maximalist answers to this question. Professor Hart is a minimalist. If there are any moral rights at all, he says, there must be at least one – the equal right of all to be free.[2] But this notion of a universal human right has not moved far from the procedural point about vocabulary already made. It asserts that we must make the assumption of human liberty in order to make sense of rights talk. If there were no such liberty, there would be nothing in which to ground human rights, no reason to protest their infraction. Another version of the minimalist position (though maximalist by comparison with Hart) is the doctrine of basic rights. Basic rights, in Henry Shue's exposition, specify the line beneath which no one should be allowed to fall, and they are defined as 'basic' in the sense that their enjoyment is a prerequisite to the enjoyment of all other rights. Subsistence, security and, less certainly, liberty are basic rights.[3]

A maximalist notion of the content of human rights specifies not merely what is required to keep everyone above some basic level, but also, in John Finnis's expression (which we met first in Chapter 2), all the requirements of practical reasonableness making possible the basic goods of human flourishing.[4] Human rights become, in this account, a modern way of expressing the principles of natural law. A less coherent and rigorous form of maximalism than this is the production of a list of human rights from the principles of all the modern conventions on the subject that have been recognized as law by the international community. What this list loses in coherence, compared with the natural law tradition, it gains in acceptability to the world community at large, and a contemporary account of the actual place of human rights in world politics would better start, as we did in the last chapter, with the United Nations than with natural law.

In the conclusion of this chapter, we shall come to a view as between minimalism and maximalism on human rights policy. But it is a chapter about human rights in international relations. Therefore, we need to take into account this political milieu in which action occurs, as well as the reasons that lead us to endorse this or that conception of human rights as a guide to political action. In this regard, we shall examine three contrasting views of the nature of the political world that confronts the advocate of human rights: the view that the only world community is a community of states, and that the rules of this community are the rules of states and not of individuals (or of any combination of individuals other than states); the view that there is a cosmopolitan community whose members are individuals, and that the purposes of these individuals must inform the construction of any political grouping; and the view that the term 'world community' is a misnomer for what is in fact a pattern of interest, and that human-rights-talk is talk of interests in disguise. By an 'examination' of these views is meant, in addition to their simple elucidation, their scrutiny from the point of view of their critics, and their line of reply. In the course of this examination we shall discover that there is less distance between the prescription of a moral principle and the description of a political milieu than might have been implied just now. Each might shape the other in a way which makes them part of the same enterprise or moral advocacy, and not separate enterprises meeting the different purposes of asserting values and gathering facts.

THE MORALITY OF STATES

The idea of a 'morality of states',[5] or of 'liberal statism',[6] as two of its critics have called it, takes states not only to be capable of moral responsibility, but also, in its classical form, to be the only bearers of rights and duties in the international society which together they form. Individuals and groups other than states have access to this society only through the agency of their states; they are objects not subjects of international law. Non-intervention, the fundamental principle of international law, is designed to prevent individuals and groups getting in the way of the relations of states.[7] What is there, morally, to support this view of the community which confronts the advocate of universal human rights?

There is, first, the idea that the principle of non-intervention is established simply by logic. If the members of international society are taken to be sovereign states acknowledging each other's rights to rule in their own domains, then it follows that intervention – the attempt to subject another state to one's will – is illegitimate as an infraction of sovereignty: if sovereignty, then non-intervention. No matter that state practice has failed to deliver a body of clear rules on the subject of intervention: the answers can be got by recourse to first principles.[8]

This is a legal argument, and only moral as well to the extent that law and

113

morality can be taken to run together. If it is part of the function of morality to provide criticisms of any legal arrangement, then it is insufficient to appeal to that arrangement as itself a moral defence. So a second, more satisfactory, line of moral defence for the principle of non-intervention lies in a judgement about the international milieu in which the principle operates.[9]

If international society is accurately described as composed of sovereign states, enclosing different political systems, guarding them jealously and always on the look-out for the next threat to them, then we may expect among its members two general attitudes towards the question of intervention (when undertaken by other members). The first is one of doubt about the motives of interveners. The second is one of scepticism about any good outcome of intervention.

As to the first, the attitude would be that the intervention was undertaken in the interest of the intervener and not in that of the community of states as a whole (though the intervener would be expected to say that it was). And even if the intervention were undertaken in the view of its perpetrator selflessly to achieve a moral purpose, others might mutter about partial conceptions of morality. As to the second, the attitude would be that intervention is unlikely to produce any good result since the vehicle of interference, bringing in outsiders, is itself morally disagreeable. And even if some moral good were achieved (Indian intervention in East Pakistan ending the slaughter of Bengalis by the army of Pakistan), there might also be less worthy outcomes to be swallowed (India's aggrandizement at the expense of its principal enemy on the subcontinent). Moreover, any principle of humanitarian intervention would issue a licence for all kinds of interference, claiming with more or less plausibility to be humanitarian, but driving huge wedges into international order. So, because of their suspicion of each other, and their worries about the causes and effects of intervention, the members of international society are united by a principle of non-intervention which bears witness to their minimal solidarity: not the absence of morality but the recognition of its limits. What makes of this argument more than just statist special pleading is the view that it is within states that a platform of order is established on which the justice we associate with the notion of human rights might be based. So anything that threatens order threatens also the possibility of achieving justice. This, as we saw in Chapter 4, was Kissinger's staple argument against allowing the question of human rights to place at risk such order as had been achieved between the United States and the Soviet Union.

This is an argument which results from a consequentialist calculation which, it might be argued, has more to do with prudence than with right. We are accustomed to treating the strongest moral arguments as those which employ the language of right and correlative obligation. In the history of international thought two arguments for non-intervention are this strong. Both arguments make use of the domestic analogy to get themselves off the ground, but once there they remain airborne under their own power. The first is the defence of non-intervention as derived from the fundamental rights of states. The second is the defence of non-intervention as a corollary of the principle of self-determination.

The first argument is most closely associated with the eighteenth century German writer Christian Wolff and his Swiss follower Emmerich de Vattel. Nations, they said, were to be considered as individual free persons living in a state of nature.[10] Since all men were naturally equal, so also were nations. Giants and dwarfs were equally men; large and small nations equally nations. Their rights and obligations were also by nature the same. Perfection of sovereignty in a nation consisted in its exercise independently of the will of any other. From this arose the obligation not to intervene and the right not to allow it. The difference between this and the straightforward legal argument for non-intervention that we noticed first above is that it anchors sovereignty and non-intervention in the obligations of natural law.

The second argument is more modern, associated in the nineteenth century with John Stuart Mill, and revived recently by Michael Walzer.[11] It too begins with the idea that states, like individuals, are to be treated as free persons, the pursuit of whose purpose requires the non-interference of others. But instead of just asserting a similarity between individuals and states, it suggests a connection between them which makes states worthy of respect because they provide collectively for the purposes of individuals. States, in one formulation, are 'associations of individuals with their own common interests and aspirations, expressed within a common tradition'.[12] The common tradition shapes a common life which it is the function of the state to protect against the outside world.[13] The moral standing of any state depends on how well it does this. But until it is shown to be utterly delinquent in this regard (by laying waste its own citizens, or by bringing on secessionist movements), it is entitled to expect that other states – concerned, as they should be, with their own communities – will refrain from intervention. Not just state sovereignty, but 'community sovereignty': the latter deepens the obligation of non-intervention already established by the former. This account of international society as a society of communities is a model of international society and not a description of it. But, Walzer asserts, most states do stand guard over the community of their citizens, at least to some degree.[14] And we might add that most citizens seem to like their states, or to dislike them less than anyone else's.

The most telling criticism of the morality of states is that which disputes the domestic analogy on which it is based, both as an empirical matter (do states resemble individuals in their moral singularity?) and as a normative one (should we make moral presumptions in favour of groups of individuals called states over the individuals who themselves compose them?). The cosmopolitanist critics of the morality of states, those who see the world as a great society of humankind, answer both these questions in the negative.[15] They see no merit in the simple assumption, made by such writers as Wolff and Vattel, that states, like individuals, are equally free. This, they argue, is an empirical question to be settled by observation of the world, and not *a priori:* one should not presume the morality of states, but investigate it. The same goes for Walzer's claims. There is no reason to assume that states as a matter of fact do protect a community of shared experiences and cooperative activity. It is more reasonable to assume that state and community do not fit neatly together in the arbitrary world of states than that they do.[16] Moreover, the communitarianism of Walzer's doctrine of self-determination is suspect. It allows the sacrifice of the individual to the group, rather than insisting that group rights derive from the specified rights of individuals which are to be protected.[17] The idea that it is better to be oppressed by one's own community than by someone else's is surely a peculiar one: oppression is oppression, whatever its source.

In other words, the cosmopolitanist criticism of the morality of states makes no concession to the state at all. States, in David Luban's phrase, are not to be loved and seldom to be trusted.[18] There is nothing to support a state's presumption of legitimacy.[19] There is good reason to doubt that citizenship is morally relevent when it comes, for example, to the question of distributive justice.[20] The appeal to community sentiment is an appeal to the *usual* system of obligation, not to the right one.[21] And it is an appeal which imagines that it is in the society of states that the great moral questions of the age are asked and disposed of. It is not. Subsistence in the face of starvation, security in the face of arbitrary violence: these are the most important moral issues which currently confront mankind, and neither of them can be met within the framework of the society of states.[22]

These are trenchant criticisms, and they especially expose the rashness of Walzer's attachment of the principle of non-intervention to that of self-determination. For the defence of the state as a shield for self-determination depends on the demonstration of both a practical and a theoretical connection between the two. As to a practical connection, Walzer's view that most states most of the time are self-determining is more a hunch than a finding. On theory, although Walzer begins – in line with liberal political tradition – with the individual, he ends up with community rights prevailing over individual rights by dint of the notion of a metaphorical contract that sanctions the community's actions by virtue of a process of association and mutuality.[23] This results in a conservative theory of political community very much like Burke's notion of 'virtual representation': 'that in which there is a community of interests, and a sympathy in feelings and desires between those who act in the name of any description of people, and the people in whose name they act, though the trustees are not actually chosen by them.'[24] Thus Walzer happens to endorse a conservative notion of self-determination. But his mistake, from the point of view of the morality of states, is to attach non-intervention to *any* particular theory of representation. By so doing he places on international society a responsibility (for judging infractions of the principle of self-determination) which is not mature enough to administer.[25] We should retreat, according to this same point of view, to the principle of state sovereignty rather than advance to that of self-determination for the defence of non-intervention.

But not to the right of state sovereignty as a matter of domestic legitimacy for this or that state. If the conditions which the cosmopolitanist critics of the morality of states lay down as necessary for any state to be considered legitimate were to become part of the constitution of the society of states, there would be few, or no, legitimate members of that society. If sovereignty, then non-intervention, is the rule of a functioning international society, for admission to which having sovereignty is the measure of international (but not domestic) legitimacy. The function of the principle of non-intervention in this society is first to protect state sovereignty as its primary constitutive rule, and then to reduce the occasions for violence, to limit the reasons for war. Intervention may be legitimate if it is consistent with these primary functions, but not if it seeks to further some municipal principle of legitimacy. Thus counter-intervention to uphold the principle of non-intervention may be legitimate, but not intervention on what is said to be the just side in a civil war, or intervention for liberalism (or democracy, or communism, or to re-establish dynastic rule). This would be legitimism.

So what non-intervention allows is pluralism. It accepts variety within states, and seeks to prevent its forceful reduction. It recognizes the foreignness of foreigners.[26] It can concede that cultural differences are in some degrees morally relevant (though not, as we sought to show in Chapter 3, exclusive). This does not mean that morality itself is bounded. Borders do not interrupt its domain. What is right is something we seek one answer to, not several, and the attention to human rights in world politics is an aspect of this search. By these standards, few governments may be legitimate. But if we made them the basis for international *conduct*, as distinct from international *criticism*, there would be no end to wars of intervention. This, I take it, is what Michael Walzer means when he writes that certain governments may not be legitimate, but that we must act *as if* they were.[27] If this is to 'yield to guns and tanks',[28] the alternative also gives way to violence, though this time that of a righteous army. And one might be sceptical, with Richard Cobden, of righteous armies pursuing the behests of the Almighty or some modern version of them.[29] This acceptance of pluralism, then, comes not from moral satisfaction with the society of states, or from the notion (ludicrous but official at the United Nations) that one state is after all as good as another, but from concern at the harmful consequences of any interventionist alternative position. In the society of states as it is, righteous intervention will be received as imperialism.

It was against imperialism, and between legitimisms, that I previously directed the principle of non-intervention.[30] Its 'neutralism' between rival ideologies I defended as a principle of international order.[31] This claim has been challenged on the grounds that the neutrality of any principle can be judged only by asking whether reasonable people would endorse it without regard to the outcome it might produce in any particular dispute.[32] I believe that in a society of states they would. But they would not necessarily endorse it if they were being asked what was reasonable as between a society of states and any other way of arranging world politics. It is to the cosmopolitanist alternative that we now turn.

COSMOPOLITANIST MORALITY

If the central idea of the 'morality of states' is that states should be desensitized to each other's domestic wrongdoings in the interest of order among them, the central idea of cosmopolitanist morality is to heighten the sensitivity of people in one place to wrongs done in another in the interest of the achievement of global justice. Thus Kant's idea of a public law of mankind, which was to make a 'violation of law and right in one place felt in *all* others'.[33] This feeling would then bear witness to the existence of a real global community, in which each individual was 'involved in Mankinde'. And this would be progress. The domain of the common good would have extended, and certain rights would have come to be regarded as located in human personality itself, rather than in attachment to this or that part of the whole, in what were merely tribal conventions.[34] And this is the challenge to reliance on the morality of states. To the pessimistic (and ahistorical) notion that the society of states allows progress within the states but among them only dismal recurrence and repetition, it opposes the arresting idea that the external relations of states are also an arena for improvement.[35] And the measure of this improvement is the extent to which 'sovereignty' and 'order' have given way to 'universalism' and a 'common good'.[36]

This cosmopolitanist morality is not put forward merely as an appeal to our better natures, or to our capacity to understand history as the working out of some moral scheme for humankind. It is an appeal also to a set of facts that has at least as much claim to our attention as that which underpins the morality of states. Against the division of the world into separate political communities, it places their amalgamation in a common economic community.[37] There is a complex network of economic interactions in contemporary world society whose existence the writers on transnationalism and interdependence (and dependence) have tried to come to terms with. The existence of this network invalidates any claim on behalf of the society of states that it marks the boundaries of social cooperation.[38] So if we are to work out principles of social justice for the world as a whole, there is no good reason to begin (and end) with the morality of states – which is founded on a doctrine of state autonomy that is no longer in touch with the facts of international life (if it ever was). Instead, it is suggested, we might begin with John Rawls's theory of justice, but apply it to the global social structure, where he applied it only nationally.[39] So the principle of equal liberty, and the difference principle by which economic inequalities were to be arranged to the benefit of the least advantaged, might be applied among individuals across the globe. And this, furthermore, might produce a model of human rights which is a closer approximation of internationally recognized human rights than that produced by the tradition of natural law.[40]

The difficulty with the argument from the fact of an economically interdependent world to the notion of human rights as the principles of social justice for the world community as a whole is, as Charles Beitz himself recognizes, the absence of a political community to match what is held to be an economic one.[41] Without a real sense of attachment to the purposes of a world community on the part of individuals and groups across the globe, the laying down of paper obligations to a notional community seems to be mere scholasticism. Or, as Michael Donelan puts it, a blend of sentimentality and intellectualism – the economists' construct of a world economy and a Global Product being mistaken for a common enterprise.[42] Moreover, if there is to be any such thing as the just distribution of the burdens and benefits of social cooperation on a global scale, this would seem to require not merely a community, but a constitution: a mature polity in and through which obligations could be formulated and made to stick.[43]

Recognizing these difficulties, Beitz has a response to them.[44] In the first place, he argues that the role of ideal theory is misunderstood if it is thought to be invalidated by the argument that its practical application is difficult. Ideal theory is to point the way. What matters, in practical terms, is that going that way be possible, not that it be easy. Secondly, there may be more routes to the destination than are dreamt of in the domestic experience of politics, and the replication of domestic institutions should not be thought of as a prerequisite for departure. Thirdly, he argues, ideal theory also has some bearing on our actions in the present and not only on our hopes for the future, so that it might give some direction to the debate on human rights in foreign policy. There is in these arguments both the notion that the absence of a world community in regard to the global achievement of human rights is a challenge to construct one and not a reason to throw up one's hands, and the idea that ideals give point to current policy. We shall return to these questions at the end of the chapter.

RIGHTS AS MERE INTERESTS

We defined rights in Chapter 1 as a particular kind of interest, and human rights as interests that are so important that everyone ought to enjoy them. They are not, in such a formulation, *mere* interests. Moral sceptics, of either a conservative or a revolutionary disposition, have not been inclined to accept the innocence of such a definition. Let us present the conservative view first, and then two kinds of more radical view.

Moral discussion, says Bruce Miller, often gives predominance to notions of universal morality.[45] But most people adhere to a group morality which is less than universal. Indeed it is a group interest in preserving itself against outsiders which gives any morality such force as it has, and morality itself is a rationalization of interest. The process of rationalization causes its exponents to speak a universalist language, so that within any society a sectional interest is represented as the interest of the whole, and in the world as a whole the interests of a particular state are represented as being to the advantage of everybody. But this should not mislead us into thinking that there is a real universal morality. It is merely that, at some level of abstraction, everybody seems to think that the establishment of such a morality would be a good idea, and there is constant nodding in its direction. Morality, then, is interest in disguise – a benevolent enough disguise, since everyone recognizes that a game of dressing-up is being played, but still a disguise. Rights, as a prominent part of the language of morality, are part of the same game.[46]

The revolutionary view of rights, as we observed in the discussion of Marx in Chapter 2, is less benevolent. It accepts that rights are mere interests. But it does not accept that they are part of a game that everybody recognizes as being played. Rather, they are part of an ideology which involves a double deception. The bourgeoisie, by speaking the universal language of rights, deceives others into attaching themselves to the purposes of bourgeois society; and it deceives itself into believing that these rights are in fact universal, the inheritance of everyone. This kind of criticism of human rights seems particularly strong when applied to the universalism, timelessness and placelessness, and absoluteness, of human rights.[47] The universalism of human rights did not survive the explosion of the eighteenth century myth of a rational, objective moral order which doled out equal rights to everyone. The idea of timelessness and placelessness (*quod semper, quod ubique*) is confronted by the commonplace observations that different societies do things differently, and that the 'same' societies have done things differently at different times. Context, in both senses, matters in evaluating so-called human rights. And there are no rights, no absolute rights, that cannot be and are not toppled by consideration of what is good for the group as a whole in bourgeois and socialist societies alike. Bourgeois human rights ideology seeks merely to entrench temporary interests by turning them into supposedly universal laws.

A second kind of more radical criticism of human rights, led by Edward S. Herman and Noam Chomsky, takes the accusation of bourgeois deceit and applies it to contemporary American foreign policy.[48] It denies the common liberal view that internal freedom makes for humane international behaviour. It argues, to the contrary, that the United States has acted in defence of non-freedom abroad in order to accommodate powerful American domestic interests whose concern is to maintain a favourable investment climate abroad. If this requires the sustaining of tyrannical regimes which use terror, among other things, to keep their economies open to American access, then the United States will go along while averting its eyes from the disagreeable consequences, and calling up in its defence the overriding need for security. The argument is that the connection between US 'security' and the infraction of human rights by client states is systematic and not accidental.[49] Accordingly the attachment, for example, of the Carter Administration to the slogan human rights is not just rhetorical in the harmless fashion of a game that all understand; it is designed to deceive. For the reality of American foreign policy has been that tyrants are accommodated to preserve the investment frontier, and their excesses excused or ignored to a sometimes breathtaking extent. Not content with merely going along with the Shah of Iran because of common economic and security interests, the United States joined him in expressions of mutual devotion to human rights.[50]

Each of these interpretations of the notion of human rights is familiar to the student of international relations from the teachings of Realism: interests determine political action; politics are a struggle for power to advance these interests; there is no right and wrong, but only opinion backed by force; the ascendancy of this or that theory of rights is merely the manifestation in doctrine of an underlying political balance. The difficulty with each of the interpretations, as with Realism, is that, in seeking to distil an essence which determines the nature of all politics, they boil away much of its substance.

The conservative dismissal of rights as interests in disguise does not sufficiently explain why it is necessary to speak the language of rights at all if everybody understands that politics is only about advantage, or about increasing the opportunities to get what one wants.[51] And as soon as an explanation is embarked upon the essence becomes impure again, as other factors are considered. Three of these stand out. The first is that existence of rights tends to be acknowledged even by those who on the grounds of interest override them. It is rare for statesmen, or others, to take canal zones, as Theodore Roosevelt did Panama, and let Congress debate. This may be merely what Grotius called the finding of pretexts for an illegal form of conduct, but even this need attests to the existence of some minimal moral community.[52] The second factor is stronger. It observes that the language of rights is available for one party against what it might be in the interest of another to do. Rights are defences (particularly strong defences in the sense that the label 'rights' indicates the existence of a social sanction) against interests as well as means by which interests are advanced. An example of this usage, as we saw in Chapter 2, is Ronald Dworkin's description of individual rights as 'political trumps held by individuals' against the imposition of collective goals.[53] The third factor is stronger still. It may be that the dismissal of rights as interests in disguise misconstrues the whole nature of political argument, which is to persuade in terms of a common tradition of discourse. Interests are a part of this discourse, and rights are another. Each plays a part in shaping the other. But to suppose that one subsumes the other is unnecessarily to confine the discussion of politics. For if advantage, and power, were all that mattered, we could abandon conversation about politics and resort to mere measurement.

The revolutionary dismissal of rights, considered above to be at its most devastating when it sought to confront the asserted universality, timelessness and placelessness, and absoluteness, of human rights, is, however, perhaps naive in its Realism. The construction of humankind as a whole as a moral community, the lawyers' reference to the 'conscience of mankind', is not intended literally. Such a community is not held to exist as Princeton, New Jersey, exists. It is a way of dramatizing and making more insistent a claim about how any individual or group ought to be treated. Rejection of such a claim on the ground that there is no such community is like a child's denial, in a theatre, that the action is real. Similarly, the assertion of timelessness and placelessness is meant, not as a statement of fact about all purportedly human rights, but, again as we argued in Chapter 2, as an attempt to provide a platform from which what is, what happens to be, can be criticized in the name of something which has resonance beyond this place, and before and after this generation. It is similar again to the assertion of the absoluteness of human rights. There are no absolute rights in the sense of claims which permit no exception. But calling them so is an attempt to make them very important even among important rights.

The argument about human rights being one of the principal frauds of US foreign policy is put powerfully, even relentlessly, by Herman and Chomsky in the sources already cited. The fraud is revealed by the demonstration that the connection between US commercial interests and human rights violations by client regimes in the Third World is systematic and not merely accidental. If this demonstration is made successfully, then the rhetoric of human rights is indeed designed to deceive. The weakness of this strongly argued hypothesis is in its assumption that US commercial interests dominate US foreign policy. Security might count as an independent variable in the shaping of US foreign policy, and not merely as a rationalization for decisions taken on economic grounds. And if that which is to be secured is defined partly in terms of rights (to individual liberty and by extension to state sovereignty), then rights play a part as a motive for foreign policy and not only as a rationalization of it. One might still object to the policy, but not because it is a policy that on a systematic basis fraudulently uses the language of human rights. Moreover, as Herman and Chomsky themselves recognize, an administration's use of the rhetoric of human rights gives an opportunity to those concerned with the failure of reality to match the rhetoric to criticize this gap and insist on its closure.[54]

The reply of the 'interests school' to these criticisms might be to accept much of what they contain as plainly true, but still to insist that the first question to ask of something asserted as a human right is whom does it benefit, or whom does it benefit most. This is indeed a useful question, and we shall make use of it in our conclusions, whose aim is to decide which of all the allegedly human rights it is reasonable for international society not merely to endorse, but also to take as the basis of a programme for action.

CONCLUSIONS

We have considered three contrasting views of the nature of international politics that bear on the advocacy of a doctrine of human rights in that arena. It is now time to make the choice just mentioned, not on the basis of placing the crown on the head of one of the three models and having its prescriptions for international conduct enthroned, but on the basis of, I hope, a judicious reading of them all. To make this possible, let us briefly recapitulate.

The 'morality of states' flows from an 'egg-box' conception of international society.[55] Sovereign states are the eggs, the goodness within contained by a (fragile) shell. The box is international society, providing a compartment for each egg, and a (less fragile) wall between one and the next. The general function of international society is to separate and cushion, not to act. It should not mistake itself for the civil societies of which it is formed. The attitude to human rights taken up by Enoch Powell is classical egg-box.[56] There are no individual rights, only social rights – rights which correlate with identifiable bearers of obligation in a particular society. Societies, or nations, or peoples, express themselves externally in states. When the Charter of the United Nations refers to peoples, it means states. When these states use the language of human rights, it is to criticize other societies, just when individuals use the language of rights within societies it is to criticize governments. So human-rights-talk is power-talk. Such episodes in international relations as the negotiations of the Helsinki Final Act, and the subsequent review conference in which the West has made a point of human rights, are to be interpreted as cultural aggression. The golden rule of international relations should be that states reciprocally recognize their right to collective liberty, and refrain from using human rights to expand their domain of collective liberty. Classical egg-box is summed up in the assertion, which Bruce Miller seems reluctant to deny, that 'in some sense, there are really no people in the world, only states'.[57]

Cosmopolitanist morality has us out of the egg-box, cracked, and into an omelette. We are all touched by a global system of economic cooperation. In another version of cosmopolitanism thought we are all part of a global ecosystem, each of us vulnerable to the four horsemen of the planetary apocalypse: nuclear disaster, resource depletion, pollution of the environment and population growth.[58] World society, as the Sprouts put it, exists in virtue of a condition of interdependence, not a cognition of it.[59] But the cognition must follow the condition, because planetary survival depends on 'drastic changes of political consciousness . . . the emergence of new belief/value orientations that reflect simultaneous emphasis on the worth of the individual person, on the solidarity of humanity, and on the value of human persistence and evolution'.[60] And if not must, then should – so long as there is the slightest hope of its realization.[61]

Then there was Realism. Here the egg is fried, or, better for our purposes, the American version – sunny side up. Rights are the rationalized interests of winners, imposing obligations on losers. Yolks convince whites that they correlate with them in the condition of fried-eggness, but still all the goodness is collected in the yolk at the centre.

What, firstly, should be rejected from each of these models? From the idea of the morality of states we should reject the notion of the exclusiveness of states, the statist ideology which allows the assertion that there are only states in the world. Otherwise the morality of states would be a doctrine rationalizing blindness to central moral issues concerned with the treatment of individuals (for example, slavery), or of groups (for example, the principle of national self-determination), or in a certain sense of the world as a whole (for example, the obligations attending travel on 'spaceship earth'). A morality giving no sight of such central issues would be a third-rate morality whatever the argument of prudence that supported it. From the idea of cosmopolitanist morality we should reject what often seems implicit in it, namely that we already inhabit a cosmopolitan world so that we can start doing world politics straightaway, or at least from tomorrow morning. This merely begs the crucial question of the establishment of global political institutions that would make projects such as those for distributive justice a possibility. From Realism we should reject the bone-headed version which would stop political conversation altogether. We keep what is left. From the morality of states we keep the cautious awareness that political power is concentrated at the level of the state, and that any scheme for moral improvement has to find its way in this world of states. Considerations of prudence do not determine the moral agenda, but they do condition its treatment. From

124

cosmopolitanist morality we keep the sense of direction. And from Realism we keep the suspicion of any purportedly universalist doctrine: it may be that there is a mere part of the whole lurking beneath the rhetoric.

What we arrive at after this exercise is modified egg-box. There are modest and more ambitious modifications. The modest version is that which is designed to make international society work better – allowing counter-intervention to uphold the principle of non-intervention, or assistance for successful secessionist movements practising the principle of self-determination.[62] The more ambitious version may presage structural change in world politics, though for the time being all it may require is a similar pattern of behaviour on fundamentals within what remain separate sovereign states. This is the doctrine of humanitarian intervention, which obliges a response from outsiders if a state by its conduct outrages the conscience of mankind.

If there is a duty of humanitarian intervention (a question we return to shortly), it may be said to correlate with a right on the part of individuals everywhere not to be treated outrageously. A right of this description may be called a 'basic right', and the basic right that has shaped the argument of this book has been the right to life – in the sense both of a right to security against violence and of a right to subsistence. Such a right is basic in the sense, following Henry Shue, that enjoyment of it is essential to the enjoyment of all other rights.[63] A right to free speech cannot be enjoyed by someone who is under physical threat, any more than a right to employment can be enjoyed by someone who is inadequately nourished.

Why should we modify the rules of international society, which allow each state to do as it wishes within its own frontiers, so as to admit this basic right which all must acknowledge? Because of a commitment to the value of human life without which the daily round would lose much of its meaning. And if it is a commitment to *human* life, then it is not reasonable to allow this value to be diluted by the mere boundaries which human beings happen to have constructed against each other. This, in my view, is the core of all cosmopolitanist arguments, and the appeal to certain facts – the existence of a global economic system, the existence of a global ecosystem – to embed it is simply to make the sermon more dramatic and persuasive for the unconverted.[64]

Is the right to life the only basic right, or should the process of modification continue? Liberty may also be a basic right: not in the heroic sense of liberty or death, but in the sense that it is essential to the enjoyment of all other rights, including the right to life. For while it is true that a benevolent despot may deliver to his or her people the substance of the right to life by providing for their security and subsistence, in the nature of despotism he or she does not deliver them as rights. As Henry Shue has persuasively shown, having a right to life means having at least the liberty to protest and mobilize opinion against its deprivation –

having some access to institutions that guarantee it.[65] Otherwise life is merely something for the provision of which one thanks the despot and hopes for the best.

This rather tentative admission of liberty as a basic right will cause pain to those followers of Hannah Arendt who take liberty to be the value that ennobles politics and gives it its great purpose. Moreover, the space given to subsistence rights would be interpreted as signing up with the sansculottes of the French Revolution who turned the rights of man into a soup-kitchen. I embrace as a project for international society what Arendt called the 'politically pernicious' doctrine derived from Marx that life is the highest good.[66] The reason for this goes back to the defence of the morality of states. International society survives as well as it does by seeking to contain revolutions within the frontiers of states, and limiting the purposes of international interaction as far as possible to procedures: on security, the balance of power; on trade, most-favoured-nation treatment; with regard to domestic matters, non-interference.[67] Liberty upheld with revolutionary enthusiasm should exhaust itself at the border, for any society that allows its intoxication with doctrine to permeate its foreign policies invites others to reply in kind, and peaceful coexistence becomes impossible. So we should allow the plural interpretation of liberty in the same spirit as we saw, in Chapter 3, C.B. Macpherson depicting three 'real worlds' of democracy.[68] This does not mean the abandonment of our own conception of liberty as a criterion by which to judge the legitimacy of foreign governments. But it does mean that we cannot act to impose such a conception on foreign communities.[69] Instead we should reach out with those communities for a conception of basic human rights which is 'neutral with respect to the main political and economic divisions in the world.'[70] And this, in my view, is the attraction of the idea of basic rights as the minimal modification of the morality of states: it seeks to put a floor under the societies of the world and not a ceiling over them.[71] From the floor up is the business of the several societies.

There remains the question of whether international society itself puts in the floor or merely endorses as a good idea the suggestion that it be built. The latter, it might be said, is relatively easy. The international community has produced a number of conventions setting standards on human rights that go well beyond the proclamation of basic rights. The hard question is whether these standards legitimize action, either by international society as a whole or by states as its agents. Or, to put it another way, does a threat to life on the New York subway or in the Sahara desert trigger an international obligation to respond? Is intervention legitimate in these circumstances?

The answer is plainly no in these circumstances. Humanitarian intervention is, as Walzer puts it, reserved for extraordinary oppression, not the day-to-day variety.[72] If the threat to life on the New York subway became the systematic killing of all commuters from New Jersey, or the threat to life in the Sahara desert reached famine proportions, in which local governments were implicated by failing to meet their responsibilities, *then* there might fall to the international community a duty of humanitarian intervention. (But even then the considerations of prudence we spoke of under the 'morality of states' would still apply.)

We return to the question of intervention in the next chapter. We conclude this one on the question of what should be done about the commonplace, as opposed to the extraordinary, deprivation of the right to life. What obligations on the part of the rest of humanity do correlate with it? This is not a small question except for those who confidently answer that there is none – which, if rights are nothing without correlative duties, does away with the right. But if the argument of this book has been at all persuasive, we cannot return this answer, or at least not with confidence. Rather, the route to follow is that pioneered by the writers who have sought to locate and measure the obligation which correlates with the right to life.[73] At the most, this obligation may require us as individuals to give aid 'up to the point at which we can do no more without sacrificing something of comparable moral importance'.[74] At the least, it may require us to avoid depriving others of the enjoyment of basic rights (which may itself imply a radical reshaping of the international economic order).[75] Whatever the precise requirement, it may be argued consistent with the wager this book has taken about the value of all human life – that a duty to respect the right to life of others falls on us all as individuals, but that we may seek to discharge it most successfully through our governments. Raising this consciousness is a task for the final chapter.

The admission of basic rights is not only a modification of the morality of states; it is also a modification of the argument that the domestic legitimacy of a state has nothing to do with its international legitimacy, which, we earlier suggested, was dependent on the fact of sovereignty and not on the right (of some entity) to be sovereign. The failure of a government of a state to provide for its citizens' basic rights might now be taken as a reason for considering it illegitimate. From which judgement might follow a decision on the part of the other members of international society not to be accomplices to this deprivation by, for example, supplying economic or military aid.[76] But this too is not a small matter. For it may be that, in regard to the failure to provide subsistence rights, it is not this or that government whose legitimacy is in question, but the whole international economic system in which we are all implicated. This, as we saw in Chapter 5, is the doctrine of the Third World advanced at the United Nations and elsewhere. So we at once encounter the cost of even a minimal form of legitimism in international relations: namely, that our enthusiasm for reform abroad (for we assume that the basic rights of our own populations are taken care of) is matched by an equal enthusiasm abroad for our reform. And we should take this seriously. For while it may be true that the claims for our reform made under the heading of the New International Economic Order are another variety of statist special pleading, in which the basic rights of individuals rate barely a mention, this does not absolve us of our responsibility to promote so far as is possible the basic rights of everyone. In this regard we should, as Richard Ullman has put it, take seriously the substance of Third World demands for resource transfer, if not their rhetoric.[77] This admission of basic rights, we might concede, sets a colossal task for international society. The minimalism which we partly embrace for realist reasons turns out to look like maximalism.

Taking this realist cue, we might step back from the current discussion about human rights in international relations and observe, with Adam Watson, that ideas about legitimacy come and go, that the anti-slavery movement which conquered international society in the nineteenth century was of small concern to it in the eighteenth, that whatever our current preoccupations they will be history in the twenty-first.[78] Moral ideas, the suggestion is, are as prone to the following of fashion as any other ideas. Moreover, with regard to our earlier Realist injunction to search for the political advantage beneath the proclaimed principle, it may be argued that the current fashion for economic rights, at least in their collective form, is very close to the interests of the Third World states in contemporary international politics, and may be the measure of their successful handling at least of the rhetoric of international politics.

The correct response to this may be, 'So what?' The claim of subsistence rights to our attention does not diminish because it is made by or on behalf of those who are most in need of their acknowledgement. And the fact of their topicality does not diminish their importance. More profoundly, the suave observation of the Realists that the wheels of diplomacy turn endlessly to grind whatever grain is produced by world society, may be missing a transformation from international relations to world politics as significant as that which established the society of states, and for which the idea of human rights is a kind of midwife. We shall return to this theme at the conclusion of this book. But first a descent into foreign policy.

8   Human rights in foreign policy

There is an inescapable tension between human rights and foreign policy. Their constituencies are different. The society of all humankind stands opposed to the club of states, and one of the primary rules of the latter has been to deny membership to the former. Foreign policy, according to these rules, should be conducted among states. It should not involve itself either with the communities enclosed by states, or with the notional global community which reformers, revolutionaries and other trouble-makers have called up to justify their enthusiasms. The society of states should and does concern itself with rights, but they are not the rights of individuals, or even of nations, but of states. And one of the points about the rights recognized by the society of states, as we saw in Chapter 8, was to allow political diversity, plural conceptions of the rights that were to apply to individuals and groups within states. The promotion of human rights, from the point of view of the morality of states, turns this doctrine inside out. It has tended to mean the attempt by one community, or group of communities, to make particular values general. This is a form of imperialism – the making of several societies one – even if it is restricted to the establishment of basic rights.

It might be argued, then, that the way for a minister of foreign affairs to resolve the 'inescapable tension' between human rights and foreign policy is to deny that human rights is part of his or her job. He or she acts for Ruritania, not the world. The rights of individuals and groups within foreign states are none of Ruritania's business. There is only a tension between human rights and foreign policy, of the kind we have described from a number of angles in this book, if a foreign minister chooses to add human rights to his or her other tasks.

Most in fact do. It is hard to think of a state that has made of states' rights an exclusive concern – though many appeal to states' rights as a defence against what others allege to be human rights. And the measure of this acceptance, on the part of international society, of obligations to non-members is the burgeoning international law of human rights that was discussed in Chapter 3. To the sceptic who scoffs, 'What human rights?', the reply is now to point to the authoritative texts on the subject, such as the International Covenants on Civil and Political Rights and on Economic, Social and Cultural Rights. To the entrenched sceptic who dismisses this as 'soft law', the reply now is to point to judicial decisions which make such basic rights as freedom from slavery and racial discrimination peremptory norms of international law binding on all states.[1] And to the moralist of states who wonders whether the international law of human rights is not itself a deodorized form of western cultural imperialism, it is now possible to reply (as was done in Chapter 3) that non-western cultures have not been slow to mark their arrival in international society by adding new international law to the corpus of doctrine received from the West. The movement for international law against apartheid, to mention a characteristic example, has not been led by the West.

What this international law of human rights suggests is that foreign ministers no longer have a choice about the inclusion of human rights. They cannot escape the tension between human rights and foreign policy simply by declaring that the former have no place in the latter. They are obliged to pay attention to human rights whether they like it or not. They are bound, according to the conventions of positivist international law, by their explicit agreements and by custom and practice. This body of doctrine forms part of their social world. There is some latitude in its interpretation, but it is not open to foreign offices to look the other way.

There is also a deeper sense in which human rights have arrived in foreign policy than that which observes the presence in foreign offices of desks bearing that title. Human rights now play a part in the decision about the legitimacy of a state (and of other actors and institutions) in international society, about whether what it is or what it does is sanctioned or authorized by law or right. It is not now enough for a state to be, and to be recognized as, sovereign. Nor is it enough for it to be a nation-state in accordance with the principle of self-determination. It must also act domestically in such a way as not to offend against the basic rights of individuals and groups within its territory. The question of what these basic rights are may not be resolved in international law (though we suggested a summary view of the matter in Chapter 3), but the argument here is that the right to life is basic if there are such things as basic rights.

So when reference is made in contemporary international politics to the notion of international legitimacy, something more is meant than a 'king's peace' of sovereign states that refrain from intervention in one another's internal affairs, but come to one another's aid when aggression takes place across international frontiers. This is the conservative, western interpretation of the fundamental principles of the United Nations Charter which Ali Mazrui sought to confront in his Third World interpretation of that document as a proclamation of global liberation in which human rights rather than state sovereignty held the first place.[2] This is to place 1945 in the tradition of 1776 and 1789 (as discussed in Chapter 6). The significance of such a location is that it legitimizes revolution. If human rights really do stand in this tradition, then they are not to be interpreted as the anodyne compromises of committee rooms at the United Nations, but as a call to arms.

This has not been the argument of this book, which is to detach basic rights from the political debate rather than engage them in it, on the ground that anyone ought to enjoy basic rights whatever their politics, that basic rights are a preface to politics. But it serves to show that the human rights, which – made much or little of in First World foreign policies – are seen as marginal to the central concerns of international relations, can be the central concern of Third World countries, or of their populations, to which the ordinary business of diplomacy is itself marginal. An awareness of this polarity is a warning against careless discussion of human rights in societies where their demands are to a large extent met. It should not be a surprise that they matter most where they are met least.

Powerful though Mazrui's statement of international legitimacy is, his conception of what it ought to consist in does not describe an international consensus – which it is the function of international law to express. A consensus so derived would indeed consist in more than a mere king's peace of the kind noticed just now, but in less than a global revolution. Human rights are more than just the cultural or ideological indicator of the rise and fall of (American) power, but they are not yet 'the idea of our time'.[3] In the contest between the principle of state sovereignty and the doctrine of universal human rights, neither side has scored a famous victory, but each sets limits to the domain of the other. In Chapter 6, which sought to plot the advance of human rights on the society of states, the conclusion was that the world society which exists in virtue or recognition of universal human rights is uneven and sometimes scarcely visible: egg-box barely modified. But, in Chapter 7, we argued for continued advance at least in regard to basic rights despite the modest achievements so far. The task now is to continue this discussion into foreign policy.

The crucial question for foreign policy in regard to human rights is how far what we have suggested to be international legitimacy penetrates, or ought to penetrate, the real world of diplomacy. Two levels of this reality are of interest here.[4] There is, first, the diplomacy of standard-setting in international relations from the conventions of the International Labour Organization to the declarations of the General Assembly of the United Nations on the reform of the international economic order. This is the level at which, it might be argued, criteria of international legitimacy are established and changed, and human rights are a prominent, if not the dominant, criterion. The size and complexity of this enterprise demands, for no more than the bureaucratic requirement of engaging in international relations, the attention of departments of foreign affairs, and other interested departments of government, around the world. Second, there is the level of standard-keeping in international relations. If states or other participants in international politics fail to meet the standards set, what are or should be the consequences? Invasion? Armed support for justifiable revolution? Economic intervention? Persuasion? Nagging? Indifference? Or a pointed stare in the opposite direction (when it comes to enforcement) in order not to ruffle sovereign feathers? A judgement on this question is the project for the conclusion of this chapter. In order to make that judgement possible, we should, in the first section, examine the argument of the professionals against too much zeal on human rights in foreign policy; in the second, subject this to scrutiny; and in the third establish some priority among the claims asserted as human rights in contemporary international politics.

GOING THROUGH THE MOTIONS

Granted that human rights are now part of the calculation of what is legitimate internationally, we might expect the hand that career diplomats extend towards them to be somewhat fastidious. If the first function of diplomacy is communication among states,[5] then it may be argued that a concern with human rights obstructs the fulfilment of that function. If a state with a poor human rights record is to be excluded socially, or, which is an alternative, lectured at, communication suffers. The professional diplomat, sensitive to cultural differences, and sensitive too to the sensitivities of other diplomats, is disinclined to allow political questions like that of human rights to upset the professionalism of his or her communication.

Moreover, diplomats are not only in the communications business; they also have an interest in maintaining *good* relations with each other. This is the point of references to the freemasonry of diplomacy: diplomats are members of a fraternity, a Grand Lodge, two of whose objects are mutual aid and the promotion of good feeling among the membership. One of the conventions of this society, accordingly, is that diplomats accommodate each other's interests wherever possible. There is a sense in which the Ruritanian Ambassador to Utopia is a representative of Utopian interests in Ruritanian decision-making. There is also a more general sense in which the Ruritanian foreign office represents the interests of foreign governments in the discussion of how Ruritania should act towards them. And Utopia is doing the same for Ruritania, and for all foreign governments (though, naturally, for some more that others). This is what has been called, in the discussion of the human rights policy of the Carter Administration in the United States, the 'clientism' of career diplomats, or their 'curator mentality'.[6] Maintaining good relations with foreign governments becomes the prime objective, rather than one among many. To meet it, there is the temptation to overlook, or to downplay, or to make excuses for, the domestic failings of clients in regard to the observation of human rights. There is an interesting Dutch example of this tendency at work. Peter R. Baehr has shown that once countries become the recipients of Dutch foreign aid, the picture painted of their human rights performance for the benefit of the Dutch parliament may be brighter than is warranted.[7] But the point here is that the tendency is neither particularly Dutch, nor peculiarly American, but systemic.

Also systemic is the preoccupation of diplomats with solving today's problem before tomorrow's crisis.[8] If all politics lies in the realm of circumstance, it might be argued that international politics is the most exposed to the contingent. Diplomats are at the mercy of the whims of their hosts as well as those of their masters, of global as well as local pressures. In this situation, the best they might hope for is an intelligible reply to the latest cable, a reasonable snapshot of the current situation for the next diplomatic bag. For these purposes, good relations with the government to which they are accredited are crucial. Any question of human rights, suggesting that good relations with this particular Utopian government might in the medium or long term be a disaster for Ruritania, is not even asked.

Moreover, for the most part, diplomats are in post only in the short term. The middle and the long term are the short terms for the next watch and the one after that. Even if there were recognition that the condition of human rights in Utopia was important for Ruritania in the medium or long term, there is no one who is interested in turning that recognition into policy now. There are no glittering prizes in diplomacy for paying attention to forces that are outside the system. So the convention which William F. Buckley mocked in the Third Committee of the United Nations – that debate was always general and never directed by name at any individual country[9] – is reproduced at the State Department. As Stephen B. Cohen reports it, there was an agreement in the Carter Administration never to determine formally that a particular government was engaged in gross abuses of human rights in case the information was leaked, which would make the government in question feel publicly insulted and thereby damage bilateral relations.[10]

Beyond the freemasonry of diplomacy, there is the fraternity of free trade. According to this argument, the societies that diplomats represent have a mutual interest in trade which would not be advanced by any notion that the failure of any one of them in regard to its human right performance should exclude it from trade, or diminish its participation in it. And the argument is extended to include aid: better to trade and aid than to make either of them dependent on human rights records. Why? First, because the interests of the manufacturing class should determine the policy of the state, as Richard Cobden argued. This should result in material advantage for all at home, and in peace, which is the best condition for trade, abroad.[11] In the second place, there is the idea, also owing something to Cobden (and before him to George Washington) that trade as a mode of contact among societies is itself a civilizing influence which governments cannot rival: 'As little intercourse as possible betwixt the *Governments*, as much connection as possible between the *nations* of the world.' One modern version of this argument is the doctrine taken up by Reagan of 'constructive engagement' (by American society) with South Africa rather than the imposition of sanctions (by the American government). And other western governments have been concerned to argue that the presence of western enterprise in South Africa is a force for progressive change in that country and not a sell-out to apartheid.[12] Thirdly, there is the extension of the free trade argument to cover aid. While aid comes from governments for the most part, and is therefore suspect from a traditional liberal standpoint, it is a good thing if it makes it possible for developing societies to gain from trade, to join this civilizing transnational society.

The tendency of these arguments is to the conclusion that in the long run trade is good for human rights. The other side of them is that the interruption of trade is unlikely to bear any human rights fruit. For one reason or another, runs the conventional wisdom, economic sanctions are prone to failure, not least because it is weakness of will in regard to the use of force that leads to resort to economic means in the first place. The arguments here are familiar: trade sanctions hurt the wrong people; they are easily circumvented; and, instead of bending the target society to the will of the outsiders, they might unite it against them.[13] So it is with suspension of aid. And here especially the argument is used that a policy which merely forces a receiver of military or economic aid to find another donor achieves nothing except damage to one's own interests and advantage for a rival.

In addition to the arguments for preferring communication, friendly relations and trade to human rights in foreign policy, but perhaps first in importance, are the arguments advocating caution on human rights for reasons of security. It is in this connection that the card of national interest is most frequently played against human rights. When it is a question of finding allies against Hitler, even devils will do, and to scrutinize domestic human rights records in this context is to court disaster by dwelling on a lesser evil.

The argument here is that even if human rights are in general a good idea, and in particular things deserving of recognition in the foreign policies of states, they are and should be trumped by considerations of national security. Thus, while the famous Section 502B of the United States Foreign Assistance Act requires that military aid not be given, and arms not be sold, to any country 'the government of which engages in a consistent pattern of gross violations of internationally recognized human rights', exceptions may be made in 'extraordinary circumstances' when 'on all the facts it is in the national interest' that such assistance should continue.[14] During the Carter Administration exceptions were made under this provision for Indonesia, Iran, the Philippines, South Korea and Zaire, countries that were the beneficiaries of military aid either because of their strategic position in the contest with the Soviet Union, or because of their natural resources, or both.[15] Once a strategic commitment is made in cases like these (for example, to military bases in the Philippines or to ground troops in South Korea), then meddling with details like local human rights records might seem a foolish distraction from grand strategy.[16]

This is the argument as applied to 'friends'. The overriding interest in security is also invoked against taking human rights too seriously in relations with adversaries. The pattern of the argument here, as we saw in Chapter 3, is that in relations between East and West a paramount interest of both sides is the avoidance of nuclear war. Given the importance of this goal, nothing comparatively trifling should be allowed to get in its way. Western governments concerning themselves with the human rights of individuals in the Soviet Union is just such an obstruction. So those rights should not be made the subject of official relations between the United States and the Soviet Union except as a matter of form. It seems, then, that for reasons of security with the Soviet Union, as well as security against it, we must be careful about human rights.

The advocate of human rights emerges from this discussion of foreign policy as an innocent abroad. Indeed, in the United States, the Bureau of Human Rights was defeated in the bureaucratic battle within the State Department during Carter's presidency because of its alleged lack of expertise on such arcane matters as that of national security.[17] But this too, to revert to our earlier theme, is systemic. It is not necessarily the heavies of the State Department pushing the good guys around for the hell of it. The State Department is charged with guarding the national interest, not the human interest. It sees it as no part of its duty to place at risk the safety or well-being of American citizens in the service of some supposed obligation to humanity. And this is a conception of its role which it shares with all foreign offices that have received the tradition of *raison d'état*. The criterion of individual morality which leads us to esteem a person who prefers another's interest to his or her own is not appropriately applied to states.[18] If states were to act like this, they would need to be criticized for neglecting the interests of their own populations, not praised.[19]

This reason to be self-centred may be especially applicable to democracies (the very political systems we associate with benevolence towards the *idea* of human rights), where policy, formally at any rate, must meet the wishes of the people.[20] What little we know about the wishes of the people in regard to human rights in foreign policy suggests that they are approved of in principle, provided they do not cost anything;[21] there is also approval for waiving them in support of repressive government if communism is the alternative.[22] In any event, domestic obligations outweigh obligations to foreigners – otherwise what is the point of citizenship? In these circumstances, human rights are a politician's graveyard. Their domestic constituency is small. They are a subject, accordingly, taken up by losers as well as on behalf of them.

If there is nothing or very little in the subject of human rights for politicians trying to get elected, there is not much in it for states either. Upsetting a foreign government on behalf of a victim does little for the state. It is a cost not a gain.[23] Given this widespread mentality of 'What's in it for us?', we might expect the issue of human rights to surface principally in two kinds of situation: when it serves the interest of the state (the provision, for example, of a stick with which to beat the Russians) and when attention to it endangers no other interest of the state (in faraway countries of which we know little).

But finding its place in the empire of circumstance is more damaging to human rights policy than it might be to other items of foreign policy, because it can be argued that it is on the substance and appearance of even-handedness that a successful human rights policy depends. If human rights are what their name suggests they are, the rights of all people, and of all people equally, then attention to the claims of Soviet minorities, or the South African majority, but not to the claims of Chinese minorities or east African Asians, brings a human rights policy into disrepute, for it is seen merely to serve interest. This is the problem of inconsistency, or double standards, about which left and right assail each other. The right accuses the left of complaining about the human rights records only of our 'friends', and of leaving the bigger target presented by our communist enemies alone. It prefers, in the now famous coupling, authoritarianism to totalitarianism.[24] The left accuses the right of absorbing the struggle for human rights into the Cold War, and not only of looking the other way when 'friends' disgrace themselves, and us, but also of being in the end responsible for their bad behaviour.[25] This argument has generated more heat than light, but the problem of consistency is so difficult, not only because of the role of ideology but also because of the role of the contingent in foreign policy, that some have despaired of including a human rights plank in it.[26]

To summarize the view of the foreign policy professionals about human rights, they are not excited by them. They are uncomfortable, even when they favour human rights in principle, about dealing with individual cases of human rights violation. They prefer the setting of universal standards.[27] They are happier that this be done in multilateral rather than bilateral diplomacy, public debate tending 'towards issues of principle' while private negotiation inclines 'towards compromise and understanding of the other man's point of view'.[28] When forced to take up a particular case, they prefer acting behind closed doors to conducting it in public, and they place great stress on the efficacy of 'quiet diplomacy', making use of their professional skills to go to the limits of the possible. And, finally, taken up reluctantly by diplomats in response to small but articulate domestic lobbies, human rights are received as a problem not a solution. They get in the way of ordinary diplomacy. They inhibit the flexibility necessary for operation in the world of states. They are enormously complex. Each new case requires different handling so that human rights policy cannot be turned into a routine. Any successes are better not claimed, while failures make the front page. There are no diplomatic triumphs to be pulled off in this area (except perhaps by the 'para-diplomacy' of the Reverend Jesse Jackson or the envoy of the Archbishop of Canterbury, whose missions to secure the release of people kidnapped by non-state groups might succeed precisely because they do not act for states). Let human rights remain on the periphery, or on the periphery of the periphery.[29] Taken in a foreign minister's baggage on a world tour, they might, as I once heard one of them say, spoil the whole trip.

TAKING RIGHTS SERIOUSLY

'Quiet diplomacy', 'keeping a low profile', 'doing the best one can in the circumstances': these are the phrases associated with going through the motions on human rights in foreign policy. No doubt, there are some non-career diplomats who would count them part of the something about the Foreign Service that 'takes the guts out of people'.[30] In the preceding section, we suggested that the primary reason for this seeming gutlessness was systemic, having to do with the structure of the diplomatic world, not the personalities of its members. But it is possible to take the systemic argument too far, so that it becomes an excuse rather than a reason for inaction on human rights. This section of the chapter investigates how far it is possible to get human rights into the system.

Human rights, we suggested earlier, might get in the way of communication among states. But states act, in some degree, for societies. In some of those societies, human rights have been taken up, notably by the non-governmental organizations we considered in Chapter 6, as questions which should inform the action of states. Their efforts have been rewarded by a good deal of publicity for human rights issues around the world, facilitated by the sophistication of systems of communication, and by questions asked about what foreign ministers are going to do about them. This is one way in which human rights have become things about which states have to communicate with each other. The professional communicators may not have accepted the brief with great enthusiasm, but as public servants they cannot refuse it. They must talk to each other about human rights because relations among their societies, over which they have incomplete control, have delivered them this issue. And sometimes it is human rights that become the absorbing questions of the day, pushing questions of security or commerce to one side. In February 1985, it is hard to imagine that the officials in the United States embassy in Seoul thought about anything other than the return to his country of the exiled leader Kim Dae-jung. In these circumstances, a protest that such an event had nothing to do with relations between the two states, South Korea and the United States, is merely silly.

Moreover, there is no reason why a concern for human rights should clog the machinery of communication. Quiet diplomacy on the matter does not have to be, as some suspect, silence. If it is defined as the business done among governments which is not brought to public attention, then a relationship might withstand a good deal of noise. Patricia Derian, Assistant Secretary for Human Rights and Humanitarian Affairs in the Carter Administration, was not prepared merely to agree with the representatives of Latin American governments that human rights were, in principle, very important. She was prepared, in conference with them, to call torture by its right name, and to identify its victims and the places where it was carried out.[31] Further, diplomats are expert in the manipulation of the symbols of communication which do not require talk: snubs at parties, the failure to appear for the National Day luncheon, returning home for 'consultation', in the end the breaking-off of relations. All these, though rarely the last, might be used to communicate displeasure at a human rights record. It is not necessary to grovel in order to be diplomatic, or to ignore human rights in order to communicate.

There remains the question, under diplomacy, of whether it is possible to maintain *good* relations among governments that draw human rights shortcomings to one another's attention. It adds another matter to those already there to dispute about, and a particularly contentious one because it touches nerves concerned with the quality of one's domestic government. So its successful handling is difficult. It tries diplomatic skill. But since it cannot be avoided, it might be better for professionals to regard the inclusion of human rights as a challenge rather than as a recipe for disaster. Certainly, the worst response is the cynical one, which tempts public servants, and members of society at large, to 'wink at' what they take to be the naive and temporary preoccupations of their masters.[32] If the enjoyment of human rights is the basis of civilized life, it is unseemly for their beneficiaries to set them at naught in societies where there are people who do not so benefit.

Also suspect is the blanket argument that we should pay no attention to human rights practice in the interest of maintaining free trade. For, in the first place, it may be that we can have both at once, patterns of trade being sufficiently resilient to withstand criticism of human rights records. If this argument is itself suspect for making morality coterminous with interest, the classical defence of free trade – offered by those who participate in it – as being productive of peace and solidarity presents even more profound difficulties in the context of human rights violations. The Cobdenite connection between trade and peace is now confronted by the idea that free trade is the doctrine of the top trading dog ('the imperialism of free trade'). And the idea that trade is the carrier of civilized values is now opposed by the notion that it can as easily buttress uncivilized ones ('funding fascism in Chile', aiding apartheid in South Africa). Moreover, in an age in which technology has allowed the multiplication of contacts among societies, in which, that is, trade no longer bears the princpal burden (along with diplomacy) of communication among them, there is less reason to regard it as untouchable: civilization need not suffer a blow at its reduction.

The general argument for free trade, then, even if it is well founded, cannot carry the day against attention to human rights in foreign policy. If, in practice, it were to prevail nevertheless, we should today call it selling out to the business lobby, who want commerce as usual whoever their trading partners may be.[33] But suspicion of the free-trade argument should not mean the manipulation of trade for political purposes at the drop of a hat. The conventional wisdom about the limitations of sanctions is well taken. The point about their limitations however, is often made more strongly in relation to human rights questions than it is in relation to security questions. It is instructive, in this regard, to compare the reaction of the United States to President Allende's regime in Chile with its reaction to that of President Pinochet: active destabilization of the Marxist regime gave way to relatively passive acceptance of the authoritarianism of the right.

Foreign aid policy is easier to manipulate, being more firmly in the hands of governments. In Congress, both before and during the Carter Administration, and in Carter's executive branch, there was the attempt to use the reduction of economic and military aid to discomfort repressive regimes, and its increase to advance progressive ones.[34] This policy did not usher in the millennium. It has been pointed out in relation to Latin America that the quality of human rights observance might follow an indigenous cycle of repression and relief more closely than an external cycle of American pressure and relaxation.[35] But at least it detached the United States from some repressive regimes and offered encouragement to domestic dissent. And it did not lead, as the sceptics said it would, straight to the deprived tyrants signing up with the opposition. In regard to arms procurement in Latin America, often it meant just less procurement.[36] The spirit of the policy of the human rights activists in the Carter Administration was not, 'We have to go on giving aid to keep them happy,' but, 'They ought to observe human rights to keep us happy.'[37]

Then there is security and the alleged inclination of human rights activists to fiddle while Rome burns. It is no doubt right that *raison d'état* should prevail in great emergencies or there may be no platform of order to which human rights may be secured. But the tendency of the argument from security against human rights is to stretch implausibly the idea of emergency: Jack crying wolf. Every tin-pot dictator requires his security defending, and the crucial moment is whenever someone mentions human rights. The argument for security is used, moreover, to blot out any other consideration. There is little sensitivity to the argument associated with Evan Luard in Britain, and with Richard Ullman in the United States, that it may be possible to have security *and* human rights.[38] Just as diplomatic communication, and trade, might survive attention to human rights, so also might security.

This point of view is sceptical of phrases like 'extraordinary circumstances in the national interest' as reasons for maintaining aid to gross human rights violators. It recognizes the weight of the forces against change when a recipient of economic and military aid is the host to American bases, in a geopolitically important position, the provider of strategic raw materials, and a regime to which the United States has attached its reputation.[39] But it is not overawed by this list of considerations. It is inclined to point out that they give the aid-recipient a bargaining advantage which it has not been slow to exploit (South Korea threatening to find arms supplies elsewhere if Washington considers their reduction in support of a human rights policy).[40] It suggests that the strategic value of aid-recipient to aid-giver might be equalled or even surpassed by the strategic value of aid-giver to aid-recipient. So that if the Shah of Iran, or President Salazar of Portugal, or President Park of South Korea, needed the western alliance more than the western alliance needed them, then this was an opportunity for the West to exploit in regard to human rights, and not a reason for silence.[41] And it draws attention to cases, like the fall of the Shah of Iran, in which exceptions were made in the name of a security which turned out to be paper-thin. This was the worst of both worlds: scant or no attention to human rights and in the end the 'loss' of Iran.

On security with adversaries, the suggestion above was that, along with the early Kissinger, we should not allow human rights to upset the stability of the strategic balance between East and West. In particular we should be wary of the Jackson–Vanik style of linkage between Soviet policy towards its citizens, and our policy towards economic and technological concessions to the Soviet Union. The argument against this linkage, as we saw in Chapter 4, is that it is unlikely to work, and that it might poison the international environment in which the strategic balance has to be preserved. But acceptance of this argument need not mean the abandonment of human rights in policy towards the Soviet Union and Eastern Europe, but merely, again as argued in Chapter 4, their cautious and unfanatical promotion.

The conclusion to this argument about security and human rights is that the use of the concept of security in foreign policy is at once too narrow and too broad: too narrow in being concentrated on safety against military threats;[42] too broad in having safety against military threats trumping all other considerations in the external relations of the state. The task is to widen the first (to include non-military threats, such as the fall of a regime in a 'friendly' state), and to narrow the second (so that the dog-eared card of security does not continue to 'win' us tricks like that of Iran). The questions that need to be asked are as follows. What are the present costs (in reputation and credibility) of locating a military base with a gangster regime? What might be the cost if it were replaced by bigger gangsters, especially if they dislike us? And what would be the present benefits of liberating ourselves from dependence on tyrants?[43] Further, in planning foreign policy, should we not decide what we are for in the world and promote it, as well as merely knowing what we are against and fighting it?[44] Planning introduces the problem of getting beyond the short term, or rather of getting consideration of the longer term into short term decision-making, a problem which was discussed above as a professionals' barrier to including human rights. Policy Planning staffs, as every realist knows, produce wise papers that nobody reads except perhaps the research staff. But if foreign policy is actually to be policy rather than merely the reaction to circumstance, the skill of its practitioner is to see beyond the short term and have this vision affect action in the short term. Sensitivity to the quality of human rights observance among both 'friends' and 'adversaries' might play a part in facilitating this vision. In any event, the appeal to *raison d'état* in the context of buttressing oppression might not be reluctant deference to the imperative of state security, but the attempt to dignify by reference to some principle what is merely convenient.

We concluded for the professionals with the argument that there was something inappropriate about dealing with human rights in foreign policy at all. It is not up to those who act for states to act for humankind. If they pretend to, we should be suspicious of them and point to the reality behind the rhetoric. And if they really have taken up humankind as a project, this is a moral fault, for they neglect thereby their citizens. This argument, we suggested, applies especially to democracies, where electorates rein in the ambition of politicians. There is a superficially appealing clarity about this point of view, for it seems to divide labour between states, which must get on with foreign policy, and individuals and groups other than states, whose imagination can run to the world as a whole. But if it is taken to mean that the list of a state's obligations includes only those to its citizens, and by virtue of international law to other states, it neither describes the practice of states in the matter of their acceptance of obligation, nor are its prescriptions reasonable. On the matter of international law, we have seen that the international law of human rights makes the obligations of states to individuals explicit. On the matter of what it is reasonable to prescribe, we may doubt whether the obligation to compensate a millionaire citizen for the appropriation of an acre of his or her property for the construction of a section of motorway is as morally pressing as its obligation to feed the starving in Ethiopia. Basic rights upset in this way the ordinary pattern of obligation, and what lies within the ordinary pattern of obligation is not morally conclusive.[45]

Moreover, the notion that democracies, by their nature, block off any attention to the whole of humankind neglects the universalistic liberalism which is also part of their tradition. This is a tradition particularly resonant in the United States, the nation established to protect the rights of man, and interested still by virtue of these origins in the rights of all men and women and not just American citizens.[46] If the establishment of the United States is regarded as a first step towards the achievement of the rights of every individual in the world, then the policy of the United States towards those not fortunate enough to be Americans must at least speak the language of rights or fall at the fence of domestic justification. In this regard, it may be argued, there is no difference between John Quincy Adams's notion of the United States as the 'well-wisher to the freedom and independence of all' but 'the champion and vindicator only of her own',[47] and Woodrow Wilson's intention to lend American influence 'of every kind' to the realization of republican principles in Latin America.[48] The American attachment to the rights of man was common to both statesmen: circumstances meant that policy was different. And although this pattern of thought is peculiarly American (no other western power needing to reproduce itself abroad in order to legitimize itself domestically), the justification of policy internally is a feature common to all democracies, and a criterion by which such justification might come increasingly to be decided is that of the attention given to human rights.

It is true that this domestic push to include human rights in foreign policy is likely to result in the human rights of some individuals and groups abroad being taken up with more enthusiasm than others. This reintroduces the issue of inconsistency and 'double standards'. The Reagan Administration is criticized (though it accepts the criticism as a description)[49] for finding fault on human rights grounds principally with communist 'enemies'. The Carter Administration was criticized for finding fault on human rights grounds principally with authoritarian 'friends'. But the point about human rights is their equal application to friends and enemies. Should we not therefore abandon governments as agencies for the improvement of human rights observance, given that their conception of rights is by definition partial, their action necessarily inconsistent? This point is not quite as show-stopping as it first appears, for it assumes a world beyond the state which it is possible to be consistent about. But it might be argued that the most elementary point about human rights issues in various parts of the world is that they are different from one another, and if unequal cases should be treated unequally, there can be no objection in justice to what critics unreasonably call inconsistency. So different treatment for different circumstances is appropriate, requiring, as David Owen put it, a very great deal of inconsistency if human rights principles are not to be abandoned altogether.[50] This may seem to make a virtue of inconsistency, which is a mistake. States should pay attention to consistency, as the BBC should to balance, but not in such a way as to allow nothing to be done. For the denial of the possibility of improvement in regard to respect for human rights anywhere on the ground that the same cannot be accomplished everywhere might be called the bloody-minded conservatism of those who would prefer that things did not get better.

To conclude this section on taking human rights seriously in foreign policy, diplomats could still be unenthusiastic about them, even after this discourse, but, given that *sang-froid* is their business, human rights are one more thing for them to be unenthusiastic about. The reason, as we have stressed, is practical as well as doctrinal. Human rights in foreign policy are not merely about standard-setting, public pronouncements, quiet words with the minister about particular cases, or finding formulae for the pacification of noisy but unimportant domestic lobbies; they are also matters which affect the great purposes of the state in securing and nourishing its citizens. This is the point of the extension of the concept of security to cover the medium and long term and the unconsidered threat. To refer back to an example we encountered in Chapter 6, the flood of refugees that might result from the denial of human rights, even from a country of whose existence we are only dimly aware, and the likelihood of their choosing the western world as a destination, should focus bureaucratic attention on the practicality of human rights observance as preventive medicine.[51] In this, and in several other respects, creative thought about the promotion of human rights might be more productive, and no more time-consuming, than the diplomatic routine of going through the motions.

THE PRIORITY OF SUBSISTENCE RIGHTS

If the idea of human rights is one that is subversive of the notion of international society,[52] what has been said here in defence of its inclusion in foreign policy hardly seems revolutionary. Indeed, the states themselves, in taking up the language of human rights, might be said to have taken some of the radical sting out of it. Great Britain, for example, makes human rights respectable when – in a lucid document of 1978 which goes far beyond the motions –[53] it accepts them as a proper goal of foreign policy. They become another item to be considered. The document draws up lists of possible actions to take in the event of glaring violations of human rights in other countries. Fourteen points are mentioned, ranging in severity from letters to politicians, through cancellation of ministerial visits, to trading sanctions. At the severe end of the list, cases are mentioned in which aid has been refused or discontinued, arms exports curtailed, or (in one case anyway) trade sanctions imposed. A strong line is taken on the need for a general and consistent posture on human rights throughout the world, coupled with the attempt to apply uniform standards. The Foreign and Commonwealth Office, the document says, should establish a systematic procedure for judging each country's human rights performance each year. And it should at least consider concentrating its human rights policy on the 'worst offenders' (as distinct, one presumes, from those over whom we have traditionally had influence, or those whose ideological predisposition against us makes a poke at their human rights record cheap). An 'obvious priority target' is those rights whose violation is 'most abhorrent to British public opinion', for example arbitrary killings and disappearances, torture and cruel or inhuman treatment, and arbitrary detention.[54]

There is little to object to in this document, which is surprisingly frank, serious-minded and realistic about its idealism (though one may doubt whether the Conservative government which followed the Labour one that wrote it was persuaded). If it is observed that it speaks of outrage in the voice of moderation, this is true, but outraged foreign offices might be less effective than moderate ones.[55] But it does slight economic and social rights, treating them as 'the Third World's theme' of a minimum guaranteed standard (the right to life) coming before everything else.[56] This book has taken a right to life, as a right to subsistence as well as security, as basic, and has to this extent signed up with the Third World. And it may even be the case that subsistence rights should be a higher priority for international society than rights to security – for reasons broached in Chapter 7 and to be returned to shortly. But first we must try to answer another question: how is it to be decided which human rights issues to promote in international society?

There are two grounds on which to base the selection. What are the worst cases? And which cases hold out the best prospect of responding positively to international attention? For a human rights issue to be taken up as international policy, a good case should be made out that it scores highly under both these headings. The difficulty, of course, is that neither of the questions prompts self-evident answers. For Elliot Abrams, the moral imperative of defeating communism, on which the Europeans are held to have gone soft, points to the infraction of liberty in the communist world as the worst case.[57] For Henry Shue, by contrast, the worst case is represented by obliviousness to the right of subsistence, what he calls the 'Holocaust of Neglect'.[58] The same antithesis is apparent in the provision of a remedy. The argument on the one hand might be that, to stop torturers, all the international community has to do is to publicize the accounts of the victims, whereas the economic and social rights associated with the provision of subsistence require the reproduction of a European welfare state on a global scale. Against this it might be said that torture is systemic rather than the product of tyrannical whim, and that building a political system civilized enough to remove it requires first the subsistence rights which are a preface to freedom.

While no answers are self-evident, some are more immediately evident than others. The Abrams argument, for example, which loses the distinctive claim of human rights in the fog of the Cold War, seems almost self-defeatingly blatant.

Not all the permutations for all the candidates can be considered here, but we shall suggest a view of subsistence rights that scores high on both scales. We have suggested from the beginning of this book that the right to life is a nonsense unless it demands sustenance against deprivation as well as protection against violence. Liberal political theory, we have seen, tended to take subsistence for granted rather than demanding it as a right. And liberal economics followed. It was not interested in such things as nutrition, health and education, Paul Streeten suggests, because in rich societies they counted as consumption and had no effect on human productivity.[59] So neither classical politics nor classical economics was equipped to deal with what, in terms of its sheer size and lack of moral ambiguity, seems the most pressing rights issue in the world today – the claim of the starving and malnourished to be properly fed. Whether the number of these people is 750 million or over a billion, to take two different estimates of the magnitude of the problem,[60] a human rights policy that ignored this problem would rightly be regarded with derision. To say that the problem of starvation is the most pressing rights issue does not mean that torture, or genocide, have less of a claim to our attention. Indeed, these great emergencies, in which people might die quickly rather than slowly, might by their immediacy turn our minds (though not those of the starving) away from that of starvation. But starvation is, so to speak, the resident emergency, and it is reasonable that seriousness about human rights should be tested by reference to it.

On the question of the effectiveness of international attention, things at first sight might seem less promising for subsistence rights. The international community (in the form of the ILO and the World Bank) has received these claims as 'basic needs', though the economic training of the officers of the bank has made them reluctant to translate them into the lawyers' language of rights.[61] The problems with basic needs as a project for international society do seem formidable. They are demandingly broad. What we have called the right to subsistence can reasonably be shown to require that progress be made not merely in food provision, but also in the supply of potable water, the maintenance of public health, and the education that makes possible the integration of these processes. They might require a radical shift in patterns of political power in order that resources can reach the submerged 40 per cent in developing societies. In the eyes of the developing world, they smack of the old imperialist routine of disguised self-interest (in, for example, dressing up the protection of northern industry as the promotion of the interest of southern peasants). In the eyes of the developed world, on the other hand, they might appear as the triumph of the welfare ethic over the work ethic, for the collectivity over the individual, and for socialism over private enterprise.

None of these problems, however, is so formidable as to dismiss the idea of basic needs. Their breadth, and the need to move forward on all fronts together, may be a strength from the point of view of development, not a weakness.

Moreover, they have a concreteness which earlier development schemes lacked. While they might require a radical shift in the pattern of political power, it is a shift that can take place only with local commitment, not external imposition. The reply to Third World suspicions is that a basic needs strategy has for the most part gone along with growth. To First World suspicions the reply is that basic needs has been successful as a strategy in capitalist and mixed economies as well as in socialist ones.

So one of the great appeals of basic needs strategy as a means of meeting the right to subsistence is that it is criticized and defended across the political spectrum. It is a communist plot, a liberal dream and a capitalist trick all at once. This might mean that there is something in it. As a programme for international society, its strength is its quasi-technical search for a pre-political programme: it does not invite the world to join up with this or that team of political developers. What is required is the bringing together of financial aid from the North to fund the programme, with provision for making allocative decisions and the monitoring of performance.

It may be that, as Roger Hansen has argued, these functions would best be fulfilled by a new international institution.[62] But even a technical programme needs leadership, and for this purpose the active and forthright involvement of the United States is essential. Is it possible to persuade any United States government to embark on a programme that requires it to do for the world what it has been prepared to do for itself only as a spasmodic response to crises: namely, involve itself in the provision of basic needs which strain the notion of limited government? If stress is placed on basic needs as in large part the provision of public goods (which involve public expenditure even in capitalist economies), on their concreteness (appealing to American pragmatism), on the 'self-evident' claim of starving children to be fed (appealing to American ideology as well as generosity), it need not be hopeless. 'All governments should accept the removal of the scourge of hunger and malnutrition, which at present afflicts many millions of human beings, as the objective of the international community as a whole, and should accept the goal that within a decade no child will go to bed hungry, that no family will fear for its next day's bread, and that no human being's future and capacities will be stunned by malnutrition.' If this is liberal utopianism it is American and from the mouth of Henry Kissinger as Secretary of State in 1974.[63]

Behind the argument that the human rights movement in international society should be focused on a single overriding goal is a comparison with the abolition of the slave trade, with the United States replacing Great Britain as the prime mover.[64] The analogy is far from complete. The United States cannot act in contemporary international society with the sublime disregard for the values of other cultures that is taken to have encouraged the British action. It cannot rely for the elimination of hunger on gunboats. It does not have the margin of power in its favour that allowed the British the command of the seas. So it must act in as wide a coalition as possible, on grounds which are regarded collectively as legitimate, relying on persuasion more than coercion. But without the leadership of the United States, and the conviction on the part of others that it means what it says, there is small prospect of success. Allies in the coalition might take the lead on particular initiatives, or do the leg-work in negotiation, but it is the commitment of the world's largest economy that might make a difference.

How? If starvation is the rough equivalent of the slave trade, where do we start? Henry Shue, as we saw in chapter 1, has distinguished three kinds of duty that correlate with the right of subsistence: the duty to avoid depriving others of subsistence; the duty to protect them if they nevertheless are deprived; and the duty to aid those incapable of providing their own subsistence.[65] The first of these duties enjoins self-consciousness and self-criticism about our own role in the world. It asks, with Noam Chomsky, 'Do we really care about the human consequences of our actions?'[66] It might require that we cease aiding a society that deprived its citizens of their basic rights. More disturbingly for us, it might require that we consider our direct responsibility for depriving people of their basic rights in foreign countries that we have economic relations with, which would raise questions about disinvestment and the like. The second duty enjoins a response to neglect on the part of others, rather than repairing our own neglect. It might require that, for example, we consider economic refugees to have an equal claim with political refugees to the hospitality of a receiving state. And the third duty might, for example, oblige us to give economic aid to drought victims.

Given the thrust of the earlier argument, it is the last of these duties that should be emphasized first in international society. For the existence of a class of global poor might be thought of as a systemic disaster to be likened to, though more massive than, a natural disaster such as an earthquake or a hurricane. It may be that this systemic disaster is not 'natural', being the product of human choice in which some of us are more culpable than others.[67] And certainly, as we saw in Chapter 5, it serves the interest of both the Second and the Third Worlds to blame the First World for its existence. But the duty to aid the deprived should be above the explanation of their predicament, and the political appeal to do so should be based on this obligation in order that a cooperative enterprise to meet human needs can start with generosity of spirit rather than mutual recrimination. The meeting of basic needs would not deliver freedom for the poor, any more than the abolition of the slave trade gave the slaves their liberty, but both are prerequisites for freedom.

Before considering some possible objections to it, let us recapitulate the case for the priority of subsistence rights as a project for international society. The size and moral clarity of the problem of starvation make it a worse case. The possibility of a technical solution to it, not engaging the major ideologies in an argument about their superiority to the others, and not requiring them to dissolve themselves for the strategy of basic needs to be put into effect, makes it score some points on the scale of practicability as an international policy. The chief problem is to engage the United States as a leader of a movement that can be likened in some respects to the abolition of the slave trade, and then to persuade it and its allies that their aid is required against a 'systemic disaster'.

Let us consider liberal, conservative and radical objections to this scheme in that order. Jack Donnelly might protest against it as a 'least-common-denominator strategy', writing off too many crucial human rights on the ground that they are controversial.[68] In reply to this, the argument is that the international community cannot be as adept in practice at keeping all the human rights balls in the air at once as Donnelly is in theory. The moral simplicity of the case is its merit. It may further be objected, from a somewhat related standpoint, that a preoccupation with subsistence rights might let go the opportunity for substantial improvements in regard to other basic rights – such as the uniquely clear target that General Amin's Uganda offered to a coffee boycott directed against a regime that was plundering the right to life in its other aspect.[69] The reply to this is to accept it: unique opportunites come only once. The argument here is that subsistence rights should in general be at the top of the agenda, not that they should always be. Then, finally, it might be objected, still from a liberal standpoint, that the priority given to subsistence rights is simply a sell-out to those who use the purported pursuit of economic and social rights as an excuse for suppressing, or ignoring, or at any rate putting off, civil and political rights. The reply to this is that we have accepted the right to liberty as a basic right (even if only the limited sense of the liberty to claim and have upheld a right to subsistence), and that it is no part of the present argument that the satisfaction of the right to subsistence *requires* an affront to civil and political rights. There is no general evidence for this proposition and it is too easy a handle to offer to tyrants.[70] It is simply that subsistence might make a more workable international programme, a more neutral undertaking for international society, than liberty.

There is also a cluster of conservative objections. The first one of these is that our scheme is too demanding, making maximalist claims of a society that has repeatedly shown its ineptitude at handling minimalist ones. Thus it might be argued that a basic needs programme of this kind would require, from the western world, the equivalent of a Marshall Plan with no political interest to prompt it; from the Third World states, the equivalent of a French Revolution with no elite interest to promote it; and supervision of the Third World by the western world amounting to neocolonialist interventionism just when the old colonialism was thrown off.[71] The reply to this might be to show that the increase in northern aid required to meet basic needs is marginal if the problem of distribution is met, and to argue along with the Brandt Report for a common global interest in growth;[72] to point out that the revolution in Third World countries is one that might buttress the position of their elites rather than undermining them; and to demonstrate that the supervision in question might be of an area which has already moved out of domestic jurisdiction. We shall return to this last point in our conclusion.

The second conservative objection questions the neutrality of basic needs. It might regard the doctrine as the logical end-product of the bias towards redistribution abroad in the world as a result of the impact of British Fabian ideas on the new states since the independence of India.[73] This is not a neutral pre-political programme, according to this point of view, but an endorsement of socialism. It is part of a new political sensibility which prefers equality to liberty and which it is the mission of the West, and especially the United States, to confront not to endorse.[74] Part of the reply to this point of view is one we have already glimpsed, namely that basic needs doctrine has been accommodated by societies across the political spectrum.[75] And the other part is to welcome the new political sensibility, if that indeed it is, as something that might be launched by the left but then defended by the right along the lines of the welfare state in Britain.

The third and most radical conservative objection to basic needs doctrine, associated with Garret Hardin's 'lifeboat ethics', suggests that it is literally a recipe for disaster.[76] The food assistance programme that would be part of meeting basic needs would merely encourage populations to multiply, speeding the eventual catastrophe as Third World swimmers were pulled aboard First World lifeboats until all sank. Societies should be made 'intrinsically responsible' for feeding themselves, and should not exceed their own 'carrying capacity' and thus become a call on other societies through slogans such as basic needs. There are a number of difficulties with 'lifeboat ethics'.[77] The doubtful assumption we might notice here is that which regards feeding the poor as necessarily a population time-bomb. It may be that the rise in living-standards associated with meeting basic needs would discourage population growth rather than encourage it, large families being no longer necessary for the security of the parents in old age. Population control might be effected without resorting to starvation.[78]

The radical objection to basic needs doctrine, which has it as a new imperialism of a peculiarly righteous kind (given, it is argued, the failure of the imperialists to meet basic needs when they were formally in charge), has a certain cynical appeal. But a stance against the doctrine of basic needs based on this ground would be a variety of bloody-minded radicalism to match the bloody-minded conservatism which we rejected earlier. There is a deeper radical criticism. We might just now have comforted a particular kind of conservative by pointing out the extent to which basic needs strategy invites states to consolidate their hold over their populations by meeting their needs through a hierarchy of regimes, rather than unloosing anarchy upon the world. If, ultimately, 'global guarantees of human rights are virtually synonymous with the quest for the next world order system',[79] then the defence of basic needs as entrenching the states-system is pointed in the wrong direction. This considerable point we come to in the conclusion of the book.

Before that, we must rule off on the priority of subsistence rights. We may note that the basic needs strategy which is designed to meet subsistence rights is also one of the strategies identified for the creation of a new international economic order.[80] But our endorsement of it here is not as part of this larger scheme. It reflects, merely, the view that basic rights ought to be met; that the plight of the global poor is the worst offence against these rights in contemporary world society; and that the project of meeting basic needs is a less profitless one for international society than, say, the global extension of a western conception of liberty. This is not a call for the extinction of liberty as a value in terms of which to judge either all foreign policy or the domestic policies of others. But it is a proposal about how progress might be made on basic rights in the international community without running into insurmountable ideological obstacles along the way.

When we suggested in Chapter 5 that such a project might transcend the East–West conflict, what was meant was not that East and West might suddenly unite in stretching out their arms to the world's poor, but that neither of them need expect to be taken seriously on 'their version' of human rights unless they meet these basic rights first. Hence our adoption of subsistence rights as a preface to politics, and also our hope of finding these rights an anchorage in interests. To those who would suggest that all this is to push against a door that is already ajar, since the ILO, the World Bank and the United States Agency for International Development have already accepted the doctrine of basic needs and it is already part of American law, the response is that what would make the difference is the acceptance of this doctrine as a doctrine of human rights imposing correlative obligation, and not merely as an option in the strategy of development.

CONCLUSION

One of the themes of this book has been to monitor, by reference to the international politics of human rights, the arrival of a world society which might unsettle the stability of international society. The advance of the one, we suggested in a number of places, might be inimical to the survival of the other. The defender of order in international relations, in particular, might cast a sceptical and at the same time apprehensive eye in the direction of human rights that might undermine it, rather like Burke on the French Revolution, listening with morbid fascination to the bell that tolled the knell of the departing system.[81]

But there has also been a theme, adding counterpoint to this one, which we introduced in Chapter 3, revisited in Chapter 6 and heard coming through strongly in this last chapter, that has human rights not as a challenge to the system of sovereign states, but as something which has added to its legitimacy, merely requiring that the shape taken by the internal systems of the members – what we have noted Suarez calling the *ius gentium intra se* – should be in some perhaps increasing degree similar. So, against the theme of international law of human rights as part of a progression away from the primitiveness of tribal attachment to the state and towards a situation in which individuals treat each other in their capacities as human beings rather than as members of tribes, there lies a counter-theme of human rights consolidating the state rather than transcending it. This counter-theme has been brilliantly described by John Boli-Bennett in his account of the 'ideology of the expanding state constantly coopting the ideology of individualism by translating human rights into citizen rights'.[82] He argues that the civil rights of the eighteenth century, the political rights of the nineteenth century, and the economic and social rights of the twentieth century have all involved a deal between individuals or groups within the state, on the one hand, and the state itself on the other. The former have gained some of their demands, and have been enmeshed in return more tightly in the net of the state. He says that it 'is no accident that the great expansion of the ideology of human rights has occurred at precisely that period in history when state power and authority have expanded most rapidly in all parts of the globe'.[83]

To use a phrase of Richard Falk's, this is the state 'controlling the terrain of legitimacy'. And for him this is a source of despair. Conservatives too might despair of human rights in international relations when they observe that the language of human rights has proliferated in an era when the European civility of the eighteenth and nineteenth centuries has declined.[84] But there is also hope, not merely in the return to a Kantian theme of liberal states that respect civil rights at home being less disposed to fight with each other abroad,[85] or in the idea that the spread of a global culture makes international society work more smoothly,[86] but also in Burke's faith in the civilizing (and not merely corrupting) power of government. If the transnational recognition of subsistence rights improves the quality of government within states, we might extend a cautious welcome both to the penetration of the state and to its strengthening itself in response. Instead of being driven out by the *moi commun*, the *moi humain* is coopted by it.

This process of cooption, it might be said, is necessary if we are to avoid the 'abstract nakedness of being nothing but human.'[87] And this notion is endorsed in contemporary international law by the view that in order for human rights to become a legal reality 'an organized society must exist in the form of a *de jure* state.'[88] But this does not mean that we simply bump up, finally, against the buffer of the state. For we have observed the reality of a transnational world from which proposals about the rights of humans come for the state to dispose of. Individuals and groups other than states have forced themselves on the attention of international society, and the international law of human rights has been both the response to this and the handle for further progress.[89] Now it maybe that the international law of human rights and its domestic reception throughout international society are connected only problematically, so that, as we argued in Chapter 6, the world society which exists in virtue of the spread of this cosmopolitan law is thin and uneven.[90] But there is now an area of domestic conduct in regard to human rights, which we have assimilated to the tradition of the *ius gentium intra se*, that is under the scrutiny of international law. This does not issue a general licence for intervention. International society is not yet as solidarist as that. But it does expose the internal regimes of all the members of international society to the legitimate appraisal of their peers. This may turn out not to have been a negligible change in international society.

Notes

1. THE IDEA OF HUMAN RIGHTS

1 See, e.g., W.N. Hohfeld, *Fundamental Legal Conceptions* (New Haven and London, Yale University Press, 1919). For the idea of a right as 'normative property', see Alan Gewirth, *Human Rights: Essays on Justification and Applications* (Chicago and London, Chicago University Press, 1982), p. 10.
2 This is adapted from Gewirth, *Human Rights*, p. 2.
3 For a discussion see Hugo Adam Bedau, 'Why Do We Have the Rights We Do?', *Social Philosophy and Policy*, vol.1 (1984), issue 2, p. 59.
4 K.R. Minogue, 'Natural Rights, Ideology and the Game of Life', in Eugene Kamenka and Alice Ehr-Soon Tay (eds), *Human Rights* (London, Edward Arnold, 1977), p. 21.
5 Ronald Dworkin, *Taking Rights Seriously* (London, Duckworth, 1977), p. xi.
6 Alan R. White, *Rights* (Oxford, Clarendon Press, 1984), p. 115.
7 See Joel Feinberg, *Social Philosophy* (Englewood Cliffs, NJ, Prentice-Hall, 1973), pp. 59–61.
8 For criticism of this doctrine, see David Lyons, 'The Correlativity of Rights and Duties', *Nous*, vol. 4 (1970), no. 1, pp. 45–55.
9 S.I. Benn and R.S. Peters, *Social Principles and the Democratic State* (London, Allen & Unwin, 1959), pp. 88–9.
10 H.L.A. Hart, 'Are There Any Natural Rights?', in A. Quinton (ed.), *Political Philosophy* (London, Oxford University Press, 1967), p. 57.
11 See Arthur C. Danto, 'Comment on Gewirth: Constructing an Epistemology of Human Rights: A Pseudo Problem?', *Social Philosophy and Policy*, vol. 1 (1984), issue 2, p. 29.
12 For treatment of a right as a justified claim, see Feinberg, *Social Philosophy*, pp. 64–7; Bernard Mayo, 'What are Human Rights?', in D.D. Raphael (ed.), *Political Theory and the Rights of Man* (London, Macmillan, 1977), p. 75; and Richard Wasserstrom, 'Rights, Human Rights and Racial Discrimination', *Journal of Philosophy*, vol. 61 (1964), p. 630.
13 See Maurice Cranston, 'Human Rights, Real and Supposed', in Raphael, *Political Theory and the Rights of Man*, pp. 51–5.
14 Jack Donnelly, *The Concept of Human Rights* (New York, St Martin's Press, 1985), pp. 16–17.
15 See Raphael, 'Human Rights, Old and New' and 'The Rights of Man and the Rights of the Citizen', in Raphael, *Political Theory and the Rights of Man*, pp. 64–5 and 112–15.

16 Henry Shue, *Basic Rights; Subsistence, Affluence, and US Foreign Policy* (Princeton, Princeton University Press, 1980), pp. 52–3.

17 See, e.g., Hedley Bull, 'Human Rights and World Politics', in Ralph Pettman (ed.), *Moral Claims in World Affairs* (London, Croom Helm, 1979); and C.B. Macpherson, *The Real World of Democracy* (New York, Oxford University Press, 1972).

18 See the Universal Declaration of Human Rights, 1948, and the International Covenant on Civil and Political Rights, 1976. Texts in Ian Brownlie (ed.), *Basic Documents on Human Rights*, 2nd edn (Oxford, Clarendon Press, 1981), pp. 21–7, 128–45.

19 See the Universal Declaration, and the International Covenant on Economic, Social and Cultural Rights, 1976. Texts in Brownlie, *Basic Documents*, pp. 21–7, 118–27.

20 See Article 1 of both International Covenants, and the International Convention on the Elimination of All Forms of Racial Discrimination, 1966 (text in Brownlie, *Basic Documents* pp. 150–63). And the Charter of Economic Rights and Duties of States, 1974, text in Robert F. Meagher, *An International Redistribution of Wealth and Power: A Study of the Charter of Economic Rights and Duties of States* (New York, Pergamon Press, 1979). For a discussion of collective rights, see Chapter 5 below.

21 The argument here is from Cranston, 'Human Rights, Real and Supposed', in Raphael, *Political Theory and the Rights of Man*, pp. 50–3.

22 The argument here is from Raphael, 'Human Rights, Old and New', in Raphael, *Political Theory and the Rights of Man*, pp. 64–5.

23 Tom Paine, *The Rights of Man* (Everyman edn, London, Dent, 1969), pp. 246–56.

24 Raphael, 'Human Rights, Old and New', p. 64.

25 *Ibid.*, p. 65.

26 Shue, *Basic Rights*, p. 7.

27 Susan Moller Okin, 'Liberty and Welfare: Some Issues in Human Rights Theory', in J.R. Pennock and J.W. Chapman (eds), *Human Rights*, Nomos XXIII (New York, New York University Press, 1981), p. 242.

28 Shue, *Basic Rights*, pp. 35–45.

29 *Ibid.*, pp. 46–51.

30 *Ibid.*, p. 27.

31 Cranston, 'Human Rights, Real and Supposed', p. 52.

32 Christian Bay, 'A Human Rights Approach to Transnational Politics', *Universal Human Rights*, vol. 1 (1979), no. 1, pp. 29–40.

33 This is explored further in Chapter 5 below.

34 See Donnelly, *The Concept of Human Rights*, p. 38.

35 Shue, *Basic Rights*, pp. 18–22.

36 Gewirth, *Human Rights*, p. 7 (emphasis in original). See also his *Reason and Morality* (Chicago, University of Chicago Press, 1978).

37 Article 2 of the Declaration of the Rights of Man and of the Citizen, the formal pronouncement of the philosophy underlying the French Revolution and published as a preface to the Constitution of 1791.

38 See Charles R. Beitz, 'Human Rights and Social Justice' in Peter G. Brown and Douglas Maclean (eds), *Human Rights and US Foreign Policy* (Lexington, D.C. Heath, 1977), pp. 53–60.

39 See A.I. Melden, *Rights and Persons* (Oxford, Blackwell, 1977), pp. 192–3.

40 Charles Fried, *Right and Wrong* (Cambridge, MA, Harvard University Press, 1978) p. 118.

41 *Ibid.*

42 See Donnelly, 'Human Rights and Natural Rights', *Human Rights Quarterly*, vol. 4 (1982), p. 405.

43 The thinking here is influenced by Margaret Macdonald, 'Natural Rights', in Anthony de Crespigny and Alan Wertheimer (eds), *Contemporary Political Theory* (New York, Atherton Press, 1970), esp. pp. 238–43. The reference to a 'rarefied level' is intended to move the discussion of human rights outside the political brawl between ideologies. In effect human rights are what every one ought to have regardless of the particular nature of the contemporary political debate. We return to this question in Chapter 7.

44 See Howard Warrender, *The Political Philosophy of Hobbes* (Oxford 1959), p. 19.

45 Hart, 'Are There Any Natural Rights?', pp. 57–8.

46 This point was suggested by my reading of Lyons, 'The Correlativity of Rights and Duties', pp. 45–55. The distinction between positive and negative liberty is from Isaiah Berlin, *Two Concepts of Liberty*, Inaugural Lecture, Oxford University, 31 October, 1958 (Oxford University Press, 1958).

47 Feinberg, 'Duties, Rights and Claims', *American Philosophical Quarterly*, vol. 3 (1966), no. 2, pp. 143–4.

48 Melden, *Rights and Persons*, p. 23.

49 De Tocqueville adds: 'But the right of the poor to obtain society's help is unique in that instead of elevating the heart of the man who exercises it, it lowers him.' Quoted in Minogue, 'Natural Rights, Ideology and the Game of Life', p. 34. This is an interesting example of the old liberal prejudice against what are now called economic and social rights.

50 Shue, *Basic Rights*, pp. 30–3.

51 Hart, 'Are There Any Natural Rights?', p. 65.

52 See Steven Lukes, *Individualism* (Oxford, Blackwell, 1973), p. 79.

53 See David Miller, *Social Justice* (Oxford, Clarendon, 1976), pp. 71–2; Richard E. Flathman, *The Practice of Rights* (New York and London, Cambridge University Press, 1976), p. 49.

54 Berlin, *Two Concepts of Liberty*, pp. 11–12.

55 Flathman, 'Moderating Rights', *Social Philosophy and Policy*, vol. 1 (1984), issue 2.

56 Bull, 'Human Rights and World Politics', pp. 89–90.

57 Michael Walzer, *Spheres of Justice* (New York, Basic Books, 1983), ch. 1.

58 *Ibid.*, p. 29.

2. HUMAN RIGHTS IN WESTERN POLITICAL THOUGHT

1 Herbert Butterfield, *The Whig Interpretation of History* (Harmondsworth, Pelican, 1973), p. 40.

2 Sir Henry Maine, *Ancient Law*, with an introduction and notes by Sir Frederick Pollock (London, John Murray, 1916), p. 174.

3 See. A.P. d'Entréves, *Natural Law*, 2nd edn (London, Hutchinson, 1970), ch. 2.

4 This is Sir Ernest Barker's account of Aristotle's definition of 'natural' as applied to man in his introduction to Otto Gierke, *Natural Law and the Theory of Society 1500 to 1800*, 2 vols., transl. and with an intro. by Ernest Barker (Cambridge, at the University Press, 1934), p. xxxv.

5 See Leo Strauss, *Natural Right and History* (Chicago, University of Chigaco Press), pp. 90–6.
6 It is with Antigone's defiance that Maurice Cranston begins his discussion of the history of human rights in *What are Human Rights?* (London, The Bodley Head, 1973), pp. 9–10.
7 See William L. Davidson, *The Stoic Creed* (Edinburgh, T. and T. Clark, 1907), pp. 142–4.
8 *Ibid.*, p. 164.
9 Cicero, *De Republica* (transl. Clinton Walker Keyes, Cambridge and London, Harvard University Press and Heinemann, 1928), bk. III, s. xxii, p. 211.
10 See d'Entrèves, *Natural Law*, p. 26.
11 See Cicero, *Laws* (transl. Keyes), bk. I, s. xii, p. 333i, and R.W. and A.J. Carlyle, *A History of Mediaeval Political Theory in the West* (3rd edn, 6 vols., Edinburgh and London, Blackwood, 1930), vol. 1, *The Second Century to the Ninth*, p. 9.
12 D'Entrèves, *Natural Law*, pp. 33–5.
13 See Barker's introduction to Gierke's, *Natural Law*, p. xxxvi.
14 De Zulueta, *Legacy of Rome*, p. 181, cited in *ibid.*, p. xi.
15 The argument that follows is from Richard Tuck, *Natural Rights Theories: Their Origin and Development* (Cambridge, Cambridge University Press, 1979), ch. 1.
16 D'Entrèves, *Natural Law*, p. 38.
17 Gierke, *Political Theories of the Middle Ages*, transl. and with an intro. by Frederic William Maitland (Cambridge, Cambridge University Press, 1951), p. 14.
18 *Ibid.*, pp. 4–5.
19 *Ibid.*, p. 87.
20 See Quentin Skinner, *The Foundations of Modern Political Thought* (2 vols, Cambridge, Cambridge University Press, 1979), vol. 1, *The Renaissance*, pp. 84–101.
21 See Skinner, *The Foundations of Modern Political Thought*, vol. 2, *The Age of Reformation*, pp. 3–9.
22 St Augustine, *City of God* (London, Dent, 1945), bk. V, ch. 17.
23 *Romans*, 13, i.
24 Skinner, *The Age of Reformation*, p. 70.
25 See Gierke, *Political Theories of the Middle Ages*, pp. 61–4; and Skinner, *The Age of Reformation*, p. 122.
26 *Ibid.*, pp. 123–4, 148–9.
27 *Ibid.*, p. 213.
28 *Ibid.*, p. 230.
29 This account derives from *ibid.*, pp. 239–338; see also Harold J. Laski, *A Defence of Liberty Against Tyrants* (London, Bell, 1924).
30 Skinner, *The Age of Reformation*, pp. 335–7.
31 Francisco Suarez, *Selections from Three Works*, vol. 2. *The Translation*, prepared by Gwladys L. Williams *et al.* (Oxford, Clarendon Press, London, Humphrey Milford, 1944), p. 30.
32 See Tuck, *Natural Rights Theories*, p. 67, and Hugo Grotius, *The Jurisprudence of Holland*, transl. and ed. R.W. Lee (Oxford, Clarendon Press, 1926), pp. 315, 293.
33 Tuck, p. 130, and Hobbes, *Leviathan*, ed. Michael Oakeshott (Oxford, Blackwell, 1945), ch. 14, p. 84.
34 Locke, *Two Treatises of Government*, ed. P. Laslett (Mentor, 1965), pp. 114–16; ch. 4, s. 22, p. 325.

35 Skinner, *The Age of Reformation*, p. 239. For the view that the seventeenth and eighteenth century German jurist Pufendorf is more important in the history of human rights than either Hobbes or Locke, see D.D. Raphael, 'The Liberal Western Tradition of Human Rights', *International Social Science Journal*, vol. 18 (1966), no. 1, p. 23.

36 D'Entrèves, *Natural Law*, ch. 4. I deal here with what is common to the American and French Revolutions. In Chapters 6 and 7 below I get to the difference between them on human rights.

37 Thomas Paine, *The Rights of Man*, 1791 (Everyman edn, London, Dent, 1969), p. 74.

38 In Paine's translation, *ibid.*, p. 94, this is an early use of the expression 'human rights'.

39 See Barker's introduction to Gierke, *Natural Law*, pp. xliv–xlv.

40 Edmund Burke, 'Speech on the Plan for Economic Reform', 11 February, 1780, in Robert A. Smith (ed.), *Edmund Burke on Revolution* (New York, Harper Torchbooks, 1968), p. 92.

41 Barker in Gierke, *Natural Law*, p. 1.

42 *Ibid.*, p. li.

43 Burke, *Reflections on the Revolution in France*, 1790, in *Works*, 6 vols (Bohn's British Classics edn, London, Bell and Daldy, 1872), vol. 2, p. 327.

44 *Ibid.*, p. 333.

45 See Charles Taylor, *Hegel* (Cambridge, Cambridge University Press, 1975), p. 385.

46 *Ibid.*, p. 376.

47 Guido de Ruggiero, *The History of European Liberalism*, transl. R.G. Collingwood (Oxford University Press, 1929; Boston, Beacon Press, 1959), p. 32.

48 Burke, *Reflections*, in *Works*, vol. 2, p. 282.

49 *Ibid.*, p. 331.

50 *Ibid.*, p. 412.

51 See Burleigh Taylor Wilkins, *The Problem of Burke's Political Philosophy* (Oxford, Clarendon Press, 1967), p. 180.

52 *Reflections*, in *Works*, vol. 2, pp. 305–6.

53 *Ibid.*, p. 306.

54 Wilkins, *The Problem of Burke's Political Philosophy*, pp. 59–60, 109–10.

55 *Ibid.*, p. 175.

56 *Reflections*, in *Works*, vol. 2, pp. 368–9.

57 *Ibid.*, p. 367.

58 See Taylor, *Hegel*, p. 423.

59 *Ibid.*, pp. 428–33.

60 Peter G. Stillman, 'Hegel's Critique of Liberal Theories of Rights', *American Political Science Review*, vol. 68 (1974), no. 3, p. 1088.

61 Taylor, *Hegel*, pp. 33 and 78–9.

62 Hegel, *Philosophy of Right*, transl. and with notes by T.M. Knox (Oxford, Clarendon Press, 1942), p. 156.

63 Taylor, *Hegel*, p. 422.

64 *Ibid.*, p. 424.

65 Jeremy Bentham, *Anarchical Fallacies*, in *Works*, vol. 2 (Edinburgh, William Tait, 1843), p. 493.

66 *Ibid.*, p. 496.

67 *Ibid.*, p. 498.

68 *Ibid.*, p. 502.

69 *Ibid.*, p. 497.
70 *Ibid.*, p. 501.
71 *Ibid.*, p. 497.
72 *Ibid.*, pp. 497 and 501.
73 *Ibid.*, p. 523.
74 *Ibid.*, p. 501.
75 Karl Marx, *On the Jewish Question*, in T.B. Bottomore (transl. and ed.), *Karl Marx: Early Writings* (London, Watts, 1963), p. 22; emphasis is in the original.
76 *Ibid.*, p. 26.
77 *Ibid.*, p. 24.
78 *Ibid.*
79 C.B. Macpherson, *The Political Theory of Possessive Individualism: Hobbes to Locke* (Oxford, Oxford University Press, 1964), p. 3.
80 *Ibid.*, p. 199.
81 Marx, *Contribution to the Critique of Hegel's Philosophy of Right*, in Bottomore, *Early Writings*, p. 43.
82 Marx, *Critique of Hegel's Philosophy of Right*, transl. A.J. and J. O'Malley, ed. J. O'Malley (Cambridge, Cambridge University Press, 1970), p. xliii.
83 *Ibid.*, p. xlv.
84 Steven Lukes, 'Marxism, Morality and Justice', in G.H.R. Parkinson (ed.) *Marx and Marxisms*, Royal Institute of Philosophy Lecture Series, No. 14: Supplement to *Philosophy* (Cambridge, Cambridge University Press, 1982), p. 198.
85 John Finnis, *Natural Law and Natural Rights* (Oxford, Clarendon Press, 1980), p. 198.
86 *Ibid.*, pp. 34–41.
87 *Ibid.*, pp. 86–9.
88 *Ibid.*, pp. 61–75.
89 *Ibid.*, p. 221.
90 Indeed, Finnis criticizes A.P. d'Entrèves for not distinguishing between discourse about natural law and discourse about doctrines of natural law, *ibid.*, p. 25.
91 H.L.A. Hart, *The Concept of Law* (Oxford, Clarendon Press, 1961), p. 189. The discussion that follows is derived from ch. 9 of this book.
92 *Ibid.*, p. 196.
93 Robert Nozick, *Anarchy, State, and Utopia* (Oxford, Blackwell, 1974).
94 *Ibid.*, p. ix.
95 John Rawls, *A Theory of Justice* (Cambridge, The Belknap Press of Harvard University Press, 1971).
96 *Ibid.*, p. 211.
97 Ronald Dworkin, *Taking Rights Seriously* (London, Duckworth, 1977).
98 *Ibid.*, pp. xi and xv.
99 *Ibid.*, p. 87.
100 *Ibid.*, p. 176.
101 *Ibid.*, p. 198.
102 Michael Oakeshott, *Rationalism in Politics* (London, Methuen, 1962), pp. 1–6 and 35.
103 John Charvet, 'A Critique of Human Rights', in J. Roland Pennock and John W. Chapman (eds), *Human Rights*, Nomos XXIII (New York, New York University Press, 1981), pp. 31–51.

104 See D.F.B. Tucker, *Marxism and Individualism* (Oxford, Blackwell, 1980), pp. 31, 57, 107.

105 Bentham, *Anarchical Fallacies*, in *Works*, vol. 2, p. 531.

106 *Galatians*, 3, 28.

107 Immanuel Kant, *on the Old Saw: That May be Right in Theory But it Won't Work in Practice*, transl. E.B. Ashton, intro. G. Millis (Philadelphia, University of Pennsylvania Press, 1974), pp. 58–9.

108 H.J. Paton, *The Moral Law: on Kant's Groundwork of the Metaphysics of Morals* (London, Hutchinson University Library, n.d.), p. 57.

109 See Taylor, *Hegel*, p. 416.

110 Paton, *The Moral Law*, pp. 56–7.

111 Oakeshott, *Rationalism in Politics*, p. 36.

112 See Judith N. Shklar, *Men and Citizens: A Study of Rousseau's Social Theory* (Cambridge, Cambridge University Press, 1969), p. 15.

113 Kant, *on the Old Saw*, pp. 75–7.

114 Gierke, *Natural Law*, p. l.

115 See Kenneth Minogue, 'The History of the Idea of Human Rights', in Walter Laqueur and Barry Rubin (eds), *The Human Rights Reader* (Philadelphia, Temple University Press, 1979), p. 14.

3. HUMAN RIGHTS AND CULTURAL RELATIVISM

1 Adda Bozeman, *The Future of Law in a Multicultural World* (Princeton, Princeton University Press, 1971), p. 183.

2 Judith N. Shklar, *Men and Citizens: A Study of Rousseau's Social Theory* (Cambridge, Cambridge University Press, 1969), p. 118.

3 John Ladd, 'Preface', in Ladd (ed.), *Ethical Relativism* (Belmont, CA, Wadsworth, 1973), p. iv.

4 Ruth Benedict, *Patterns of Culture* (London, Routledge, 1935), pp. 200–1.

5 Ernest Gellner, *Legitimation of Belief* (Cambridge, Cambridge University Press, 1974), pp. 47–8.

6 Clifford Geertz, *The Interpretation of Cultures* (London, Hutchinson, 1975), pp. 52–3.

7 Text in *International Legal Materials*, vol. 21 (1982), no. 1.

8 See the discussion by Rhoda Howard in 'Is There an African Conception of Human Rights?' in R.J. Vincent (ed.), *Foreign Policy and Human Rights: Issues and Responses* (Cambridge, Cambridge University Press, 1986). See also B. Obinna Okere, 'The Protection of Human Rights in Africa and the African Charter on Human and Peoples' Rights: A Comparative Analysis with the European and American Systems', *Human Rights Quarterly*, vol. 6 (1984), no. 2, pp. 145–6.

9 Asmarom Legesse, 'Human Rights in African Political Culture' in Kenneth W. Thompson (ed.), *The Moral Imperatives of Human Rights: A World Survey* (Washington, University Press of America, 1980), pp. 125–6.

10 Ali A. Mazrui, *Towards a Pax Africana* (London, Weidenfeld & Nicolson, 1967), esp. ch. 8.

11 For texts, see Ian Brownlie (ed.), *Basic Documents on Human Rights*, 2nd edn (Oxford, Clarendon Press, 1981), pp. 28–30, 150–63.

12 Respectively UN General Assembly resolutions 2158 (XXI), 1966, 3281 (XXIX), 1974.
13 Edward Kannyo, 'Human Rights in Africa', *Bulletin of the Atomic Scientists* (December 1981), p. 16.
14 Chung-Shu Lo, 'Human Rights in the Chinese Tradition' in UNESCO, Jacques Maritain (intro.), *Human Rights: Comments and Interpretations* (London and New York, Allan Wingate, n.d.), p. 187.
15 *Ibid.*, p. 186.
16 Bozeman, *The Future for Law*, pp. 144–45.
17 Hungdah Chiu, 'The Nature of International Law and the Problem of a Universal System' in Shao-Chuan Leng and Hungdah Chiu (eds), *Law in Chinese Foreign Policy and Selected Problems of International Law* (Dobbs Ferry, New York, Oceana, 1972), pp. 1–2.
18 'Notes on the Human Rights Question', *Beijing Review*, no. 45 (9 November, 1979), pp. 17–18.
19 *Ibid.*, pp. 17, 19.
20 *Ibid.*, pp. 19–20.
21 Quoted in Donal J. Munro, 'The Malleability of Man in Chinese Marxism', *China Quarterly*, no. 48 (1971), p. 617.
22 Samuel S. Kim, *China, The United Nations and World Order* (Princeton, Princeton University Press, 1979), pp. 484–6.
23 *Ibid.*, pp. 161, 484–6, 493.
24 Jerome Allen Cohen and Hungdah Chiu, *People's China and International Law: A Documentary Study*, 2 vols (Princeton, Princeton University Press, 1974), vol. 1, pp. 91–3, 166–7.
25 Alice Ehr-Soon Tay, 'Marxism, Socialism and Human Rights', in Eugene Kamenka and Tay (eds), *Human Rights* (London, Edward Arnold, 1978), p. 112.
26 Majid Khadduri, *War and Peace in the Law of Islam* (Baltimore, Johns Hopkins University Press, 1955), p. 3.
27 Abdul Aziz Said, 'Precept and Practice of Human Rights in Islam', *Universal Human Rights*, vol. 1 (1979), no. 1, pp. 64–5.
28 *Ibid.*, p. 63.
29 Khadduri, 'Human Rights in Islam', *The Annals of the American Academy of Political and Social Science*, vol. 243 (1946), p. 78.
30 Seyyed Hossein Nasr, 'The Concept and Reality of Freedom in Islam and Islamic Civilization', in Alan S. Rosenbaum (ed.), *The Philosophy of Human Rights* (Westport, CT, Greenwood Press, 1980), pp. 95–7.
31 Khadduri, 'Human Rights in Islam', p. 78.
32 *Ibid.*, p. 79.
33 *Ibid.*, p. 79.
34 J.N.D. Anderson, *Islamic Law in the Modern World* (London, Stevens, 1959), p. 98.
35 Khadduri, 'Human Rights in Islam', p. 78; Said, 'Precept and Practice', p. 66.
36 James P. Piscatori, 'Human Rights in Islamic Political Culture', in Thompson, *Moral Imperatives of Human Rights*, p. 143.
37 See the view of L. Oppenheim, cited in Louis B. Sohn and Thomas Buergenthal (eds), *International Protection of Human Rights* (Indianapolis, Bobbs-Merrill, 1973), pp. 1–3.

38 See F.V. Garcia-Armador, cited in *ibid.*, pp. 124–32; and Richard B. Lillich (ed.), *Humanitarian Intervention and the United Nations* (Charlottesville, University Press of Virginia, 1973), foreword by John P. Humphrey, p. vii.

39 See generally, Sohn and Buergenthal, *International Protection of Human Rights;* C.A. Norgaard, *The Position of the Individual in International Law* (Copenhagen, Munksgaard, 1962); Ian Brownlie, *Principles of Public International Law*, 3rd edn (Oxford, Clarendon Press, 1979), ch. 24; and Brownlie (ed.), *Basic Documents on Human Rights*, 2nd edn (Oxford, Clarendon Press, 1981).

40 Norgaard, *The Position of the Individual*, pp. 216–21.

41 Humphrey, in Lillich, *Humanitarian Intervention*, p. vii.

42 Lillich, *Humanitarian Intervention*; John Norton Moore (ed.), *Law and Civil War in the Modern World* (Baltimore, Johns Hopkins University Press, 1974); and R.J. Vincent, *Nonintervention and International Order* (Princeton, Princeton University Press, 1974), pp. 283 4, 344–9.

43 The text on this position is Myres S. McDougal, Harold D. Lasswell and Lung-Chu Len, *Human Rights and World Public Order: The Basic Policies of an International Law of Human Dignity* (New Haven and London, Yale University Press, 1980).

44 J.G. Starke, 'Human Rights and International Law', in Kamenka and Tay, *Human Rights*, p. 116.

45 Sohn and Buergenthal, *International Protection of Human Rights*, p. 519.

46 See G. David Fensterheim, 'Toward an International Law of Human Rights Based Upon the Mutual Expectations of States', *Virginia Journal of International Law*, vol. 21 (1981), pp. 185 and 197–8.

47 See the extract in Sohn and Buergenthal, *International Protection of Human Rights*, pp. 18–19, from which the quotations following are taken.

48 There is an interesting parellel here with D.D. Raphael's distinction between human rights that are universal in the strong sense (*viz.* held against everyone else) and those that are universal in the weak sense (*viz.* held against particular governments). See above Chapter 1 and 'Human Rights, Old and New', in Raphael (ed.), *Political Theory and the Rights of Man* (London, Macmillan, 1967), p. 65.

49 Brownlie, *Principles*, pp. 596 and 512–15.

50 Garcia-Amador, in Sohn and Buergenthal, *International Protection of Human Rights*, pp. 129–32.

51 See Vincent, *Nonintervention and International Order*, pp. 113–14.

52 J.E.S. Fawcett, *The Law of Nations* (London, Allen Lane, 1968), p. 154.

53 Brownlie, *Principles*, pp. 596–8 and 513.

54 C. Wilfred Jenks, *The Common Law of Mankind* (London, Stevens, 1958), pp. xi and 1. See also H. Lauterpacht, *International Law and Human Rights* (London, Stevens, 1950).

55 See Vincent, *Nonintervention and International Order*, pp. 294–310.

56 Rosalyn Higgins, 'Conceptual Thinking about the Individual in International Law', *British Journal of International Studies*, vol. 4 (1978), no. 1, p. 11.

57 See, e.g., C.H. Waddington, *The Ethical Animal* (London, Allen & Unwin, 1960).

58 Barrington Moore, Jr, *Reflections on the Causes of Human Misery and Upon Certain Proposals to Eliminate Them* (London, Allen Lane, 1972), p. 11.

59 Adamantia Pollis and Peter Schwab, 'Human Rights: A Western Construct with Limited Applicability', in Pollis and Schwab (eds), *Human Rights: Cultural and*

Ideological Perspectives (New York, Praeger, 1979), p. 1. For an interesting precursor of this approach, see Jeanne Hersch (ed.), *Birthright of Man* (New York, Unipub for UNESCO, 1969).

60 See, e.g., Rhoda Howard, 'Evaluating Human Rights in Africa: Some Problems of Implicit Comparisons', *Human Rights Quarterly*, vol. 6 (1984), no. 2; and Harry M. Scoble and Laurie S. Wiseberg, 'Problems of Comparative Research on Human Rights', in Ved P. Nanda, James R. Scarritt and George W. Shepherd, Jr (eds), *Global Human Rights: Public Policies, Comparative Measures, and NGO Strategies* (Boulder, Colo., Westview Press, 1980).

61 See, e.g., Richard P. Claude (ed.), *Comparative Human Rights* (Baltimore and London, Johns Hopkins University Press, 1976); and Schwab and Pollis (eds), *Toward a Human Rights Framework* (New York, Praeger, 1982).

62 See, e.g., Jorge I. Dominguez, 'Assessing Human Rights Conditions', in Dominguez *et al.*, *Enhancing Global Human Rights* (New York, McGraw-Hill for the Council on Foreign Relations, 1979).

63 This is a measure of life expectancy, infant mortatlity and literacy developed at the United States Overseas Development Council. M.D.M. and F.B. Liser, 'The PQLI: Measuring Progress in Meeting Human Needs', *Communiqué on Development Issues*, no. 32 (Washington, ODC, 1977), cited in Paul Streeten with others, *First Things First: Meeting Basic Human Needs in Developing Countries* (New York, Oxford University Press for the World Bank, 1981) ch. 3.

64 See the yearbook *Freedom in the World*, produced under the auspices of Freedom House, in which Raymond D. Gastil rates countries on their political rights and civil liberties performance.

65 Of course the enterprise might produce very little, as it has for Edmund Leach, who asserts that 'it is extremely difficult to detect *any* moral principle which is *universally* held to be valid'. 'The Integration of Minorities' in Ben Whitaker (ed.), *Minorities: A Question of Human Rights?* (Oxford, Pergamon, 1984), p. 27. For the opposite tendency to Leach, asserting a good deal of common ground among cultures on human rights, see Willem A. Veenhoven and Winifred Crum Ewing, *Case Studies on Human Rights and Fundamental Freedoms: A World Survey*, 5 vols. (The Hague, Martinus Nijhoff, 1975, 1976).

66 See, e.g., F.S.C. Northrop, 'Towards a Bill of Rights for the UN', in UNESCO, *Human Rights: Comments and Interpretations;* and Asmarom Legesse, 'Human Rights in African Political Culture', in Thompson, *Moral Imperatives*, p. 123.

67 Alex Inkeles, 'The Emerging Social Structure of the World', *World Politics*, vol. 27 (1975), no. 4; and Vincent, 'The Factor of Culture in the Global International Order', *Year Book of World Affairs*, 1980.

68 Jack Donnelly, 'Human Rights and Human Dignity: An Analytical Critique of Non-Western Conceptions of Human Rights', *American Political Science Review*, vol. 76 (1982), pp. 312–13.

69 C.B. Macpherson, *The Real World of Democracy* (New York and Oxford, Oxford University Press, 1972).

70 Macpherson, 'Natural Rights in Hobbes and Locke', in D.D. Raphael (ed.), *Political Theory and the Rights of Man* (London, Macmillan, 1976), pp. 1–2.

71 *Ibid.*

72 Bernard Williams, *Morality: An Introductions to Ethics* (Harmondsworth, Penguin, 1973), pp. 34–9.

73 Gellner, *Legitimation of Belief*, pp. 48–50.

74 What is being criticized here is a *strong* version of cultural relativism. Jack Donnelly has shown that universal human rights are compatible with a weak version of cultural relativism; see 'Cultural Relativism and Universal Human Rights', *Human Rights Quarterly*. vol. 6 (1984), no. 4. Herbert Kelman calls the strong version 'vulgar relativism'; 'The Conditions, Criteria and Dialectics of Human Dignity', *International Studies Quarterly*, vol. 21 (1977), no. 3, p. 543.

75 Benedict, *Patterns of Culture*, pp. 200–1.

76 Geertz, *Interpretation of Cultures*, p. 44.

77 Gellner, *Legitimation of Belief*, p. 51.

78 See Sohn and Buergenthal, *International Protection of Human Rights*, pp. 124–32.

79 John Stuart Mill, *On Liberty*, in Mary Warnock (ed.), *Utilitarianism* (London and Glasgow, Collins/Fontana, 1962), p. 201.

80 *Ibid.*, p. 144.

81 *Ibid.*, pp. 144–7.

82 *Ibid.*, p. 136.

83 Shao-Chuan Leng and Hungdah Chiu (eds), *Law in Chinese Foreign Policy and Selected Problems of International Law* (Dobbs Ferry, New York, Oceana, 1976), p. 8. For use of this argument against the Chinese regime, see Simon Leys, 'Human Rights in China', *Quadrant*, November 1978.

4. HUMAN RIGHTS IN EAST–WEST RELATIONS

1 It is of course true that practice matches doctrine in neither the West nor the East. It has also been argued by some that the West outperforms the East in economic and social rights as well as civil and political rights, and by others the opposite. My purpose here is not to pursue these interesting questions, but to capture the essence of the official debate between East and West on human rights.

2 Edward L. Keenan, 'Human Rights in Soviet Political Culture' in Kenneth W. Thompson (ed.), *The Moral Imperatives of Human Rights: A World Survey* (Washington, DC, University Press of America, 1980).

3 Jane Degras (ed.), *Soviet Documents on Foreign Policy*, 3 vols (London, Oxford University Press, 1951, 1952, 1953), vol. I, *1917–24*, pp. 1–3.

4 E.H. Carr, *The Bolshevik Revolution 1917–1923*, 3 vols, (Harmondsworth, Penguin, 1966), vol. 3, pp. 32–3.

5 See Tracy B. Strong, 'Taking the Rank With What is Ours: American Political Thought, Foreign Policy, and Questions of Rights', in Paula R. Newberg (ed.), *The Politics of Human Rights* (New York and London, New York University Press, 1980), pp. 51–4.

6 See R.J. Vincent, *Nonintervention and International Order* (Princeton, Princeton University Press, 1974), ch. 4.

7 Richard N. Dean, 'Beyond Helsinki: The Soviet View of Human Rights in International Law', *Virginia Journal of International Law*, vol. 21 (1981), p. 58.

8 Mary Hawkesworth, 'Ideological Immunity: The Soviet Response to Human Rights Criticism', *Universal Human Rights*, vol. 2 (1980), no. 1, p. 71.

9 *Ibid.*, p. 72.

10 N. Khrushchev, quoted in *ibid.*, p. 73.

11 See Louis Henkin, *The Rights of Man Today* (Boulder, Colo., Westview, 1978), p. 61.

12 Article 50 of the Soviet Constitution, *ibid.*, pp. 61–2.

13 H.L.A. Hart, 'Are there Any Natural Rights?', in A. Quinton (ed.), *Political Philosophy* (London, Oxford University Press, 1967), p. 53.

14 Cyrus Vance, 'Human Rights and Foreign Policy', *Georgia Journal of International and Comparative Law*, vol. 7, Suppl. (1977), p. 223.

15 For argument that it should not see Part Three below.

16 Peter Reddaway, *Uncensored Russia; The Human Rights Movement in the Soviet Union* (London, Cape, 1972), pp. 20–1.

17 *Ibid.*, p. 22.

18 Abraham Brumberg, 'Dissent in Russia' *Foreign Affairs*, vol. 52 (1974), no. 4; Richard N. Dean, 'Contacts with the West: The Dissidents' View of Western Support for the Human Rights Movement in the Soviet Union', *Universal Human Rights*, vol. 2 (1980), no. 1; and Reddaway, *Uncensored Russia*, intro.

19 David Kowalewski, 'Human Rights Protest in the USSR: Statistical Trends for 1965–1978', *Universal Human Rights*, vol. 2 (1980), no. 1, pp. 8–11.

20 Reddaway, *Uncensored Russia*, pp. 23–5.

21 Kowalewski, 'Human Rights Protest', p. 6.

22 *The Current Digest of the Soviet Press*, vol. 33, no. 11 (15 April, 1981), p. 17.

23 Harvey Fireside, 'The Conceptualization of Dissent: Soviet Behaviour in Comparative Perspective', *Universal Human Rights*, vol. 2 (1980), no. 1, p. 39.

24 Hawkesworth, 'Ideological Immunity', p. 81.

25 *Ibid.*, pp. 81–2.

26 *Ibid.*, p. 82.

27 Reddaway, *Uncensored Russia*, p. 39.

28 Fireside, 'The Conceptualization of Dissent', p. 36. The notion that totalitarianism is a condition from which one cannot return is famously expounded in Jeane Kirkpatrick, 'Dictatorship and Double Standards', *Commentary*, November 1979.

29 For text, see Ian Brownlie (ed.), *Basic Documents on Human Rights*, 2nd edn (Oxford, Clarendon Press, 1981), pp. 320–77.

30 Louis Henkin, 'Human Rights and "Domestic Jurisdiction"', in Thomas Buergenthal, assisted by Judith R. Hall (ed.), *Human Rights, International Law and the Helsinki Accord* (Montclair, NJ, New York, Allanheld, Osmun/Universe Books, 1977), p. 37.

31 Buergenthal, 'International Human Rights Law and the Helsinki Final Act: Conclusions', *ibid.*, p. 8.

32 Henkin, 'Human Rights and "Domestic Jurisdiction",' pp. 22, 25, 36.

33 For a discussion of international agreements that are not law, see Oscar Schachter, 'The Twilight Existence of Nonbinding International Agreements', *American Journal of International Law*, vol. 71 (1977), no. 2, pp. 296–304.

34 Virginia Leary, 'The Implementation of the Human Rights Provisions of the Helsinki Final Act: A Preliminary Assessment: 1975–1977', in Buergenthal, *Human Rights, International Law and the Helsinki Accord*, pp. 112–27.

35 *Ibid.*, pp. 150–1.

36 Dean, 'Beyond Helsinki', pp. 73–4.

37 Leary, 'The Implementation', p. 149.

38 *Ibid.*, pp. 142–3.

39 Suzanne Bastid, 'The Special Significance of the Helsinki Final Act', in Buergenthal,

Human Rights, International Law and the Helsinki Accord, p. 15; and Henkin, 'Human Rights and "Domestic Jurisdiction"', p. 37.

40 G. Arbatov, 'Soviet–American Relations Today', *Pravda*, 3 August, 1977, *Current Digest of the Soviet Press*, vol. 29, no. 31, p. 1.

41 William B. Husband, 'Soviet Perception of US "Positions of Strength" Diplomacy in the 1970s', *World Politics*, vol. 31 (1979), no. 4, pp. 505–6.

42 Dean, 'Beyond Helsinki', p. 78.

43 Hawkesworth, 'Ideological Immunity', p. 76.

44 Harold S. Russell, 'The Helsinki Declaration: Brobdingnag or Lilliput?', *American Journal of International Law*, vol. 70 (1976), no. 2, p. 268.

45 This argument is set out at greater length in Vincent, *Nonintervention*, ch. 9, and 'Western Conceptions of a Universal Moral Order', *British Journal of International Studies*, vol. 4 (1978), no. 1, pp. 40–4. It is criticized in Richard Falk, *Human Rights and State Sovereignty* (New York, Holmes and Meier, 1981), and Charles R. Beitz, *Political Theory and International Relations* (Princeton, Princeton University Press, 1979), Pt. II. This question is returned to in Chapter 7 below.

46 Hugh M. Arnold, 'Henry Kissinger and Human Rights', *Universal Human Rights*, vol. 2 (1980), no. 4, p. 57.

47 *Ibid.*, pp. 62–3.

48 William F. Buckley, 'Human Rights and Foreign Policy: A Proposal', *Foreign Affairs*, vol. 58 (1980), no. 4, pp. 782–3.

49 Aleksandr Solzhenitsyn, 'Misconceptions about Russia are a Threat to America', *Foreign Affairs*, vol. 58 (1980), no. 4, p. 822.

50 The discussion of Solzhenitsyn's views here is based on Dean, 'Contacts with the West', pp. 56–7. A useful additional source is Donald R. Kelley, *The Solzhenitsyn–Sakharov Dialogue* (Westport, CT, and London, Greenwood Press, 1982).

51 Dean, 'Contacts with the West', p. 57.

52 Sakharov, quoted in *ibid.*, p. 58.

53 See esp. Sakharov, *Alarm and Hope*, ed. E. Yankelevich and A. Friendly, Jr. (New York, Knopf, 1978), chs. 1, 7 and 11.

54 Andrei D. Sakharov, *Progress, Coexistence, and Intellectual Freedom* (New York, Norton, 1968), pp. 41–3.

55 Roy Medvedev, 'Problems of Democratization and Détente' in Medvedev, *et al.*, *Détente and Socialist Democracy* (New York, Monad Press, 1976), p. 25.

56 Arnold, 'Henry Kissinger and Human Rights', pp. 65–9.

57 Dean, 'Contacts with the West', p. 50.

58 Medvedev, 'Problems of Democratization and Détente', pp. 26–7.

59 This is the argument, in relation to US foreign policy towards the Soviet Union, of Hawkesworth, 'Ideological Immunity'.

60 Dean, 'Contacts with the West', pp. 59–65.

61 Quoted in *ibid.*, p. 49.

62 Bastid, 'The Special Significance of the Helsinki Final Act', p. 16.

5. HUMAN RIGHTS IN NORTH–SOUTH RELATIONS

1 W.A. Malik, to plenary meeting of VIIth Special Session of the United Nations General Assembly, 3 September, 1975. Quoted in Robert F. Meagher, *An Inter-*

national Redistribution of Wealth and Power: A Study of the Charter of Economic Rights and Duties of States (New York, Pergamon Press, 1979), p. 99.

2 J.-P. Cot, 'Winning East–West in North–South', *Foreign Policy* no. 46 (Spring 1982).

3 Douglas Williams, 'Human Rights, Economic Development and Aid to the Third World: an Analysis and Proposal for Action', *ODI Review*, no. 1 (1978), pp. 14–15.

4 Kenneth E. Boulding, 'The Shadow of the Stationary State', *Daedalus*, vol. 102 (1974), no. 4, pp. 100–101.

5 Richard Falk, 'Comparative Protection of Human Rights in Capitalist and Socialist Third World Countries', *Universal Human Rights*, vol. 1 (1979), no. 2, p. 5.

6 John Locke, *Two Treatises of Government*, ed. Peter Laslett (Cambridge, Cambridge University Press, 1960), p. 303.

7 Fouad Ajami, 'Human Rights and World Order Politics', *Alternatives*, vol. 3 (1978), no. 3, p. 365.

8 *Ibid.*, p. 381.

9 Jack Donnelly calls this the predominant view at the UN; see 'Recent Trends in UN Human Rights Activity: Description and Polemic', *International Organization*, vol. 35 (1981), no. 4, p. 640.

10 Article 1(2).

11 Article 73(b) and Article 76(b).

12 Antonio Cassese, 'The Self-Determination of Peoples', in Louis Henkin (ed.), *The International Bill of Rights* (New York, Columbia University Press, 1981), pp. 92–3. Both international covenants entered into force in 1976.

13 Resolution 1514(XV); text in Ian Brownlie (ed.), *Basic Documents on Human Rights*, 2nd edn (Oxford, Clarendon Press, 1981), pp. 28–30.

14 Cassese, 'The Self-Determination of Peoples', p. 101.

15 *Ibid.*, p. 109.

16 Resolution 2106(XX), B; text in Brownlie, *Basic Documents*, pp. 162–3.

17 Resolution 3068(XXVIII); text in *ibid.*, pp. 164–70.

18 Article 55.

19 See preamble to the Declaration on the Granting of Independence, Brownlie, *Basic Documents*, p. 29.

20 General Assembly Resolution 2158(XXI) on Permanent Sovereignty over Natural Resources; text in *Year Book of the United Nations 1966* (New York, 1968), pp. 333–4.

21 See Raul Prebisch, *Towards a New Trade Policy for Development* (UN Doc.E/Conf.46/3 UN Sales No.64, II, B.4), excerpts cited in Brownlie, *Basic Documents on Human Rights*, pp. 489–98.

22 Preamble to the Charter, cited in Meagher, *An International Redistribution of Wealth and Power*, p. 181.

23 Paragraph 13 of the Proclamation, cited in Donnelly, 'Recent Trends in UN Human Rights Activity', p. 634.

24 General Assembly Resolution 32/130; text in *Year Book of the United Nations 1977* (New York, 1980), pp. 734–5.

25 Karel Vasak, Director of UNESCO's Division of Human Rights and Peace, *UNESCO Courier*, November 1977, cited in Tony Godfrey Smith, 'The Right to Development: Human Right, Socioeconomic Strategy or Letter to Santa Claus', unpublished paper, Canberra, 1983.

26 Draft Declaration of the Right to Development (UN Doc. E/CN.4/AC.39/1983/L.2). The quotations that follow are from Article 1 and Article 8 of the Draft.

27 See B. Malinowski, *The Scientific Theory of Culture and Other Essays* (Chapel Hill, NC, 1944), A. Maslow, 'A Theory of Human Motivation', *Psychological Review*, vol. 50 (1943). For an excellent defence of the doctrine of human needs as the basis for a theory of social welfare, see Raymond Plant, Harry Lesser and Peter Taylor-Crosby, *Political Philosophy and Social Welfare* (London, Routledge and Kegan Paul, 1980), Pt. I.

28 C.B. Macpherson, 'Needs and Wants: an Ontological or Historical Problem', in Ross Fitzgerald (ed.), *Human Needs and Politics* (Rushcutters Bay, NSW, Pergamon Press, 1977), p. 29.

29 K.R. Minogue, *The Liberal Mind* (London, Methuen, 1963), p. 103.

30 Neil McInnes, 'The Politics of Needs – or, Who Needs Politics?', in Fitzgerald (ed.), *Human Needs and Politics*, p. 229.

31 Fitzgerald (ed), 'Introduction', in *Human Needs and Politics*, pp. ix–x, xiii.

32 Maslow, 'A Theory of Human Motivation', pp. 372–82.

33 Notably Paul Streeten; see his *The Frontiers of Development Studies* (London, Macmillan, 1972), ch. 9, and 'Basic Human Needs', *Millennium*, Special edition, Autumn 1978. The arguments that follow are taken from these sources. See also Streeten *et al.*, *First Things First. Meeting Basic Human Needs in Developing Countries* (New York, Oxford University Press for the World Bank, 1981).

34 See, for example, Philip Alston, 'Human Rights and Basic Needs: A Critical Assessment', *Revue des droits de l'homme*, vol. 13 (1979), pp. 1–20.

35 Richard Falk, 'Comparative Protection of Human Rights in Capitalist and Socialist Third World Countries', *Universal Human Rights*, vol. 1 (1979), no. 2.

36 Alston, 'Human Rights and Basic Needs', pp. 29–34.

37 *Ibid.*, pp. 47–9. For a clear statement, from a liberal perspective, of the interdependence of 'needs' and 'rights', see Emanuel de Kadt, 'Some Basic Questions of Human Rights and Development', *World Development*, vol. 8 (1980).

38 See, e.g., Maslow, 'A Theory of Human Motivation', p. 383.

39 Alston, 'Human Rights and Basic Needs', p. 55.

40 *Ibid.*, p. 55.

41 See the British paper to the North–South Round Table in Rome, 18–20 May 1978, cited in Johan Galtung, 'The New International Economic Order and the Basic Needs Approach', *Alternatives*, vol. 4 (1979), no. 4, pp. 461–2.

42 Galtung, 'The NIEO and the Basic Needs Approach', pp. 463–7.

43 See above, Chapter 3.

44 Tom J. Farer (ed.), *Toward a Humanitarian Diplomacy: A Primer for Policy* (New York, New York University Press, 1980), p. 28.

45 Antony G.N. Flew, 'Wants or Needs; Choices or Commands', in Fitzgerald, *Human Needs and Politics*, pp. 217–18.

46 Alston, 'Human Rights and Basic Needs', pp. 40–1.

47 Galtung, 'The NIEO and the Basic Needs Approach', p. 463.

48 See Henry Shue, *Basic Rights* (Princeton, Princeton University Press, 1980), ch. 3. See also Chapter 7 below.

49 See on this Philip Alston, 'The Alleged Demise of Political Human Rights at the UN: A Reply to Donnelly', *International Organization*, vol. 37 (1983), no. 3; and J.A.

Ferguson, 'Human Rights and the Third World', in R.J. Vincent (ed.), *Foreign Policy and Human Rights; Issues and Responses* (Cambridge, Cambridge University Press, 1986).

50 See Cot, 'Winning East–West in North–South', *Foreign Policy*, no. 46, (Spring 1982).

51 W. Brandt *et al.*, *North–South: A Programme for Survival* (London, Pan, 1980).

6. HUMAN RIGHTS IN CONTEMPORARY WORLD SOCIETY

1 Article 56 of the UN Charter.

2 The classic statement of this position in regard to individuals is H. Lauterpacht, *International Law and Human Rights* (London, Stevens, 1950). For the interpretation of the arrival of human rights as *the* most revolutionary development in the theory and practice of international law and of the Universal Declaration as 'the Magna Carta of the World', see John P. Humphrey, *Human Rights and the United Nations: A great adventure* (New York, Dobbs Ferry, Transnational Publishers, 1984), pp. 46, 63.

3 See Sir Samuel Hoare, 'The UN Commission on Human Rights', in Evan Luard (ed.), *The International Protection of Human Rights* (London, Thames and Hudson, 1967). As we saw in Chapter 3, there are particular precursors of this general acceptance: most notably the work of the International Labour Organization.

4 On the UN and human rights, see *United Nations Action in the Field of Human Rights* (ST/HR/2: Sales number E.74.XIV.2); Philip Alston, 'The Alleged Demise of Political Human Rights at the UN: A Reply to Donnelly', *International Organization*, vol. 37 (1983), no. 3; and Egon Schwelb and Philip Alston, 'The Principal Institutions and Other Bodies Founded Upon the Charter', in Karel Vasak (gen. ed.; rev. edn Alston), *The International Dimensions of Human Rights* (2 vols, Westport, Conn., Greenwood Press, for UNESCO, 1982), vol. 1, pp. 231–302.

5 For an excellent brief discussion of formal means of implementing human rights instruments, see David P. Forsythe, *Human Rights and World Politics* (Lincoln and London, University of Nebraska Press, 1983), pp. 43–61. For a good general discussion of the problem of implementation, see Vernon Van Dyke, *Human Rights, The United States and the World Community* (New York, Oxford University Press, 1970), Section IV. For an equally good review of the functions carried out by human rights institutions from disseminating information to imposing sanctions, see Vasak, 'The Distinguishing Criteria of Institutions', in Vasak (ed.), *The International Dimensions of Human Rights*, vol. 1, pp. 215–30.

6 For text, see Ian Brownlie (ed.), *Basic Documents of Human Rights*, 2nd edn (Oxford, Clarendon Press, 1981), pp. 16–18; and see Schwelb and Alston, 'The Principal Institutions', pp. 269–77.

7 See A.H. Robertson, *Human Rights in the World*, 2nd edn (New York, St Martin's Press, 1982), esp. chs. 3, 4 and 5; and Vasak, 'Introduction' to Sub-Part II, in Vasak, *The International Dimensions*, vol, 2, pp. 215–30.

8 Robertson, *Human Rights in the World*, p. 83.

9 Texts of American documents in Brownlie, *Basic Documents*, pp. 382–416.

10 Text in *International Legal Materials*, vol. 21 (1982), no. 1, pp. 59–68.

11 For a useful discussion, see Laurie S. Wiseberg and Harry M. Scoble, 'Recent Trends in the Expanding Universe of NGOs Dedicated to the Protection of Human Rights', in Ved. P. Nanda *et al.*, *Global Human Rights: Public Policies, Comparative Measures, and NGO Strategies* (Boulder, Colo., Westview Press, 1980).

12 For an excellent brief discussion, see Peter Archer, 'Action by Unofficial Organiza-tions on Human Rights', in Luard, *International Protection*, pp. 162–4.

13 John P. Humphrey, 'The UN Charter and the Universal Declaration of Human Rights', in Luard, *International Protection*, p. 40; and Humphrey, *Human Rights and the United Nations*, pp. 12–13.

14 See the summary of activities of the International League for Human Rights in Archer, 'Action by Unofficial Organizations', in Luard, *International Protection*, pp. 110–12.

15 See Forsythe, *Human Rights and World Politics*, pp. 66–70.

16 And also of ICRC, though it acts privately and the sanction is to go public with a full report if governments seek to quote selectively. For a discussion of the relative merits of the public and the private in this field, see J.D. Armstrong, 'Non-governmental Organizations', in R.J. Vincent (ed.), *Foreign Policy and Human Rights: Issues and Responses* (Cambridge, Cambridge University Press, 1986). On Amnesty and public opinion, see Martin Ennals, 'Amnesty International and Human Rights', in Peter Willetts (ed.), *Pressure Groups in the Global System* (London, Frances Pinter, 1982), pp. 78–80.

17 John Gerard Ruggie, 'Human Rights and the Future International Community', *Daedalus*, vol. 112 (1983), no. 4, p. 103.

18 See *Human Rights International Instruments*, UN Document (ST/IIR/4/Rev.4, New York, 1982), pp. 18–19.

19 Richard Falk, *Human Rights and State Sovereignty* (New York, Holmes and Meier, 1981), p. 33.

20 For a helpful collection of readings on this, see Richard B. Lillich and Frank C. Newman, *International Human Rights: Problems of Law and Policy* (Boston, Little, Brown, 1979), pp. 317–88.

21 See J. Carey, *UN Protection of Civil and Political Rights* (Syracuse, Syracuse University Press, 1970), ch. 9.

22 Falk, *Human Rights and State Sovereignty*, p. 48.

23 *Ibid.*, p. 5.

24 Robertson, *Human Rights in the World*, pp. 174–5

25 See Falk, *Human Rights and State Sovereignty*, p. 154.

26 Jonathan Power, *Against Oblivion* (Fontana, 1981), p. 24.

27 Cosmas Desmond, *Persecution East and West* (Harmondsworth, Penguin, 1983), pp. 26–8.

28 *Ibid.*, pp. 37, 78.

29 *Ibid.*, p. 53.

30 *Ibid.*, pp. 24–5.

31 *Ibid.*, p. 24.

32 Text in Falk, *Human Rights and State Sovereignty*, pp. 225–28. For a similar criticism that the charitable foundations in the West exist in the interest of donors not receivers, see Ben Whitaker, *The Philanthropoids, Foundations and Society* (New York, William Morrow, 1974), pp. 14, 31–2.

33 E. Schwelb, 'The Influence of the Universal Declaration of Human Rights on International and National Law', cited in Lillich and Newman, *International Human Rights*, pp. 60–5; Schwelb and Alston, 'The Principal Institutions', p. 245. A. Glenn Mower reports that 22 states in Africa, between 1948 and 1964, adopted constitutions expressly referring to the Universal Declaration. *The United States, The United*

Nations, and Human Rights (Westport, CT, Greenwood Press, 1979), p. 58.

34 Cited in Lillich and Newman, *International Human Rights*, p. 99.

35 See Richard Pierre Claude, 'The Case of Joelito Filártiga and the Clinic of Hope', *Human Rights Quarterly*, vol. 5 (1983), no. 3, pp. 275–301.

36 Cited in *ibid.*, p. 291.

37 Cited in *ibid.*, p. 293.

38 For a recent account, see Paul Sieghart, *The International Law of Human Rights* (Oxford, Clarendon Press, 1983).

39 For a forthright statement of this view, see Michael Akehurst, *A Modern Introduction to International Law*, 5th edn (London, Allen & Unwin, 1984), p. 76.

40 See, e.g., Michael S. Teitelbaum, 'Right versus Right: Immigration and Refugee Policy', *Foreign Affairs*, vol. 69 (1980), no. 1; and Animeslo Ghoshal and Thomas M. Crawley, 'Refugees and Immigrants: A Human Rights Dilemma', *Human Rights Quarterly*, vol. 5 (1983), no. 3.

41 Sandy Vogelgesang, *American Dream, Global Nightmare: The Dilemma of US Human Rights Policy* (New York, Norton, 1980), pp. 18–20.

42 See R.J. Vincent, 'Edmund Burke and the Theory of International Relations', *Review of International Studies*, vol. 10 (1984), no. 2.

43 See Gaston V. Rimlinger, 'Capitalism and Human Rights', *Daedalus*, vol. 112 (1983), no. 4, p. 68.

44 Hannah Arendt, *On Revolution* (London, Faber, 1958), p. 68.

45 See C.B. Macpherson, 'Natural Rights in Hobbes and Locke', in D.D. Raphael (ed.), *Political Theory and the Rights of Man* (London, Macmillan, 1967), pp. 1–2.

46 Arendt, *On Revolution*, p. 54.

47 Peter L. Berger, 'Are Human Rights Universal?', *Commentary* (September 1977).

48 Peter C. Reynolds, *On the Evolution of Human Behavior: the Argument from Animals to Man* (Berkeley, University of California Press, 1981), p. 2.

49 Andrew Linklater, *Men and Citizens in the Theory of International Relations* (London, Macmillan, 1982), p. 54.

50 Michael Oakeshott, *Rationalism in Politics and Other Essays* (London, Methuen, 1962), p. 198.

7. HUMAN RIGHTS AND THE THEORY OF INTERNATIONAL RELATIONS

1 This was a theme of Part Two of this book. It is well expressed in J.A. Ferguson, 'The Third World', in R.J. Vincent (ed.), *Foreign Policy and Human Rights: Issues and Responses* (Cambridge, Cambridge University Press, 1986).

2 H.L.A. Hart, 'Are there any Natural Rights?', in A. Quinton (ed.), *Political Philosophy* (London, Oxford University Press, 1967), p. 53, and Chapters 2 and 4 above.

3 Henry Shue, *Basic Rights: Subsistence, Affluence, and US Foreign Policy* (Princeton, Princeton University Press, 1980), esp. ch. 1. See also Chapter 1 above.

4 John Finnis, *Natural Law and Natural Rights* (Oxford, Clarendon Press, 1980), p. 198, and Chapter 3 above.

5 See Charles R. Beitz, *Political Theory and International Relations* (Princeton, Princeton University Press, 1979), pp. 63–6.

6 Richard A. Falk, *Human Rights and State Sovereignty* (New York, Holmes and Meier, 1981), ch. 1.

7 See Vincent, *Nonintervention and International Order* (Princeton, Princeton University Press, 1974), ch. 9.
8 *Ibid.*, ch. 2.
9 *Ibid.*, ch. 9, and Vincent, 'Western Conceptions of a Universal Moral Order', *British Journal of International Studies*, vol. 4 (1978), no. 1.
10 Vincent, *Nonintervention*, ch. 2.
11 J.S. Mill, 'A Few Words on Non-Intervention', in *Dissertations and Discussions: Political, Philosophical and Historical*, 4 vols. (London, 1875), vol. 3, pp. 153–78; and Michael Walzer, *Just and Unjust Wars* (London, Allen Lane, 1977).
12 S.I. Benn and R.S. Peters, *Social Principles and the Democratic State* (London, Allen and Unwin, 1959), p. 361.
13 Walzer, *Just and Unjust Wars*, p. 54.
14 *Ibid.*
15 Beitz, *Political Theory and International Relations*, Pt II.
16 Beitz, 'Nonintervention and Communal Integrity', *Philosophy and Public Affairs*, vol. 9 (1980), no. 4, p. 384.
17 Beitz, 'Bounded Morality: Justice and the State in World Politics', *International Organization*, vol. 33 (1979), no. 3, p. 414.
18 David Luban, 'Just War and Human Rights', *Philosophy and Public Affairs*, vol. 9 (1980), no. 2, p. 173.
19 Beitz, 'Nonintervention and Communal Integrity', p. 385.
20 Beitz, 'Bounded Morality', p. 417.
21 *Ibid.*, p. 421.
22 Luban, 'Just War and Human Rights', pp. 174–5.
23 Walzer, *Just and Unjust Wars*, p. 54.
24 Edmund Burke, from the letter to Sir Hercules Langrishe, 1792, cited in A.M.D. Hughes (ed.), *Edmund Burke: Selections* (Oxford, 1921), p. 75.
25 This is spelled out in Vincent, *Nonintervention*, pp. 379–81.
26 This is Walzer's argument in his reply to his critics, 'The Moral Standing of States: A Response to Four Critics', *Philosophy and Public Affairs*, vol. 9 (1980), no. 3, p. 213.
27 *Ibid.*, p. 217.
28 Luban, 'The Romance of the Nation-State', *Philosophy and Public Affairs*, vol. 9 (1980), no. 4, p. 397.
29 Richard Cobden, Speech to House of Commons, 5 June, 1855, in John Bright and James E. Thorold Rogers (eds.), *Speeches by Richard Cobden on Questions of Public Policy*, 2 vols (London, Macmillan, 1870), vol. 2, p. 27.
30 Vincent, *Nonintervention*, ch. 9.
31 *Ibid.*
32 Beitz, *Political Theory and International Relations*, pp. 88–9.
33 Immanuel Kant, 'On Eternal Peace', trans., in Carl J. Friedrich, *Inevitable Peace* (Cambridge, MA, Harvard University Press, 1948), pp. 257–9.
34 Andrew Linklater, *Men and Citizens in the Theory of International Relations* (London, Macmillan, 1982), p. 31.
35 *Ibid.*, pp. 10–14, 38–54.
36 *Ibid.*, pp. 188, 196–7.
37 Beitz, *Political Theory and International Relations*, pp. 143–53.
38 *Ibid.*, p. 149.
39 *Ibid.*, pp. 128–36, and John Rawls, *A Theory of Justice* (Cambridge, Harvard

University Press, 1971).

40 Beitz, 'Human Rights and Social Justice', in Peter G. Brown and Douglas Maclean (eds.), *Human Rights and US Foreign Policy* (Lexington, DC, Heath, 1979), pp. 58–9, and Chapter 1 above.

41 Beitz, *Political Theory and International Relations*, pp. 154–5.

42 Michael Donelan, 'A Community of Mankind', in James Mayall (ed.), *The Community of States* (London, Allen & Unwin, 1982), p. 144.

43 James Mayall, 'The Liberal Economy', in Mayall, *The Community of States*, p. 110.

44 Beitz, *Political Theory and International Relations*, pp. 155–61, 169–76. I refer here also to private correspondence with Professor Beitz.

45 J.D.B. Miller, 'Morality, Interests and Rationalization', in Ralph Pettman (ed.), *Moral Claims in World Affairs* (London and Canberra, Croom Helm, 1979), p. 36. The argument that follows is taken from this chapter.

46 Bruce Miller's work is used here because of the clarity of its statement of the realist position. I should note, however, that there are important disagreements within the realist school. Hans J. Morgenthau, for example, would deny the proposition that all morality was interest in disguise, and argues that moral principles have some autonomous application to all political conduct including foreign policy. He agrees with Miller, however, that there is no mission for a country to apply its own moral principles to the rest of humanity. See Morgenthau, *Human Rights and Foreign Policy*, First Distinguished CRIA Lecture on Morality and Foreign Policy (New York, Council on Religion and International Affairs, 1979), pp. 1–4. For a similar position, see Kenneth W. Thompson, 'Implications for American Foreign Policy', in Thompson (ed.), *The Moral Imperatives of Human Rights: A World Survey* (Washington, DC, University Press of America, 1980). For a fuller discussion of variation within the realist position, see Vincent, 'Realpolitik', in Mayall, *The Community of States*, pp. 74–5.

My own view is that the sophisticated realist position of Morgenthau exists in unstable equilibrium between the 'morality of states' (where rules of law and morality are acknowledged as external constraints on state action whatever their strength) and 'morality as mere interests' (where no external moral constraint is recognized). Sophisticated realism has the former's recognition of constraint, and the latter's egotism, and the two sit uneasily together.

47 For an excellent treatment, see Tom Campbell, *The Left and Rights: A Conceptual Analysis of the Idea of Socialist Rights* (London, Routledge & Kegan Paul, 1983), ch. 6. The following passage is based on this source and the material cited above in Chapter 2.

48 See generally Edward S. Herman and Noam Chomsky, *The Political Economy of Human Rights*, 2 vols (Boston, MA, South End Press, 1979). For a crisp statement of a similar view in relation to Latin America see William L. Wipfler, 'Human Rights Violations and US Foreign Assistance: The Latin American Connection', in Brown and Maclean, *Human Rights and US Foreign Policy*.

49 Herman and Chomsky, *The Washington Connection and Third World Fascism*, vol. 1, p. 33.

50 *Ibid.*, pp. 35–6.

51 This is Brian Barry's definition of 'interest' in *Political Argument* (London, Routledge & Kegan Paul, 1965), p. 176.

52 See Hedley Bull, 'The Grotian Conception of International Society', in H. Butterfield

and M. Wight (eds.), *Diplomatic Investigations* (London, Allen & Unwin, 1966), p. 73; and *The Anarchical Society* (London, Macmillan, 1977), p. 138.

53 Ronald Dworkin, *Taking Rights Seriously* (London, Duckworth, 1977), pp. xi and xv; and Chapter 2 above.

54 Herman and Chomsky, *The Washington Connection*, p. 36.

55 This is a conception developed by my colleague Hidemi Suganami and myself in a joint lecture on non-intervention that we give annually to students at the University of Keele - though I think that Mr Suganami invented it. To our chagrin, something like it has been published by Stanley Hoffmann in *Primacy or World Order: American Foreign Policy Since the Cold War* (New York, McGraw-Hill, 1978), p. 117.

56 What follows is mainly based on the 1982 English-Speaking Union Chester Lecture, delivered by J. Enoch Powell on 10 December, 1982.

57 J.D.B. Miller, *The World of States* (London, Croom Helm, 1981), p. 16.

58 Richard A. Falk, *This Endangered Planet* (New York, Random House, 1971).

59 Harold and Margaret Sprout, *Toward a Politics of the Planet Earth* (New York, Van Nostrand, 1971), p. 19.

60 Falk, *The End of World Order: Essays in Normative International Relations* (New York, Holmes and Meier, 1983), p. 249.

61 See Lucien Goldman, *Immanuel Kant* (London, New Left Books, 1971), p. 171.

62 These are subtly dealt with in Walzer, *Just and Unjust Wars*, ch. 6.

63 Shue, *Basic Rights*, p. 19.

64 For Beitz's acceptance of this view, see his 'Cosmopolitan Ideals and National Sentiment', *Journal of Philosophy*, vol. 80 (1983), no. 10.

65 *Ibid.*, pp. 74–8. The difficulty with this argument, which I cannot explore here, is that it seems to be inherently expansive: basic rights requiring for their actual enjoyment the establishment of all the institutions that we associate with a mature liberal democracy, which may then also be called basic rights if they are essential to the enjoyment of basic liberty. Any interdiction of this institutional creep, in an attempt to rehabilitate the idea of basic rights, might then appear to be as arbitrary as other (rightly) criticized distinctions, such as that between civil and political rights and economic and social aspirations.

66 Hannah Arendt, *On Revolutions* (London, Faber, 1958), p. 58.

67 For a recent argument in this spirit, see Terry Nardin, *Law, Morality and the Relations of States* (Princeton, Princeton University Press, 1983).

68 C.B. Macpherson, *The Real World of Democracy* (New York, Oxford University Press, 1972).

69 Walzer, 'The Moral Standing of States', pp. 214–18.

70 Thomas M. Scanlon, 'Human Rights as a Neutral Concern', in Brown and Maclean (eds.), *Human Rights and US Foreign Policy*, p. 83.

71 See Stanley Hoffmann, *Duties Beyond Borders* (Syracuse, Syracuse University Press, 1981), pp. 121–2.

72 Walzer, 'The Moral Standing of States', p. 218.

73 Shue, *Basic Rights*, ch. 2; Peter G. Brown and Henry Shue (eds), *Food Policy: The Responsibility of the US in the Life and Death Choices* (New York, Free Press, 1977); and Brown and Shue (eds), *Boundaries: National Autonomy and its Limits* (Totowa, NJ, Rowan and Littlefield, 1981).

74 Peter Singer, 'Reconsidering the Famine Relief Argument', in Brown and Shue, *Food Policy*, p. 37.

75 Shue, *Basic Rights*, Pt. II.

76 Shue, *Basic Rights*, ch. 7.

77 Richard H. Ullman, 'Introduction', in Jorge I. Dominguez *et al.*, *Enhancing Global Human Rights* (New York, McGraw-Hill, 1979), p. 17.

78 Adam Watson, *Diplomacy: The Dialogue Between States* (New York, McGraw-Hill, 1983), pp. 47–50.

8. HUMAN RIGHTS IN FOREIGN POLICY

1 See Ian Brownlie, *Principles of International Law*, 3rd edn (Oxford, Clarendon Press, 1979), pp. 596 and 512–15; and Chapter 3 above.

2 Ali Mazrui, *Towards a Pax Africana* (Chicago, University of Chicago Press, 1967), ch. 8.

3 For the first of these ideas, see Samuel P. Huntington, 'Human Rights and American Power', *Commentary* (September 1981). For the second, see Louis Henkin, 'Introduction', in L. Henkin (ed.), *The International Bill of Rights* (New York, Columbia University Press, 1981), p.l.

4 This division was suggested by my reading of Tom Campbell, *The Left and Rights* (London, Routledge & Kegan Paul, 1983), pp. 119–20.

5 Alan James, 'Diplomacy and International Society', *International Relations*, vol. 6 (1980), no. 6, pp. 942–8.

6 See Stephen B. Cohen, 'Conditioning US Security Assistance on Human Rights Practices', *American Journal of International Law*, vol. 76 (1982), p. 257: Lars Schoultz, *Human Rights and United States Policy Towards Latin America* (Princeton, Princeton University Press, 1981), p. 123; and Laurence H. Silberman, 'Toward Presidential Control of the State Department', *Foreign Affairs*, vol. 57 (1979), no. 4, pp. 882–3.

7 Peter R. Baehr, 'Concern for Development Aid and Fundamental Human Rights: The Dilemma as Faced by the Netherlands', *Human Rights Quarterly*, vol. 4 (1982), no. 1, pp. 46–9.

8 Cohen, 'Conditioning US Security Assistance', p. 257.

9 William F. Buckley, *UN Journal: A Delegate's Odyssey* (New York, Putnam, 1974), p. 198.

10 Cohen, 'Conditioning US Security Assistance', p. 264.

11 See R.J. Vincent, *Nonintervention and International Order* (Princeton, Princeton University Press, 1974), pp. 47–8.

12 See Philip Alston, 'International Trade as an Instrument of Positive Human Rights Policy', *Human Rights Quarterly*, vol. 4 (1982), no. 2, pp. 165–6.

13 For good discussions, see Christopher Hill and James Mayall, *The Sanctions Problem: International and European Perspectives*, European University Institute Paper No. 59 (San Domenico, Italy, 1983); Margaret Doxey, *Economic Sanctions and International Enforcement* (London, Oxford University Press, 1971); and James Barber, 'Economic Sanctions as a Policy Instrument', *International Affairs*, vol. 55 (1979), no. 3.

14 Cited in Cohen, 'Conditioning US Security Assistance', pp. 247–8.

15 *Ibid.*, p. 270.

16 See Richard H. Ullman, 'Both National Security and Human Rights Can be Served Simultaneously', *The Center Magazine*, March/April 1984, p. 22.

17 Cohen, 'Conditioning US Security Assistance', p. 271.

18 See Reinhold Niebuhr, *Moral Man and Immoral Society* (New York, Scribner's, 1941), p. xi.

19 See Vincent, 'Realpolitik' in James Mayall (ed.), The *Community of States* (London, Allen & Unwin, 1982), pp. 74–5; and generally F. Meinecke, *Machiavellism* (London, Routledge & Kegan Paul, 1962).

20 Margaret Grayden, 'Human Rights and United States Foreign Policy: The Neglected Political Dimension', unpublished paper, Department of Politics, Princeton University, p. 8.

21 *Ibid.*, pp. 17–20.

22 Schoultz, *Human Rights and United States Policy Towards Latin America*, pp. 24–6.

23 Elliot Abrams, Assistant Secretary of State for Human Rights and Humanitarian Affairs, Lecture at Princeton University, 26 November, 1984.

24 Jeane Kirkpatrick, 'Dictatorships and Double Standards', *Commentary*, vol. 68 (1979), no. 5.

25 See generally Noam Chomsky and Edward S. Herman, *The Political Economy of Human Rights*, 2 vols. (Boston, MA, South End Press, 1979), and Chapter 7 above.

26 As Richard Falk says the exponents of 'liberal statism' have done; see *Human Rights and State Sovereignty* (New York, Holmes and Meier, 1981), ch. 1.

27 David Owen, *Human Rights* (London, Cape, 1978), p. 44.

28 Adam Watson, *Diplomacy: The Dialogue Between States* (New York, McGraw-Hill, 1983), p. 80.

29 That is, under the heading UN affairs, and at the bottom of that list. See Henkin, 'The United States and the Crisis of Human Rights', *Virginia Journal of International Law*, vol. 14 (1974), p. 666.

30 See the remarks of Ambassador Evan G. Galbraith on leaving the United States embassy in Paris, as cited by Flora Lewis in the *New York Times*, 15 February, 1985.

31 See Schoultz, *Human Rights and United States Policy Towards Latin America*, pp. 126–8.

32 See Ullman, 'Introduction' to Jorge I. Dominguez *et al.*, *Enhancing Global Human Rights* (New York, McGraw-Hill, 1979), p. 16.

33 See Schoultz, *Human Rights and United States Policy Towards Latin America*, pp. 66–73.

34 *Ibid.*, pp. 204–7.

35 *Ibid.*, p. 363.

36 *Ibid.*, p. 248.

37 See Cohen, 'Conditioning US Security Assistance', p. 257.

38 See Evan Luard, 'Human Rights and Foreign Policy', *International Affairs*, vol. 56 (1980), no. 4, pp. 585–6; Ullman, 'Both National Security and Human Rights', *passim*.

39 Ullman, pp. 22–3.

40 See David N. Ranard, 'Korea, Human Rights and United States Foreign Policy', in Tom J. Farer (ed.), *Toward a Humanitarian Diplomacy* (New York and London, New York University Press, 1980), p. 209.

41 Luard, 'Human Rights and Foreign Policy', p. 586.

42 This is the argument of Ullman, 'Redefining Security', *International Security*, vol. 8 (1983), no. 1. For an analysis of the concept of international security, see Barry Buzan, *People, States and Fear* (Brighton, Harvester Press, 1983).

43 These questions were prompted by Ullman, 'Both National Security and Human Rights', pp. 24–5.

44 This is the argument of Vincent, 'The Reagan Administration and America's Purpose in the World', *Year Book of World Affairs*, vol. 37 (1983).

45 See Henry Shue, *Basic Rights* (Princeton, Princeton University Press, 1980), ch. 6.

46 For an excellent treatment of this view, see Tracy B. Strong, 'Taking the Rank with What is Ours: American Political Thought, Foreign Policy and Questions of Rights', in Paula R. Newberg (ed.), *The Politics of Human Rights* (New York and London, New York University Press, 1980).

47 Quoted in Samuel Flagg Bemis, *John Quincy Adams and the Foundations of American Foreign Policy* (New York, Knopf, 1949), pp. 364–5.

48 J.W. Gantenbein, *The Evolution of our Latin American Policy: A Documentary Record* (New York, Columbia University Press, 1950), pp. 94–5.

49 Elliot Abrams, speech at Princeton, 26 November, 1984.

50 Owen, *Human Rights*, p. 2.

51 For a strong argument on the practicality of human rights, See Sandy Vogelgesang, *American Dream Global Nightmare: The Dilemma of US Human Rights Policy* (New York, Norton, 1980). For the use of the idea of 'preventive medicine' in a different human rights context, see Alan Tonelson, 'Human Rights: The Bias We Need', *Foreign Policy*, no. 49 (Winter 1982–3), p. 67.

52 See Hedley Bull, *The Anarchical Society* (London, Macmillan, 1977), p. 83; Vincent, 'Western Conceptions of a Universal Moral Order', *British Journal of International Studies*, vol. 4 (1978), no. 1, p. 28.

53 *British Policy Towards the United Nations*, Foreign Policy Documents no. 26 (London, HMSO 1978), pp. 14–26. The summary that follows is of these pages.

54 *Ibid.*, p. 22.

55 The fortitude to be content with marginal gains in this area is one of Rosalyn Higgins's themes. See, for example, *Human Rights Prospects and Problems*, 34th Montagu Burton Lecture on International Relations (Leeds University Press, 1979).

56 *British Policy*, p. 22.

57 Abrams, Lecture at Princeton, 26 November, 1984.

58 Shue, *Basic Rights*, p. 201. Shue actually applies this image to the 6 million Asians being allowed to die of starvation at the same time as 6 million Jews were being killed in Europe, but the image applies, in terms of numbers, with even greater reason today.

59 Paul Streeten, *First Things First: Meeting Basic Human Needs in Developing Countries* (New York, Oxford University Press, for the World Bank, 1981), p. 13.

60 Streeten, p. vii; Shue, p. 183.

61 See Streeten's interesting Appendix on 'Basic Needs and Human Rights', which denies the irresistible. The discussion of the pros and cons of basic needs in the text is derived from Streeten, *First Things First*, *passim*.

62 Roger D. Hansen, *Beyond the North–South Stalemate* (New York, McGraw Hill, 1979), p. 300.

63 Quoted in Peter G. Brown and Henry Shue, *Food Policy* (New York, Free Press, 1977), p. 3. For liberal and radical sensitivity to the need to win over conservatives on this subject, see Farer, *Toward a Humanitarian Diplomacy*, ch. 1; and Falk, *Human Right and State Sovereignty*, ch. 2.

64 For this comparison (but deployed for a different purpose), see Charles H. Fairbanks, Jr., with Eli Nathans, 'The British Campaign Against the Slave Trade', in Marc F.

Plattner (ed.), *Human Rights in Our Time: Essays in Honor of Victor Baras* (Boulder, Colo., and London, Westview Press, 1984.)

65 Shue, *Basic Rights*, pp. 52–3.

66 Chomsky, in 'Human Rights and American Foreign Policy: A Symposium', *Commentary*, vol. 72 (1981), no. 5, p. 30.

67 For a questioning of the distinction between natural and man-made disasters on the ground that the failure to take precautions against disaster is man-made, see Onora Nell, 'Lifeboat Earth', *Philosophy and Public Affairs*, vol. 4 (1975), no. 3. For a persuasive argument that starvation is a function of entitlements to food (that is, a social product), and not of food availability (that is, the product of nature), see Amartya Sen, *Poverty and Famines: An Essay on Entitlement and Deprivation* (Oxford, The Clarendon Press, 1981). For the practical reception of this argument, see Independent Commission on International Humanitarian Issues, *Famine: A Man-made disaster* (London, Pan, 1985).

68 Jack Donnelly, 'Human Rights and Foreign Policy', *World Politics*, vol. 34 (1982), no. 4, p. 584.

69 See Ullman, 'Human Rights and Economic Power: The United States versus Idi Amin', *Foreign Affairs*, vol. 56 (1978), no. 3.

70 See Rhoda Howard, 'The Full Belly Thesis: Should Economic Rights Take Priority over Civil/Political Rights? A Discussion from Sub Saharan Africa', University of Toronto, Development Studies Programme, Working Paper No. 3, (April 1983).

71 For two excellent statements of the problem, and scrutiny of solutions, see Roger D. Hansen, *Beyond the North–South Stalemate* (New York, McGraw-Hill, 1979), esp. chs. 3, 8 and 9; and Michael W. Doyle, 'Cultivating Disaster: Local and International Contexts Affecting the Provision of Food in Natural Disasters', in Lynn H. Stephens and Stephen J. Green (eds.), *Disaster Assistance: Appraisal, Reform and New Approaches* (New York, New York University Press, 1979).

72 Willy Brandt *et al.*, *North–South: A Programme for Survival* (London, Pan Books, 1980).

73 This is an extrapolation from the argument of Daniel P. Moynihan, 'The United States in Opposition', *Commentary*, vol. 59 (1975), no. 3.

74 For the 'new political sensibility', see Robert W. Tucker, *The Inequality of Nations* (New York, Basic Books, 1977). For a more sympathetic treatment of it, see Arthur Schlesinger, Jr, 'Human Rights and the American Tradition', *Foreign Affairs, America and the World* (1978).

75 See Farer, *Toward a Humanitarian Diplomacy*, ch. 1.

76 Garret Hardin, 'Lifeboat Ethics: The Case Against Helping the Poor', *Psychology Today*, vol. 8 (1974), reprinted in William Aiken and Hugh La Follette, *World Hunger and Moral Obligation* (Englewood Cliffs, NJ, Prentice-Hall, 1977).

77 For a general critique of Hardin, see Marvin S. Soroos, 'Coping with Resource Scarcity: A Critique of Lifeboat Ethics', in Charles W. Kegley, Jr., and Eugene R. Wittkopf, *The Global Agenda: Issues and Perspectives* (New York, Random House, 1984).

78 See Singer, 'Famine, Affluence, and Morality', *Philosophy and Public Affairs*, vol. 1 (1972), no. 3, reprinted in Aiken and La Follette, *World Hunger and Moral Obligation*, pp. 31–2.

79 Falk, 'Responding to Severe Violations', in Dominguez, *Enhancing Global Human Rights*, p. 253.

80 Michael Doyle calls it the strategy of 'the neofunctionalist reformers'; see 'Stalemate in the North–South Debate: Strategies and the New International Economic Order', *World Politics*, vol. 35 (1983), no 3.

81 See Michael Freeman, *Edmund Burke and the Critique of Political Radicalism* (Oxford, Blackwell, 1980), p. 167; and Vincent, 'Edmund Burke and the Theory of International Relations', *Review of International Studies*, vol. 10 (1984), no. 2.

82 John Boli-Bennett, 'Human Rights or State Expansion? Cross-National Definitions of Constitutional Rights, 1870–1970', in Ved P. Nanda *et al.* (eds.), *Global Human Rights, Public Policies, Comparative Measures, and NGO Strategies* (Boulder, Colo., Westview Press, 1980), p. 173.

83 *Ibid.*, p. 176.

84 Hans J. Morgenthau, *Human Rights and Foreign Policy*, First Distinguished CRIA Lecture on Morality and Foreign Policy (New York, Council on Religion and International Affairs, 1979). For a general treatment of this question, see Hedley Bull and Adam Watson *The Expansion of International Society* (Oxford, Clarendon Press, 1984).

85 See Michael W. Doyle, 'Kant, Liberal Legacies, and Foreign Affairs', Pt. I, *Philosophy and Public Affairs*, vol. 12 (1983), no. 3.

86 See Ronald Dore, 'Unity and Diversity in Contemporary World Culture', in Bull and Watson, *The Expansion of International Society*.

87 Hannah Arendt, *The Origins of Totalitarianism*, new edn (New York, Harcourt, Brace, 1973), p. 299.

88 Karel Vasak, 'Human Rights: As a Legal Reality', in Vasak (gen.ed.; rev.edn P. Alston), *The International Dimension of Human Rights* (Greenwood Press, Westport, Conn., 1982), p. 4.

89 See Stanley Hoffmann, 'Reaching for the Most Difficult: Human Rights as a Foreign Policy Goal', *Daedalus*, vol. 112 (1983), no. 4, p. 21.

90 See also the pessimistic conclusion about the domestic reception of human rights reached by Ernst B. Haas in his pioneering study of the International Labour Organization, *Human Rights and International Action* (Stanford, Stanford University Press, 1970).

Index

Abrams, Elliot, 144
absolutism, *see* states
Adams, John Quincy, 142
Afghanistan
  Soviet imperialism in, 69
Africa
  human rights institutions, 96
  interpretations of human rights, 47–8; of the individual, 42
  regional conception of rights, 39–41, 42, 47–8, 64; in enforcement of global standards, 101
Africa, east
  Asians in, 136
Africa, southern, 95; *see also* South Africa
African Commission on Human and People's Rights, 96
Agency for International Development (US), 150
American Convention on Human Rights (1978), 95–6
aggression, 82
  cultural, 123
aid, foreign, 133, 139, 146
  strategies of, 134–5
  recipient/giver values, 140
Alexander the Great, 21
Algiers Declaration, 103
Alien Land Law (US), 103
Alien Tort Statute (US) (1789), 104
aliens
  admission and expulsion, 46–7
American Revolution, *see* United States of America
Americas
  American Convention on Human Rights (1978), 95–6
  American Declaration of the Rights and Duties of Man (1948), 96
  Central American Court of Justice, 44
  North America, discovery of rights of man in, 31

Organization of American States, 96
  regional enforcement of global standards, 101
  see also Latin America; United States of America
Amin, General, 148
Amnesty International, 97–8, 102
  beliefs, 98–9
  Statute (1980), 97
anarchy, 30
anthropology, 54
  'practical', 35, 39, 53
Antigone, 21
'antique-modern theory', 23
Anti-Slavery Society, 97
apartheid, 80, 82, 100, 134, 139
Aquinas, St Thomas, 24
Arab world
  regional enforcement of global standards, 101
Arendt, Hannah, 107, 126
Aristotle, 21
Asians
  in east Africa, 136
Augustine, St, 23, 24

Baehr, Peter R., 133
Baltic states
  separatism, 64
Banjul Charter on Human and People's Rights, 39–41, 96
Barcelona Traction case, 46
Barker, Ernest, 36
Bay, Christian, 14
Beitz, Charles, 119
Belgrade Conference on Security and Cooperation in Europe (1977), 67
Benedict, Ruth, 54
Bentham, Jeremy, 31, 34, 35
  and theory of natural rights, 30
Berlin
  four-power agreement on (1971), 70